DICKENS'S FICTION

DICKENS'S FICTION

Tapestries of Conscience

Stanley Friedman

AMS Press
New York

Library of Congress Cataloging-in-Publication Data

Friedman, Stanley, 1933-
  Dickens's Fiction: Tapestries of Conscience / Stanley
Friedman.
       p. cm. – (AMS Studies in the Nineteenth Century –
    ISSN 0196-657x; no. 30)
    Includes bibliographical references and index.
    ISBN 0-404-64460-0 (alk. paper)
    1. Dickens, Charles, 1812-1870—Technique.   2. Didactic
    fiction, English—History and criticism.   3. Dickens,
    Charles, 1812-1870—Ethics.   4. Conscience in literature.
    5. Ethics in literature.   6. Fiction—Technique.   7.
    Narration (Rhetoric).   I. Title.   II. Series.
PR4591.F75   2003
823'.8—dc21   2002034241
                                                               CIP

All AMS books are printed on acid-free paper that meets the guidelines
for performance and durability of the Committee on Production
Guidelines for Book Longevity of the Council on Library Resources.

AMS Press, Inc.
Brooklyn Navy Yard
63 Flushing Avenue, Bldg. 292, Suite 417
Brooklyn, NY 11205, USA

MANUFACTURED IN THE UNITED STATES OF AMERICA

To Lita,
David and Jennie,
and Jeremy,
and
to the memory of my parents,
Yetta and Henry Friedman

Contents

List of Illustrations

Documentation and Abbrevations

For the eight books by Dickens discussed in detail, I cite the book number when relevant, followed by chapter and page numerals (except for *A Christmas Carol*, for which I offer the stave and page numbers). I use the following editions, for which full bibliographical information is provided in the "Works Cited" section:

Oliver Twist: Norton, ed. Fred Kaplan
Nicholas Nickleby: Penguin, ed. Mark Ford
A Christmas Carol: *The Christmas Books*, Volume 1, Penguin, ed. Michael Slater
David Copperfield: Norton, ed. Jerome H. Buckley
Bleak House: Norton, ed. George Ford and Sylvère Monod
Hard Times: Norton, 2nd ed., ed. George Ford and Sylvère Monod
Great Expectations: Norton, ed. Edgar Rosenberg
Our Mutual Friend: Penguin, ed. Adrian Poole

I use the following abbreviations for the texts listed below, with full bibliographical information appearing in my "Works Cited" section:

DCH: *Dickens: The Critical Heritage*, ed. Philip Collins
DWN: *Dickens' Working Notes for His Novels*, ed. Harry Stone
PL: The Pilgrim Edition of *The Letters of Charles Dickens*
PR: *The Public Readings*, ed. Philip Collins

Preface

During a long career, Dickens made extensive use of diverse reiterative techniques to increase the complexity and appeal of his fiction. His employment of these tactics, which are prevalent in many popular works, especially the Bible, fairy tales, and Shakespeare, is remarkably extensive. By focusing on such techniques, we enhance our comprehension of his temperament and of his great skills as a literary artist. Through detailed discussions of such duplicating devices as repetition, paradox, and multiple perspectives in eight of Dickens's books composed at various stages in his life, this study observes some of the ways in which narrative structures may reflect moral concerns. The works examined are *Oliver Twist, Nicholas Nickleby, A Christmas Carol, David Copperfield, Bleak House, Hard Times, Great Expectations,* and *Our Mutual Friend.*

The sixth chapter, "Sad Stephen and Troubled Louisa: Paired Protagonists in *Hard Times,*" appeared in a slightly different form in *Dickens Quarterly* 7: 2 (June 1990): 254–62, and is reproduced with the permission of The Dickens Society. Chapter 7, "Estella's Parentage and Pip's Persistence: The Outcome of *Great Expectations,*" was originally published in a slightly different version in *Studies in the Novel* 19: 4 (Winter 1987): 410–21, copyright 1987 by the University of North Texas, and is reproduced with the permission of the publisher.

I wish to thank my friend and colleague Michael Timko for advice generously given over many years and for his reading of my manuscript. I am also grateful to Gabriel Hornstein, President of AMS

Press, for consistent encouragement, and to Jack Hopper, Editor-in-Chief at AMS Press, for his editorial skills and for his preparation of the index to this book.

I take pleasure in acknowledging the assistance of various family members. My wife, Lita, read the entire manuscript while it was in progress and made numerous valuable suggestions regarding both substance and syle. My sons, David and Jeremy, gave me instruction in computer techniques, and Jeremy also offered helpful comments on three chapters. David's wife, Jennifer Sun, often displayed enthusiastic interest. My brother, Arthur, read four chapters and proposed useful emendations, while his wife, Barbara, frequently provided moral support.

I am also pleased to acknowledge the cheerful assistance that Geraldine Ricciotti, of the Syosset Public Library, gave me in handling problems with computer scanning. In addition, I am indebted to an anonymous reviewer for AMS Press for suggestions concerning style and presentation. Although I have not accepted all of these recommendations, many have been helpful.

Chapter 1

Weaving Stories

In the 1857 preface to *Little Dorrit* and in a postscript to *Our Mutual Friend*, Dickens describes himself as weaving a story's "threads" into a completed "pattern," a metaphor for fiction-writing that aptly suggests the intricacy of design in his books and also reminds us of his need to anticipate developments long beforehand and to supervise the placement of minute details in these gigantic, complicated tapestries.[1] Under Dickens's control, characters are introduced into the story, then disappear, and later reenter, in a pattern that is repeated and places them in various juxtapositions with other persons. In similar ways plot strands, settings, and themes come into view, vanish, and become visible again. By carefully managing these many appearances and concealments, Dickens creates a slowly emerging, elaborate picture in ways that give us the pleasures of suspense and discovery. We enjoy recognizing parallels, grouping them, and comprehending relationships. Readers gain a sense of mastery by perceiving likenesses as well as meaningful distinctions among types of characters, places, or events.

This narrative complexity is largely attributable to many different types of repetition, including doubles of characters, parallelism in situations or events or settings, and reiterated motifs. Two other rhetorical techniques that Dickens favors, closely related to each other, may also be seen as modes of recurrence: paradox and the employment of diverse perspectives.[2]

These artistic duplicating devices help gain an audience's involvement and are, of course, especially common in many kinds of literature with widespread appeal, such as fairy tales, the Bible, and the plays of Shakespeare, all of which, especially the works of Shakespeare, greatly appealed to Dickens.[3] Nevertheless, the extensiveness of repetition, paradox, and multiple perspectives in Dickens's fiction seems extraordinary. Repetition, the most basic means of gaining emphasis, commands our attention, since we instinctively compare the later version with the first, watching for deviations and wondering why material is being duplicated. Often, repetition tends to universalize an effect, as in the double plot of *King Lear*. At other times, the facsimile modifies the original in subtle or obvious ways, and on occasion echoing even subverts, as when Shakespeare's Mark Antony protests far too much that Brutus is "an honorable man."

Recurrence—either within one book or among different texts—becomes itself a motif. Indeed, repetition may be suggested by a wide variety of features: ghosts and other revenants; statues and portraits; patterns of revenge and also of detective work; coincidences; hereditary resemblances; foreshadowings; prophecies (as well as blessings and curses), when fulfilled; rituals; déjà vu experiences; doppelgängers or doubles; mirrors; the cycles of the seasons and of human life; stage performances; reiterated imagery; and the inclusion of visual illustrations of characters, settings, and incidents described in the text. Indeed, recurrence is remarkable for its prevalence and complexity: it is basic to life itself in breathing, pulse, heartbeat; it is present in memory and in the habitual acts of our daily routines; and it is found in the metrical features of verse, the multiple meanings of puns and wordplay, the various types of rhyme and alliteration, and in elements of many other rhetorical devices. It is also inherent in any kind of mimesis, including parody and mimicry, for these are forms of simulation, and in all types of figurative expression, whether in the tenor and vehicle of metaphor, in the components of simile, in symbolic and emblematic references, in analogies evoked by allusions, or in parable and allegory.

In considering psychological reasons for repetition, Freud, after attributing duplication to an instinctive, regressive longing for return to an earlier state, a death-wish, moved to the idea that repetition in some cases could also be an attempt to achieve mastery or control over problems and feelings that appear threatening.[4] Repetition often seems a response to intense desires and fears regarding sexuality and death and at times is akin to complicated obsessive compulsive rituals intended to reduce anxiety by either warding off or else bringing about particular events.[5] Indeed, Frank J. Sulloway proposes that Freud sought to demonstrate "an organic compulsion to repeat" by referring to "phenomena of heredity and the facts of embryology" (402). Wordsworth, in his Preface to *Lyrical Ballads, with Pastoral and Other Poems* (1802), states that among the main causes of our enjoyment of metrical language is "the pleasure which the mind derives from the perception of similitude in dissimilitude," a "principle" that he terms "the great spring of the activity of our minds, and their chief feeder," the "principle" from which "the direction of the sexual appetite, and all the passions connected with it, take their origin" (57). In a lecture on drama, Coleridge remarks, "one great principle is common to all [the fine arts], a principle which probably is the condition of all consciousness. . . . I mean . . . the perception of identity and contrariety, the least degree of which constitutes *likeness*, the greatest [,] absolute difference" (1: 181). In *Rhythm in the Novel*, E. K. Brown maintains that repetition is "the strongest assurance an author can give of order," while the "extraordinary complexity of the variations is the reminder that the order is so involute that it must remain a mystery" (115).

   J. Hillis Miller, in *Fiction and Repetition: Seven English Novels*, considers "Two Forms of Repetition," based, respectively, on underlying samenesses and on intrinsic differences (5–17), forms that may in some texts be joined by "intertwining" (69, 127). For Miller, the variations accompanying repetitions may induce readers to find "undecidability" in a narrative, to have a feeling that the story's meaning is not clear (68–69, 108). But attempts to generalize, even by critics as subtle as Miller, must be treated with caution, since readers respond in subjective ways and since various types of recurrence may be included for diverse reasons by different authors or even by the same writer at different times.

   Dickens in his fiction often returns to situations and incidents in his own past, for these experiences continued to trouble him. In the autobiographical fragment given to John Forster, Dickens tells of his aversion years after to going near the site where the blacking factory at which he worked when twelve was located (*Life* 1: 3: 35). Evidently, in his fiction some recurrent features that dealt with experiences like those involved in his own past sufferings perhaps provided for him a way to control deep feelings of anger and resentment regarding his childhood and his parents. Although we at times cannot determine the extent to which the repetition of details within one narrative or between two novels is deliberate or unconscious, the recurrence seems to fulfill a psychological need for Dickens, who felt strongly attracted to particular motifs, characters, and incidents. As the autobiographical fragment indicates, he saw the blacking house employment as an abandonment by his parents, felt envy over his sibling Fanny's favored position as a music student, bitterly could "never forget" that after his release his mother wanted to have him sent back (*Life* 1: 2: 25–35), and retained in later life a sense of identification "with the very poor and unprosperous" (*Life* 1: 3: 39).

Another instance of this attraction to recurrence is found in Monroe Engel's reminder that Dickens, when starting to write a new story, had "the curious habit of reading his own work for inspiration" (12). Engel, however, cites just one instance of this, a comment in a letter to Forster on February 12, 1840, in which Dickens mentions that he had "been reading Oliver, Pickwick, and Nickleby to get" his "thoughts together for the new effort [*The Old Curiosity Shop*], but all in vain" (Engel 12 [n. 26]; PL 2: 24). Throughout Dickens's lengthy career his involvement with new editions of his novels and later with preparing adaptations to be used in his own public readings led him frequently to return to earlier materials. Just as Shakespeare's membership in a repertory company kept him immersed in prior efforts, so Dickens would remain always mindful of his preceding work. Kathleen Tillotson suggests that, in general, Dickens was "perhaps chiefly a re-reader—going back and back to that shelf of boyhood favourites lovingly enumerated in *David Copperfield*" ("Writers and Readers" 309); and he certainly often reread his own previously published books.

Forster tells us that when Dickens was to begin work on *Great Expectations*, in October 1860, he realized that there might be resemblances between Pip and David Copperfield, since each character was to present a first-person narrative describing a boy's development from childhood on. In order to avoid "unconscious repetitions," Dickens reread the earlier narrative (*Life* 9: 3: 734). Despite this precaution—or perhaps because of it—Dickens's tendency to repeat predominates, for many parallels are evident between David and Pip.[6] Just as we cannot always know if recurrences within a novelist's canon are intended or inadvertent, we often cannot determine how aware a writer may be of similarities between features in his or her book and details in a work by a predecessor. Similarly, we may remain in doubt when considering the extent to which an author is conscious of subtle implications or covert situations in a text. Although any writer is his or her own first reader, intensity of emotion may distract attention from what is obvious to a more detached observer—for instance, Forster reports that Dickens, in deciding on a name for David Copperfield, did not realize that "the [character's] initials were but his own reversed" (*Life* 6: 6: 524).

Of course, repetition may be seen as inherently paradoxical, for it seems theoretically impossible: in Heraclitus's terms, we cannot enter the same stream twice—not only because the water has changed, but because the time is not the same (Rimmon-Kenan 153; Naddaff 160). The experience would be made different by our inability to erase the memory of the first entry, even if this recollection remains unconscious.

If recurrence brings up paradox, paradox, in turn, involves repetition, for one main type of paradox is a statement that appears contradictory but becomes acceptable when regarded from two distinct viewpoints: when Hamlet tells Gertrude he must be cruel in order to be kind, the seeming conflict does not remain a problem, for we are induced to look twice at his behavior—that is, to repeat our evaluation—and to conclude that Hamlet's words are cruel because they are intentionally wounding but also kind since they are designed to lead to his mother's repentance and subsequent salvation. Even the other basic kind of paradox—an insoluble puzzle like the question of whether we should believe a Cretan who asserts that all Cretans always lie—forces a repeated consideration, for if we deny the Cretan's generalization we must concede that he has been indeed lying, and if we accept his maxim we must acknowledge that he has provided an exception to the general rule. Both varieties of paradox demand that we give a double look, and both also invite us to change from one perspective to another. Elizabeth Hankins Wolgast, referring to Plato's consideration of paradox in the *Republic* (bk. 7, secs. 523–25), remarks, "apparent contradictions force the mind to reflect in unaccustomed ways" (18).

Dickens continually engages in repetition, often presenting an abused child, a sadistic authority-figure, a benevolent godparent, and he frequently offers paradoxes—for a time Fagin is both Oliver's worst enemy and his best friend, since the old man is simultaneously a treacherous predator and the person who gives Oliver kinder treatment than he has ever previously received. Moreover, as we have just noticed, closely related to one kind of paradox is the penchant for exploring different—even conflicting—perspectives. Although Dickens avoids moral relativism, he nevertheless insists on complications. In finding Fagin less repugnant than the members of the workhouse board, readers may remember the comment of Lear when he reacts to Regan's outdoing Goneril in limiting his right to have his own retainers: "Those wicked creatures yet do look well-favor'd / When others are more wicked" (2: 4: 256–57). Indeed, Badri Raina finds in the novels a "dialectic" in which the narrator assumes different roles (10), and Dickens is always conscious of the importance of viewpoint. In one preface to *Martin Chuzzlewit* he offers the following comment: "What is exaggeration to one class of minds and perceptions, is plain truth to another. That which is commonly called a long-sight, perceives in a prospect innumerable features and bearings non-existent to a short-sighted person" (41).

In Dickens's first novel, *Pickwick Papers*, the importance of diverse perspectives is emphasized early in the narrative. Mr. Pickwick, after being called a "humbug" by Mr. Blotton, is readily mollified when the latter explains that the word was being used "in its Pickwickian sense," instead of "in a common sense"; for the expression employed by Blotton, if understood from "a Pickwickian point of view," is wholly inoffensive (1: 71–72). In the next chapter Mr. Jingle, offering a warning about the need for passengers on the top of the coach to lower their heads when the vehicle goes under a low archway, remarks, "Terrible place—dangerous work—other day—five children—mother—tall lady, eating sandwiches—forgot the arch—crash—knock—children look round—mother's head off—sandwich in her hand—no mouth to put it in—head of a family off—shocking, shocking!" (2: 79). A grisly fatal accident is made amusing by Jingle's staccato-like style and by his absurd pun ("head of a family off"), demonstrating the possibility of finding a perspective that will make even a pathetic and painful subject seem funny.

Horace Walpole's assertion that "*this world is a comedy to those that think, a tragedy to those that feel*" (7: 166 [letter to Sir Horace Mann, Dec. 31, 1769]) appears questionable, since for an event like Macbeth's murder of Duncan to be perceived as comic, we must not merely think of the irony in a kind man's being betrayed by someone he trusts, but must find this reversal amusing, a response that depends on our suppressing all pity and also all fear of being similarly victimized. Total detachment from feeling is needed, and this can usually be achieved only when we react to the world of farce, a realm in which characters are flat, disconnected from others, lacking any past, and often impervious to serious injury or death. The frequent interconnection between thought and emotion is presupposed by expressions like "a sad premonition" or "a happy idea." Indeed, the power of Shakespeare's Sonnet 30, "When to the sessions of sweet, silent thought," depends on our accepting the speaker's belief that some of his thoughts can make him depressed and that then thinking of his dear friend can cheer him totally. Of course, differing viewpoints are significant in determining responses. The mother in Jingle's little story is carefully kept distant and unreal. Despite the bizarre humor in examples like this, Dickens asserts in the "Preface to the Original Edition, 1837," the belief that throughout *Pickwick Papers* "no incident or expression occurs which could call a blush into the most delicate cheek, or wound the feelings of the most sensitive person" (42).

Sudden shifts in perspective keep the reader off-balance in Dickens's second novel, *Oliver Twist*. On the opening page the narrator refers to his protagonist as an "item of mortality" and proceeds to joke about infant death (an extremely distressing social problem in Victorian Britain) by stating that, for "a long time" after Oliver's birth, there was "considerable doubt whether the child would survive to bear any name at all; in which case it is somewhat more than probable that these memoirs would never have appeared" (1: 17). We then find the humorously ironic affirmation that while "being born in a workhouse" is not "in itself the most fortunate and enviable circumstance that can possibly befal a human being, . . . in this particular instance, it was the best thing for Oliver Twist that could by possibility have occurred" (1: 17). The ensuing explanation cynically maintains that, for an infant trying to breathe, the solicitous attention of godmothers, aunts, nurses, and doctors would "inevitably and indubitably" have been fatal (1: 18). While such a perspective seems whimsically yet bitterly ironic, the same narrator, of course, can at other times be entirely straightforward and direct: "For the next eight or ten months, Oliver was the victim of a systematic course of treachery and deception" (2: 19).

Throughout Dickens's life, this concern with diverse perspectives persisted. In *Dombey and Son*, for example, two important passages appear late in the novel: the narrator exclaims, "Oh for a good spirit who would take the house-tops off, with a more potent and benignant hand than the lame demon in the tale [the demon Asmodeus in LeSage's *Gil Blas*], and show a Christian people what dark shapes issue from amidst their homes, to swell the retinue of the

Destroying Angel as he moves forth among them" (47: 738), and Mr. Morfin speculates, "how will many things that are familiar, and quite matters of course to us now, look, when we come to see them from that new and distant point of view which we all must take up, one day or other?" (53: 841). The theme of varying perspectives is developed with exceptional thoroughness and depth in such novels as *David Copperfield, Bleak House,* and *Great Expectations,* the first and the third of these being presented by a narrator who recaptures the viewpoint of his earlier years and juxtaposes this with his mature vision, while *Bleak House* includes two tellers with differing personalities and outlooks.

Dickens's interest in multiple perspectives may be in part attributable to his fascination with the changing viewpoints of Swift's Gulliver and with the satire of England provided by Goldsmith in his *The Citizen of the World,* a collection of letters supposedly written by Lien Chi Altangi, an alien observer from China. But the inclination also stems from Dickens's absorption at an early age in Shakespeare and in the theater. In January 1842, when Dickens was embarking on his first trip to America, his close friend Forster gave as a farewell gift a pocket edition of Shakespeare's plays (Johnson 1: 362; PL 3: 165–66 [to Forster, 22–23 March]); and years later, in an after-dinner speech, the novelist asserted, "every writer of fiction, though he may not adopt the dramatic form, writes in effect for the stage" (*Speeches* 262 [3 / 29 / 1858]). Many Victorian writers shared an interest in exploring subjectivity in responses, as we see from the growing fascination with the dramatic monologue as a poetic form, an interest culminating in a work like Browning's *The Ring and the Book.* Jacob Korg proposes that "the nineteenth century turned to the hypothesis that the mind was a dualism which could accommodate contradiction" and that, consequently, "doubling invaded literature as a theme, a pattern, a ubiquitous unconscious inference" (75). Indeed, Korg maintains, "There can never have been such a convergence of forces favouring the hypothesis of dualism as there was in Europe generally during the Victorian period" (80–81).

Although Dickens gained extraordinary popularity among virtually all social classes in his own era, he is often surprisingly demanding of his readers. The difficulty of responding to his narratives is caused not only by his extensive use of such complicating devices as repetition, paradox, and multiple perspectives—techniques employed by many of his contemporary novelists—but also by other features common to Victorian fiction.

The most obvious of these is the length of the narratives. George Ford and Sylvère Monod, in their edition of *Hard Times*, estimate that each of the longer Dickens novels—the eight works published in nineteen monthly numbers, the last number being a double installment—is some 350,000 words long (ix). We might note that this length is nearly 40% of the total word count (884,647) that one authority gives for Shakespeare's complete extant writings (Spevack v). For those in Dickens's audience who read the original serialized versions, each of these eight narratives could not be read in under eighteen months, the time between the appearance of the opening installment and the publication of the concluding double-number. Furthermore, Dickens expected his readers to be extremely attentive and retentive. For instance, in *David Copperfield* we learn early in Chapter 1, first published in May 1849, that Aunt Betsey's husband went off to India (1: 11). Dickens clearly wished his original audience to recall this detail five months later, in October 1849, when Chapter 16 refers to Jack Maldon's going to India (16: 207); for we are to assume that Jack would have been as unsatisfactory a husband as Aunt Betsey's spouse, had Annie Strong married him instead of the doctor.[7]

The length of the novels is attributable to Dickens's weaving of his story—the inclusion of a number of plot strands, the gradual unfolding of these, and careful attempts to connect them. These strands are diverse in nature, since Dickens juxtaposes tragic and comic elements and also ranges from urban to pastoral settings and from one social class to another. In each of the eight longer novels, moreover, we encounter close to fifty characters who are relatively memorable and who must be considered if we are to comprehend fully the events that are developing. Although this large number of personages may try a reader's memory,[8] the variety also affords interest and pleasure.

Indeed, Dickens's novels resemble the popular Gothic architecture found in the homes of many wealthy Victorians: large, highly ornamented buildings, with a complex symmetrical balance of both large and small features—rooms, gables, bay windows, alcoves, and connecting passages. The many groupings of two or more like or opposed characters in an enormous novel resembles the correspondences among various components in a Gothic residence, since Dickens is frequently drawn to what E. K. Brown refers to as "repetitions with intricate variations" (115) and Dorothy Van Ghent calls "antithetical parallelisms" (*English Novel* 10). In *David Copperfield*, for instance, we find a triad of villains—Murdstone, Steerforth,

Heep—each of whom harms David by injuring a woman of whom
he is fond. In Clara Copperfield and Clara Peggotty the child David
has two mothers. He is later victimized by two deceptive minor
figures, the friendly waiter he encounters on the trip to Salem House
and the young man with a donkey-cart who steals his box at the
beginning of the escape from London. As a schoolboy David meets
two antithetical headmasters—Creakle and Dr. Strong—and becomes friendly with two fellow students who later reenter his
life—Steerforth and Traddles. The protagonist finds two eccentric
but benevolent paternal substitutes in Wilkins Micawber and Mr.
Dick, as well as two unsatisfactory parental surrogates in Mrs.
Crupp and Mr. Spenlow.

Other pairs include Jane Murdstone and Aunt Betsey (two spin-
sters), Dora and Agnes (the protagonist's two wives), Wickfield and
Spenlow (each a widower with a motherless daughter), Mrs. Heep
and Mrs. Steerforth (widowed mothers devoted to errant sons), Emily and Rosa Dartle (two young women attracted to Steerforth), and
Miss Mowcher and Martha Endell (two women from the periphery
of society who reveal far more merit than they initially seem to
possess and are the characters referred to in the title of Chapter 22,
"Some old Scenes, and some new People"). All of these sets, as well
as other "couples" in the book, reflect the intricacy of balancings
found in Dickens's fiction, as he weaves numerous characters, diverse settings, and many events into complicated patterns involving
moral concerns.

Dickens's extensive canon invites readers to make comparisons
of protagonists, villains, themes, and plots. For while the novels
remain discrete, with no sequels and no characters actually reap-
pearing as some do in the fiction of James Fenimore Cooper, Balzac,
Thackeray, and Trollope,[9] character-types and situations recur, of
course, with great frequency. Dickens often echoed himself, for he
reread not only his favorite classic literary texts, but also, as we have
previously noticed, his own novels. Indeed, Bret Harte amusingly
registers a complaint in his parody "The Haunted Man. A Christmas
Story. By Ch_r__s D_ck_ns" in *Condensed Novels* (1871)—the charge
that each new novel presents the "old story," a narrative including
"a most unnatural child" that dies, "a good woman, undersized,"
"a haughty, proud and wicked lady" (98) and extensive use of foreshadowing (99). But repetition is used by Dickens within individual
novels and within the canon for subtle and sophisticated purposes,
prompting Edmund Wilson to state boldly, "Dickens never really
repeats himself: his thought makes a consistent progress, and his

art . . . keeps on going to new materials and effects" (74). This assertion notwithstanding, Dickens does employ repetition, as well as paradox and diverse perspectives, to complicate his tales and thereby engage his readers. Moreover, the intricate structural patterns in Dickens's novels help convey important moral implications, ideas that simultaneously reassure and challenge readers concerned with basic problems of human behavior.

Although George Orwell, in his admiring and influential essay, maintains, "The outstanding, unmistakable mark of Dickens's writing is the *unnecessary detail*" (450), this opinion seems questionable, since often in reading Dickens we can only see the forest clearly if we look closely at the individual trees. For details develop associations, links, contexts, and overall patterns. Dorothy Van Ghent, who states that Dickens presents "a world visibly disintegrated into things," believes that his "indefatigable attention to detail" may be seen as "one way to find" a "coherence": "No thing must be lost, as it is doubtless essential to the mysterious organization of the system" ("The Dickens World" 426). In Dickens's narratives, a realistic touch may encourage suspension of disbelief in an improbable story, while a fantastic detail may lull a reader into approaching moral issues that he or she would prefer to avoid. David Copperfield, describing how—just prior to the death of Dora—he sat thinking of "every little trifle" between himself and her, concludes, "trifles make the sum of life" (53: 647).

I question, too, Virginia Woolf's idea that Dickens's facility at creating characters leads him to make "his books blaze up . . . by throwing another handful of people upon the fire," that when "interest flags" he simply introduces another figure, so that his narrative "is apt to become a bunch of separate characters loosely held together" (194). Such an opinion entirely disregards the pleasure that readers may take in perceiving the intricate interrelationships among the hordes of figures in a given narrative. Indeed, many of us would tend to accept for Dickens the apostrophe that De Quincey addresses to Shakespeare at the end of "On the Knocking at the Gate in *Macbeth*": "Thy works are . . . like the phenomena of nature, . . . which are to be studied . . . in the perfect faith that . . . the further we press in our discoveries, the more we shall see proofs of design and self-supporting arrangement where the careless eye had seen nothing but accident!" (244). As Jerome Meckier remarks, discussing Victorian multiplot novels, although the fiction composed by Dickens and his contemporaries is "multidimensional" and "complex," the narratives are also "unified" (*Hidden Rivalries* 10).

In the last half-century many scholars and critics have carefully examined Dickens's impressive ability to synthesize diverse materials through the use of parallels among characters, recurrent situations, and iterative imagery. Although numerous previous studies have considered repetition, especially doubling of characters, as well as paradox and the use of multiple perspectives, I believe that my succeeding chapters offer a number of new, detailed observations that cumulatively enhance our awareness of the ways in which Dickens employs these intricate techniques to support his moral vision. Style and form, especially duplication, shape overall significance.

Chapter 2 examines the effects of repetitive patterns regarding identity, heredity, and guilt in *Oliver Twist* and *Nicholas Nickleby*. In Chapter 3, I consider the paradoxical doubling of characters and viewpoints discernible in *A Christmas Carol*, a story exploring alternative or potential lives. Moving to the middle of Dickens's long career, I examine in Chapter 4 the ways in which several rhetorical devices, including equivocal chapter-titles, induce us to take double looks at many features of *David Copperfield*. Chapter 5 seeks reasons both artistic and personal for the extraordinary number of echoes of *Oliver Twist* in *Bleak House*, which began appearing more than thirteen years after the earlier novel was written. Chapter 6 views Stephen Blackpool and Louisa Gradgrind as co-protagonists whose likenesses, in *Hard Times*, reveal the social needs of mid-Victorian England. I then proceed in Chapter 7 to discuss coincidence as a recurrent motif that strongly influences the expectations of both Pip and his readers in *Great Expectations*. In the next chapter, Mr. Boffin and Mr. Riah are seen as doubles, covert and complementary partners, in *Our Mutual Friend*. Finally, Chapter 9, by examining the ways in which some of the conflicts Dickens presents are resolved (and, in some cases, re-solved), seeks to explore more fully the relationship between the strategies of duplication employed by Dickens and the moral ethos he expresses in his fiction. Of special significance are the implications that the narratives convey regarding the consequences of virtuous actions and of immoral ones, implications that are complicated by noteworthy ambiguities concerning moral issues.

In weaving extremely intricate fictions, Dickens was concerned with conscience in both the customary and the older senses—offering guidance on how to behave and increasing our consciousness of the complexity of human life.

Notes

1. This figure of weaving as writing is also, of course, employed in other places by Dickens. For example, in *Oliver Twist* the narrator, nearing the end of his story, expresses the desire to "weave, for a little longer space, the thread of these adventures" (53: 359), and in *David Copperfield* the penultimate chapter opens with the statement by David that he plans to report an "incident . . . without which one thread in the web" he has "spun, would have a ravelled end" (63: 727): he refers here to Mr. Peggotty's visit to England and the account of the lives of those who migrated to Australia. Moreover, Dickens's working notes for various novels (available in H. Stone's edition, DWN), jottings intended only for his own personal use, at times introduce language suggestive of this figure of weaving: "To carry on the thread of Uriah, carefully, and not obtrusively; also of David and Agnes" for No. 13 of *David Copperfield*; "Carry through" [doubly underlined] for No. 15 and "Wind up" for Chapter 64 of the same novel; "Carry on" for No. 4 of *Bleak House*; "Carry through" for No. 6 and "Carry on" for Chapter 39 of *Bleak House*; "Wind Up——" for Chapter 67 of that novel; in the notes for *Little Dorrit* "Run the two ends of the book [Book II] together" for Chapter 22 of Book II; and in the notes for *Our Mutual Friend* "Work in two witnesses" and "Work in the girl" for No. 1, "Work out the story" for No. 3, "Take up Wrayburn and Lightwood?" for No. 4, and "Wind up the book I" for No. 5. In a letter to Bulwer-Lytton on June 24, 1861, Dickens comments on revising the conclusion of *Great Expectations* and refers to beginning "to unwind the thread that I thought I had wound for ever" (PL 9: 428). For remarks on Dickens's interest in this figure, see Monod 82, 379 (n. 6), 436, 437 and Garrett 31. Bates comments on the antiquity of this use of weaving as a metaphor for writing and also points to the relationship between the terms *textile* and *text* and to the connection between *fabric* and *fabricate* (52–56). Writing about fairy tales, Warner observes, "Spinning a tale, weaving a plot: the metaphors illuminate the relation; while the structure of fairy stories, with their repetitions, reprises, elaboration and minutiae, replicates the thread and fabric of one of women's principal labours—the making of textiles from the wool or the flax to the finished bolt of cloth" (23). Scheid and Svenbro consider weaving as one of "the metaphors that has been used in the West—and elsewhere—to designate linguistic activity" (111).

2. For considerations of complexity in Dickens, see esp. Hardy ("Complexity") and Sucksmith. For Dickens's use of repetition, see Coolidge, Daleski, and Watkins. Among those noticing paradox or apparent contradiction in the novels are Engel, who refers to Dickens's "enigmatic mixture of radicalism and conservatism" (34); Henkle, who discusses

paradox in Dickensian comedy (179–82); Watkins, who points to Dickens's inconsistency (85; see, also, 2–3, 12, 84, 86, 87); and Flint, who mentions "unresolvable contradictions" (29; see, also, 30–46, 93, 133). For Dickens's interest in diverse perspectives see Raina, as well as Garrett and Sucksmith.

3. For the influence of fairy tales, see Kotzin, Grob, and H. Stone, *Dickens and the Invisible World*; for the Bible, see Vogel and Larson; for Shakespeare, see Fleissner, Harbage (*A Kind of Power* and "Shakespeare and the Early Dickens"), and Gager.

4. In "The 'Uncanny' " (1919) Freud regards the compulsion to repeat as "instinctual" (17: 238); in *Beyond the Pleasure Principle* (1920) he reaffirms the belief that this drive is of "an instinctual character," but states that children, while playing, "repeat unpleasurable experiences for the additional reason that they can master a powerful impression far more thoroughly by being active than they could by merely experiencing it passively" and adds, "Each fresh repetition seems to strengthen the mastery they are in search of" (18: 35). See, too, the comments by Kawin 16, 18, 26; Erikson 41–42; and Rimmon-Kenan 154. For a discussion of psychoanalytic explanations of the déjà vu phenomenon as an attempt to control an anxiety-inducing situation or a disturbing desire by projecting it backwards into the past (a past in which the problem has presumably been dealt with), see Friedman, "Dickens' Mid-Victorian Theodicy" 137–39.

5. The double has been regarded as signifying a wish for immortality, a fear of mortality, and a desire for incest (a form of self-extension), overlapping motives. Rank maintains that the double, although "originally conceived of as a guardian angel, assuring immortal survival to the self, . . . eventually appears as precisely the opposite, a reminder of the individual's mortality, indeed the announcer of death itself" ("The Double as Immortal Self" 75–76). Elsewhere, Rank also emphasizes the complexity of this device: "the double, who personifies narcissistic self-love, becomes an unequivocal rival in sexual love; or else, originally created as a wish-defense against a dreaded eternal destruction, he reappears in superstition as the messenger of death" (*The Double* 86). Irwin sees in "the brother / sister relationship a kind of doubling" (41).

6. For considerations of these similarities, see Engel 146–47, Pearlman 190–202, and H. Stone, *Dickens and the Invisible World* 299.

7. Aunt Betsey's husband and Jack Maldon are linked in another way, for in No. 16 we encounter two mysteries, each of which involves one of these figures. Chapter 16 records the puzzlement over the disappearance of Annie Strong's cherry-colored ribbon, an item that David has seen Jack carry off as a keepsake (16: 211–12), while in Chapter 17 Mr. Dick tells David of the strange man who frightens Aunt Betsey (17: 216–17). These two mysteries are later solved in adjacent installments, Nos. 15 and 16: in the former we learn that Annie has remained faithful

despite being tempted by Maldon (45: 558–59), and in the latter Aunt Betsey reveals that the stranger is her long-lost, disreputable husband (47: 580).

8. Geoffrey Tillotson offers some astute comments on the experience of reading Dickens: "Quite apart from the immensity of twenty parts, readers were slowed down by the Dickensian intensity that burned on almost every page" (138). Tillotson adds, "To read him . . . was to be taxed extraordinarily" (138) and to incur "a danger . . . of being overwhelmed by Dickens's 'multitudinousness' " (147).

9. Although Mr. Pickwick, Sam Weller, and the latter's father appear in some of the early installments of *Master Humphrey's Clock* (chs. 3–6), these sections do not form part of any novel.

Chapter 2

Oliver Twist and *Nicholas Nickleby*: Primal Secrets

> Now no matter, child, the name:
> Sórrow's spríngs áre the same.
> —Hopkins, "Spring and Fall"

Between mid-February 1836 and mid-September 1839, Dickens wrote the three long narratives that launched his amazing career: *Pickwick Papers*, *Oliver Twist*, and *Nicholas Nickleby*. In providing this continuous monthly flow of serialized major fiction, he wrote approximately the first quarter of *Oliver* concurrently with the last 40% of *Pickwick*, and he composed the final 60% of *Oliver* while preparing the first 40% of *Nickleby*. During these early years, moreover, the youthful author also frenetically immersed himself in such other literary activities as editing *Bentley's Miscellany*, revising Thomas Egerton Wilks's edition of *The Memoirs of Joseph Grimaldi*, assembling a collection entitled *The Pic Nic Papers* to benefit the widow and children of John Macrone (publisher of *Sketches by Boz* in February 1836), and anonymously writing *Sketches of Young Gentlemen* in 1838.[1]

The nearly simultaneous creation of parts of *Pickwick* and *Oliver* and the overlapping in the composition of sections of *Oliver* and

Nickleby might lead us to expect duplication—or recycling—of characters and events, and despite the great differences in the three protagonists—a wealthy old bachelor, an impoverished orphan child, and a young gentleman seeking to find his way in the world—commentators have pointed to noteworthy parallels. For example, Morris Golden sees Oliver as "the innocent self in incriminating circumstances hunted and misunderstood by all, like Dickens' other projections at this time, notably Pickwick and the Nickleby siblings" ("Dickens, Oliver, and Boz" 69). But although the three novels are also linked in various other ways, a relationship to be considered later in this discussion, the closest ties are between *Oliver* and *Nickleby*, and many of the resemblances involve the two characters who emerge as each book's emotional center, the two figures that most stir our concern and compassion—Oliver himself and not Nicholas, but Smike, whom Beth F. Herst calls a "surrogate for his more fortunate cousin" (14). Each of these young victims, Oliver and Smike, suffers because of mysterious, hidden actions perpetrated by others in a distant past, deeds not disclosed until very late in each story and then described in a disjointed manner that emphasizes the importance of these discoveries but also strangely distracts us and reduces the chances of our retaining wholly clear recollections. In *Oliver Twist* and *Nicholas Nickleby*, the similarities in narrative strategies, as well as the likenesses in situations, are significant in that they form a complex of motifs that endured as constants in Dickens's art over the succeeding three decades, motifs that reflect some of the deepest psychological concerns not only of the author but also of his legions of devoted readers.

When we meet Oliver and Smike, the former soon becomes and the latter already is a resident in a harshly run institution, a place ostensibly benevolent but actually a scene of deprivation, cruelty, and hellish confinement—the parish workhouse and Dotheboys Hall. We quickly find each youngster violating either an implicit or a clear rule: Oliver, chosen when the boys cast lots, asks for more gruel, while Smike, distressed because of Squeers's increasing abuse and the apprehension that Nicholas will soon leave, tries to run away. Oliver is imprisoned in a "dark and solitary room" (3: 29) and "carried every other day" into the dining-hall to be "sociably flogged" before the other boys (3: 30); Smike, after being apprehended, is "securely locked up in a cellar" (13: 155) and then brought forth to be whipped in front of all the school, a punishment interrupted by Nicholas. Both boys are pathetic victims, and even though Oliver is only in his ninth year (2: 21), while Smike is 18 or 19 (7: 90), they are nearly equivalent, since we learn that the latter cannot "master some task" that could easily be accomplished by "a child of nine years old, possessed of ordinary powers" (12: 148). But both boys escape these hostile institutions: Oliver, after being sent to work for the undertaker Sowerberry, pummels Noah Claypole and eventually flees, walking alone some 75 miles to London (8: 59); Smike, after Nicholas thrashes Squeers, joins his friend (13: 162), and they walk over 250 miles to London.

In *Oliver Twist*, the protagonist finds refuge with Fagin, a histrionic figure who, with the Dodger and Charley Bates, "played at a very curious and uncommon game, which was performed" by his acting as an old gentleman walking "about the streets," while the boys try to pick his pockets (9: 69–70). In a sense, Fagin runs a theatrical school, for he keeps an "inexhaustible stock" of costumes (13: 93), and Nancy rehearses the part of Oliver's older sister (13: 93), a role she later assumes in public (13: 94; 15: 107–08). In *Nickleby* we find a much more benevolent example of an acting school when Smike and Nicholas, after leaving London, join Vincent Crummles's troupe. Just as Fagin believes that Oliver, because of his innocent appearance, has great potential as a thief, unlike most other boys, whose "looks convict 'em when they get into trouble" (19: 137), so Crummles remarks that Smike, because of his "capital countenance," would "make such an actor for the starved business as was never seen in this country" (22: 275).

Although Oliver never performs satisfactorily for Fagin, we should recall the boy's earlier success when acting for Sowerberry as a "'mute" mourner at children's funerals (6: 50–51), a role that Oliver's "melancholy" facial appearance suggested to the undertaker (5: 45). Smike, because of his "haggard" look, proves highly successful as the Apothecary in *Romeo and Juliet* (22: 275; 25: 318).

Other parallels are also noticeable between these two characters, each ignorant of his true parentage, each answering to a name given by a stranger. Each manages to escape from a diabolic instructor who feigns benevolence but is actually a greedy predator—Fagin and Squeers. Afterwards, walking on a London street, each youngster is noticed and kidnapped in order to be returned to captivity, Oliver by Nancy and Sikes (15: 107–08), Smike by Squeers and his son, young Wackford (38: 471–72). Both victims are utterly distraught, since each finds himself forcibly separated from the first true home he has ever known: Oliver has previously pleaded with Mr. Brownlow to be allowed to stay ("Don't turn me out of doors to wander in the streets again" [14: 98]), while Smike has movingly implored Nicholas not to send him away ("You are my home—my kind friend—take me with you, pray" [13: 162]). Then, too, Oliver and Smike are traduced and wrongly described as reprobates by, respectively, Bumble (17: 123–24) and Squeers (38: 474–75; 45: 561). Each figure also is persecuted by a close relative: Monks seeks to bring disgrace to his half-brother, Oliver, while Ralph Nickleby, unaware that Smike is his son, tries to harm the young man by separating him from Nicholas. Each of these villains enlists the aid of a wicked teacher—Monks uses Fagin, while Ralph employs Squeers.

After the aborted attempt by Bill Sikes and Toby Crackit to break into the Maylie household, Oliver again finds freedom and refuge and becomes attached to the beautiful young Rose Maylie, later identified as his aunt, but subsequently claimed by him as a closer relation, "my own dear sister" (51: 348). Similarly, Smike is attracted to Kate, who is eventually discovered to be his first cousin, but, unlike the younger Oliver, he feels "dejection," since he knows his romantic inclinations are doomed because of his mental infirmity (38: 463). Of course, the difference in the kinds of interest developed by Oliver and Smike leads to dissimilar reactions when each young-ster realizes that the young lady has a highly eligible suitor—for Rose, Harry Maylie (34: 224–25), and for Kate, Frank Cheeryble (43: 534–35).

In the rural retreat to which the Maylie group takes him, Oliver finds pleasure in tending the garden (32: 216), while Smike, living with the Nicklebys in their suburban cottage at Bow, makes "the garden a perfect wonder to look upon" (35: 436): in each case, gar-dening is used to express gratitude and love. When Smike becomes desperately ill (49: 601–02; 55: 687–88), Nicholas takes him to Dev-onshire, where the sinking young man is terrified by seeing, behind a tree, the face of the man who first took him to Dotheboys Hall (58: 713–14). Nicholas wonders if this vision is "the mere delusion of an imagination affected by disease" (58: 713) and searches in vain for the man (58: 715), but later discovers that this mysterious person, subsequently identified as Brooker, Ralph Nickleby's former clerk, had indeed spied on Smike (60: 739). The incident, of course, closely resembles the experience of Oliver, who, after being taken by the Maylies to the country to convalesce, looks outside a window and, in his half-awake state, fearfully notices that he is being spied upon by Fagin and Monks (34: 231), intruders that afterwards cannot be

found (35: 232–33). Just as Nicholas wonders if Smike is hallucinat-
ing, so Harry Maylie tells Oliver, "It must have been a dream" (35:
232). But just as Smike's report is later confirmed, so Oliver's
sighting of Fagin and Monks is subsequently verified by Brownlow
during Monks's public confession (51: 345).

Late in both novels, we realize that the two young victims, despite
their weakness, have ironically brought about the defeat of the villains. Sympathy for Oliver induces Nancy to eavesdrop twice on
Fagin and Monks (26: 178–79; 39: 261–62; 40: 268–69), and her revelations to Rose and Brownlow (46: 308–09) make possible the discovery of Oliver's identity and also lead to the murder of Nancy herself
and the subsequent destruction of Fagin and his gang. As the crazed
Fagin, in the death cell, remarks of Oliver when the boy visits, "He
has been the—the—somehow the cause of all this" (52: 355). In
Nicholas Nickleby Ralph Nickleby is undone because of Smike, his
own lost son, for Ralph's desire to harm Nicholas by taking Smike
from him (34: 420) induces the villain to enlist the services of Snawley to pose as Smike's father; later, Snawley, to assure his own
safety, accuses Ralph (59: 729). Ralph's other major scheme, involving the marriage of the old miser Arthur Gride to young Madeline
Bray, has been thwarted through eavesdropping comparable to
Nancy's, done in this case by Newman Noggs (47: 577–86; 51:
638–39); for Nicholas, informed of the plot by Noggs, has a confrontation with Bray (53: 655–57) that may well be a contributing cause
of the latter's sudden death. Although Noggs eavesdrops only once
on his employer, he later gains added information when he is able
to read Ralph's confidential letter to Gride (51: 634).

The extraordinary number of parallels suggests that, for Dickens,
Oliver and Smike are nearly the same character. Of course, Smike
does bear permanent damage from being abused—a limp, slowness
of intellect, problems with memory—while Oliver emerges unscathed; and Smike dies, while Oliver lives. But in each novel we
find a complementary surrogate: little Dick dies in place of Oliver;
Nicholas triumphs in Smike's stead. Just as Oliver at the end of the
story enjoys peaceful security in a rural area where the home of his
adoptive father, Mr. Brownlow, is "within a mile of the parsonage-
house" inhabited by Rose and Harry Maylie and Harry's mother
(53: 357), so Smike is buried in a churchyard near the home later
reacquired by Nicholas (58: 712), who lives there with Madeline,
and "within a stone's-throw" is "another retreat," that of Kate and
her husband, Frank Cheeryble (65: 777).[2] In each book, Dickens appears to have wanted to blend tragic pathos and triumphant resil-
ience in one character but to have decided that decomposition was

a more suitable technique—little Dick and Oliver, Smike and Nicholas. Although Steven Marcus comments, "In Smike on the one hand and Nicholas on the other, a life such as Oliver Twist's is divided into its principal components" (121), Oliver's life also, as I have suggested, appears to be split, with little Dick serving as a tragic surrogate for the protagonist. In addition, one further intriguing likeness between Oliver and Nicholas deserves attention. Just as Oliver resists attempts to make him a pickpocket, so in another sense does Nicholas, for the latter decries the practices of hack playwrights who adapt "the uncompleted books of living authors": Nicholas claims to see no difference "between such pilfering as this, and picking a man's pocket in the street" (48: 598).

The most significant similarities, however, are between Oliver and Smike. But perhaps even more important than these parallels are the resemblances to be seen in the underlying causes of the two characters' respective stories and in the ways in which these details come to light. Late in each narrative, a villain's confession provides important revelations. In *Oliver Twist*, after Nancy tells the information gleaned from her eavesdropping to Rose and Brownlow, the latter intimidates Monks into describing the events that led to Agnes Fleming's giving birth to Oliver in a workhouse, while in *Nicholas Nickleby* the return of the transported convict Brooker and his becoming acquainted with Noggs, Ralph's disaffected clerk, bring about the novel's dénouement. In the resolutions of the two novels, significant assistance is provided by the future husbands of Rose Maylie and Kate Nickleby: Harry Maylie helps in the hunt for Sikes after Nancy's murder (49: 331; 50: 337–38), and Frank Cheeryble aids Noggs in obtaining the will Squeers has received from Peg Sliderskew, who stole it from Arthur Gride (57: 707–10).

In each novel the reasons for the early sufferings of the young male victim—Oliver and Smike, respectively—are disclosed only very late in the narrative. Not until *Oliver Twist* is approximately 90% over do we start to get a clear sense of the secrets behind the tale, when Brownlow for the first time describes the troubled marriage of his friend Edwin Leeford, Monks's father, the subsequent affair Edwin Leeford had with Agnes Fleming, and the providential discovery of Oliver, the issue of this liaison (49: 326–28). Then Brownlow coerces Monks into agreeing to divulge what he knows (49: 329–31), but these extremely complex revelations are presented only in the novel's following monthly installment (51: 343–48). Robert Tracy remarks that by the time "we do hear the story of Oliver's parentage . . . it does not really seem to have very much to do with the novel we have been reading" (1).

The mystery of Oliver's birth, however, has been introduced in the novel's first chapter, in the remark of Mrs. Thingummy (Old Sally) about Agnes Fleming: "where she came from, or where she was going to, nobody knows" (1: 19). Our interest in this matter is then sustained by a long series of details, introduced at various points in the narrative: conjectural references by Bumble, Noah Claypole, and Mrs. Bedwin to Oliver's mother, the portrait in Brownlow's home, a picture that Oliver resembles and is strangely attracted to, Old Sally's deathbed confession, the appearance of Monks and his purchase of the gold locket from Mr. and Mrs. Bumble, and Nancy's disclosures to Rose and Brownlow of the statements overheard during eavesdropping on conversations between Monks and Fagin. Dickens, therefore, especially by his use of the portrait owned by Brownlow and of the strange behavior of Monks, keeps the mystery of Oliver's birth almost continually before us, while delaying a clear explanation. When Mr. Losberne seeks to persuade Mrs. Maylie's servants, Giles and Brittles, that Oliver was not the boy who participated in the attempt to break into the house, the doctor asserts, "It's a simple question of identity" (30: 201). Taken in another sense, this comment describes the central problem of the novel.

When we do learn Oliver's story, we realize that the originating event behind it was the forcing of Edwin Leeford, when he was not even twenty, to marry a woman chosen by his father (49: 326–27). After the separation of Leeford from his wife, who was ten years his senior, he fell in love with Agnes Fleming, to whom he promised marriage (51: 343–44). Because of Leeford's premature death, however, and his wife's destruction of his will and concealment of a letter to Agnes (51: 344), the latter was left alone to face the consequences of her pregnancy and ran away, seeking "to die near the grave of the father of the child" (51: 346), since she had evidently learned of her lover's death. Although Leeford died in Rome (49: 327), he was buried, we assume, in England, and Agnes learned, perhaps through newspaper accounts (but this is not made clear), of the site of his grave. Through the malice of Leeford's estranged wife, the legitimacy of Rose, Agnes's younger sister, was called into question after her father's death from grief, and the girl was saved from wretchedness only when Mrs. Maylie saw her "by chance, pitied her, and took her home" (51: 347–48).

Interestingly, Harry Maylie receives a gentle admonition from his mother, who cautions that if he were to marry Rose the "stain" of her supposed illegitimacy might "one day" lead him to have regrets (34: 226). Mrs. Maylie's advice, however, should be distinguished from coercive interference by parents or their surrogates in a young person's marital choice. Harry does face such interference, for, as Rose remarks, he has "powerful connexions" who "can help men in public life," but are "proud" and would resent an alliance with her (35: 236). When Mr. Losberne later refers to Harry's wealthy relatives as "the great nobs," Harry mentions his "most stately uncle" (36: 237). We learn only later that the reason Oliver's father, Edwin Leeford, was "forced" into a "wretched marriage" was to increase the "importance" of "rich relations" (49: 326–27). Unlike Edwin Leeford, however, Harry eventually defies his "relatives of influence and rank," renounces his political aspirations, and chooses to become a country parson in order to persuade Rose to accept him (51: 349).

Discussing Chapter 51 of *Oliver Twist*, a chapter in which Oliver's and Rose's true identities are revealed, S. J. Newman suggests that the sentence, "A father, sister, and mother, were gained, and lost, in that one moment" (51: 348), carries "unmistakeable echoes" of Shakespeare's *The Winter's Tale*, a play presenting in its last scenes the restorations of Perdita and Hermione (Newman 43). We may add to Newman's observation the point that in *Oliver Twist* the narrator's following comment, "Joy and grief were mingled in the cup" (51: 348), evokes recollections of the emphasis in *The Winter's Tale* on the mingling of "joy" and "sorrow" (5.2.15–19, 43–46, 72–76). Dickens, as Newman observes, had seen his friend William Charles Macready perform in a production of this drama in September 1837 (Newman 43). I would propose, however, that *Oliver Twist* also appears to show the influence of Shakespeare's play in other respects that Newman does not discuss. Just as Shakespeare's Florizel is willing to relinquish his position as heir apparent in order to marry Perdita, so Harry Maylie chooses to abandon his hopes for a political career so that he can gain Rose. Both Perdita and Rose have been adopted, Rose by Mrs. Maylie, whom she regards as an "aunt" (30: 198), Perdita by the old Shepherd, whom the young woman considers her father. This elderly man mistakenly believes that Perdita is illegitimate (3.3.71–76), while Rose's legitimacy has been falsely questioned by Monks's mother (51: 347). Perdita is eventually identified by tokens, items left with her when she was abandoned as an infant (3.3.114–22), while proof of Oliver's identity depends on the locket and ring left by his dying mother (51: 345–46).

Other points of similarity between the novel and the play also deserve attention. Early and late in *The Winter's Tale* we find interest in close facial resemblance between parent and child: Leontes seeks to reassure himself of his young son Mamillius's legitimacy by referring again and again to the boy's likeness to himself (1.2.121-22, 128–30, 134–35, 153–60, 208), while in the final act of the play Leontes notices Prince Florizel's resemblance to King Polixenes (5.1.124–29), while the Third Gentleman, describing the discovery of Perdita's identity, mentions "the majesty of the creature [Perdita] in resemblance of the mother [Hermione]" (5.2.35–36). Old Sally, before she dies, observes that Oliver grew very much "like his mother" (24: 165), and we have already noted the boy's resemblance to the woman in the portrait, who is later revealed to be his mother. But Oliver, as Burton M. Wheeler (53–54) and Goldie Morgentaler (40–43) notice, also looks very much like his father, since only such a close resemblance could account for the ability of Monks to identify a youngster whom he has never previously seen (26: 179; 40: 268; 49: 329). The inheritance of facial features from both parents explains, too, Brownlow's earlier feeling of having seen "something like that look before" (11: 76): Brownlow may be recalling the features of Agnes in the portrait, or of his dead fiancée, Edwin Leeford's sister, or of Leeford himself, since the latter, Brownlow later remarks, "had his sister's soul and person" (49: 327).

Then, too, in *The Winter's Tale* Antigonus, just before he abandons Perdita, addresses the infant and describes a vision he has had of her mother, Hermione:

> I have heard (but not believ'd) the spirits o' th' dead
> May walk again. If such thing be, thy mother
> Appear'd to me last night; for ne'er was dream
> So like a waking. . . .
>   (3.3.16–19)

In *Oliver Twist* the narrator, in his final paragraph, reports that in the village church "stands a white marble tablet" bearing Agnes's name, comments, "There is no coffin in that tomb," and then adds,

> But, if the spirits of the Dead ever come back to earth, to visit spots hallowed by the love—the love beyond the grave—of those whom they knew in life, I believe that the shade of Agnes sometimes hovers round that solemn nook.   (53: 360)

Some of these similarities are common to many romances and melodramas, but one additional resemblance between *The Winter's Tale* and *Oliver Twist* seems very much worth considering. In the penultimate scene of the former, the First Gentleman, while describing how the old Shepherd told Leontes and Polixenes of the discovery years before of Perdita, remarks, "I make a broken delivery of the business" (5.2.9). Certainly, Dickens's narrator in *Oliver Twist* makes "a broken delivery"—an interrupted presentation—in telling how the backgrounds of Oliver and Rose are discovered. In Chapters 49 and 51, we find a complex interweaving of details offered by Brownlow, Monks, and the two old women (Anny and Martha) that attended the dying Old Sally, a workhouse inmate who had been present years before when Oliver's mother died. The indirect, fragmented, and protracted revelations by different characters increase the complexity of the tale of Edwin Leeford's unhappy marriage, separation from his wife, affair with Agnes Fleming, unexpected death, and destroyed testament. Indeed, the obfuscatory manner of narration creates a sense that arcane, deeply hidden secrets are being gradually and with great difficulty brought to light. Dianne F. Sadoff, who calls attention to Dickens's "intense curiosity about origins" (11), asserts, "his narrative structures seek ... the father's secret of the son's birth" (11).

In *Nicholas Nickleby* the causal events behind the plight of Smike and also the narrative technique employed seem very similar to those in the prior novel. The initiating actions underlying Smike's story are not described until the novel is about 95% completed, but, as in *Oliver Twist*, the reader has been made aware of the mystery early in the novel and has been reminded very frequently of this matter. Shortly after Smike first appears, Nicholas notices the youngster's eager interest in whether any mail has been received concerning him and Squeers's reply, "Not a word," to which the schoolmaster adds, "and never will be," followed by the comment that many years have passed with no message regarding the boy (7: 90). We later learn that this eighteen- or nineteen-year-old (7: 90) has been at Dotheboys Hall ever since he was, in his own words, "a little child, younger than any that are here now" (8: 105), and that Smike recalls no comforting prior home (8: 106), an anticipation of his later cry to Nicholas, "You are my home" (13: 162). In the sixth monthly installment, the mystery of Smike's origin is emphasized by Nicholas's remark about the boy to Ralph, "I would that I knew on whom he has the claim of birth" (20: 247), a statement that becomes bitterly ironic when Smike's identity is finally revealed in the novel's concluding double-installment. As the narrative progresses, we find, in the seventh monthly number, Smike's dim recollection that before being sent to Squeers's school he "slept in . . . a large lonesome room at the top of a house, where there was a trapdoor in the ceiling," a room that returns to him in "terrible dreams" (22: 268). In the eleventh installment, Squeers tells Ralph that Smike had been at Dotheboys Hall for fourteen years, having arrived at the age of five or six and being kept without payments after "six or eight" years (34: 419–20). Still later, the fraudulent claim of Snawley that he is Smike's father is supported by Ralph's fictitious statement about a false account of the youngster's death (45: 557–59). Ralph's fabrication about a deceiving estranged wife ironically foreshadows his later discovery that long ago his alienated clerk, Brooker, created a false report of Smike's death (60: 738–39).[3] Before this revelation, the declining Smike, who has been taken by Nicholas to Devonshire, has told of seeing the man who brought him years before to Dotheboys Hall (58: 713–15), and after Brooker's confession Ralph hangs himself in the garret that had haunted his son (62: 754). Throughout *Nickleby*, various details like these do not allow us to forget the mystery of Smike's origin.

In the story told by Brooker, we receive an explanation of the circumstances that enabled this man to succeed in vindictively depriving Ralph of his son. We learn that Ralph had married secretly, since his wife, by "a clause in her father's will," would lose the property left to her should she marry "without her brother's consent," a consent that would have to be purchased (60: 737–38). When Smike was born, he was sent away, presumably to preserve the secret of his parents' marriage (60: 738), and when Ralph, because of greed, refused the urging of his wife that they reveal their relationship, she eventually "eloped with a younger man" (60: 738). Brooker, who had been mistreated by Ralph, took Smike to Yorkshire and falsely reported the boy's death as part of a plan to extort money from Ralph at some future time (60: 739).

Just as Oliver's early distresses arose because his paternal grandfather compelled Edwin Leeford to marry a woman who proved entirely incompatible, so Smike's suffering and early death are attributable to a clause in the will of his maternal grandfather. It was this will that led Smike's father, Ralph Nickleby, to insist on keeping his marriage a secret. Moreover, just as the causes of Oliver's story are offered to us only very late in the novel and in a very disjointed fashion, so the background describing Smike's abandonment is revealed only near the conclusion of *Nicholas Nickleby* and, although presented just by one character rather than by several, as is the case in *Oliver Twist*, this explanation is nevertheless also related in a distracting way. Brooker has appeared or been mentioned in earlier chapters, yet his importance has never before been clearly indicated (44: 539–43, 550; 51: 636–37). Furthermore, our attention has been diverted by such matters as the death of Walter Bray (which saves Madeline), the demise of Smike, and Ralph's plotting about the deed of bequest that Gride has withheld from Madeline, a document subsequently stolen by Peg Sliderskew, then given by her to Squeers, from whom it is taken by Frank Cheeryble and Newman Noggs. Only after all of these events do we hear Brooker's tale. In both *Oliver* and *Nickleby*, therefore, a mysterious villain—Monks in one book, Brooker in the other—eventually discloses the hidden background, while admitting his own criminal actions that caused the truth to be so long concealed—for over twelve years in the case of Oliver (37: 245) and for fourteen years in that of Smike (60: 739). In each novel the contorted disclosure adds suspense and realism, but may seem annoyingly confusing.

As we observed previously, in *Oliver Twist* the younger generation—represented by Harry Maylie and Rose—does not suffer because of interference by parents or surrogates, since Harry willingly abandons a political career to gain freedom. In *Nicholas Nickleby* the younger generation also escapes harm from interference when the opportune death of Walter Bray prevents him from inducing his daughter Madeline to sacrifice herself by marrying the odious miser Arthur Gride. In each book the parents of a boy or young man—Oliver and Smike—have been severely damaged by familial interference, and the youthful victim suffers greatly; but in each novel some members of the younger generation—Rose and Frank, Madeline and Nicholas—are spared. Moreover, both Oliver and Nicholas—a surrogate for Smike in gaining triumph over adversity—are assisted by benevolent parental figures: Mr. Brownlow adopts Oliver (53: 357), while the Cheeryble brothers act as fathers to Nicholas. Interestingly, both Brownlow and Charles Cheeryble have experienced extreme sorrow in love, the former having watched his fiancée, the older sister of Edwin Leeford, who would later become Oliver's father, die on the morning of the day they were to have been married (49: 325), and the latter having been rejected by the woman he loved when she chose Walter Bray, who would become Madeline's father (46: 565–66). In addition, Charles reveals that his brother Ned (Edwin) was engaged to this woman's sister, "but she died" (46: 565). We assuredly get the sense that neither Brownlow nor either of the Cheeryble brothers has ever fully recovered from his loss and that each man's suffering has served to increase his compassion for others. Moreover, the age and celibacy of each benefactor seem to remove him as a possible competitor in any Oedipal struggle.

In each novel, too, the actions of a character hostile to the young sufferer ironically lead to the disclosure of the latter's identity. Monks, who recognized Oliver by chance on the day the boy accompanied the Dodger and Charley Bates, is led by hatred not only to pay Fagin to corrupt the boy (51: 345) but also to search out Bumble in hopes of finding tokens that can be destroyed (37: 243–47). But Monks's success in this venture backfires, since his boasting to Fagin, overheard by Nancy, is reported to Rose and Brownlow and enables them to establish Oliver's identity and to learn the contents of Edwin Leeford's destroyed will. In *Nicholas Nickleby* Ralph extends his hostility from Nicholas to Smike, but the villain's refusal to assist the impoverished returned convict, Brooker, leads the latter to confide in Newman Noggs, who thereby gains assurance that Snawley's claim to be Smike's father is false (44: 550; 59: 727). Moreover, Brooker , now remorseful, indicates to Noggs a willingness to testify (59: 727).

While Newman, as we have observed, sees the influence of *The Winter's Tale* on *Oliver Twist*, we may also notice possible traces of another Shakespearean romance, *Cymbeline*, in both *Oliver* and *Nicholas Nickleby*. In May 1837, when Chapters 7–8 of *Oliver Twist* were published, Macready, whom Dickens had not yet met, appeared as Posthumus in a production of *Cymbeline* (Macready 1: 394), and while there is no record that Dickens attended a performance, his lifelong devotion to theater-going make this at least a possibility. Even if he did not, Dickens, because of his intense interest in Shakespeare, perhaps had read the play or seen another production.

In *Cymbeline* Belarius's vindictive abduction and concealment for twenty years of Cymbeline's sons may have suggested Brooker's kidnapping of Smike. Moreover, the theme of parental interference in marital selection is prominent both in *The Winter's Tale*, in which Polixenes objects to his son Florizel's engagement to Perdita, and in *Cymbeline*, in which the title-figure refuses to accept his daughter Imogen's marriage to Posthumus. In addition, details at the end of *Cymbeline* may be reflected in *Oliver Twist*. In the final act of Shakespeare's play, the imprisoned Posthumus has a dream in which the ghosts of his dead parents and dead brothers appear and ask assistance for him from Jupiter, who offers reassurance.

Dickens's Oliver, also a posthumous child, tells Mrs. Bedwin that he at times feels as if his dead mother has sat by him during his illness and, "if she knew" of his condition, "must have pitied" him (12: 82). Furthermore, in *Cymbeline* the physician Cornelius, late in the play, informs Cymbeline that his queen, whose malicious behavior was designed to aid her son, has died (5.5.25–27, 31–33): this despairing death seems to resemble the demise of Monks's mother (51: 344–45).

I suggest, too, that there is significance in the fact that Nicholas and Smike excel for Vincent Crummles in a production of *Romeo and Juliet*, the most famous case in British literature of parental interference in marital choice. Like Shakespeare's young lovers, Nicholas and Madeline Bray appear to fall in love at first sight—certainly, Nicholas does—and the couple seems to be "star-cross'd," doomed because of Walter Bray's selfishness. This motif of parental intrusion is also not only noteworthy in such other Shakespearean plays as *A Midsummer Night's Dream, Hamlet*, and *Othello*, but is prevalent, too, in nineteenth-century melodrama: in *Nicholas Nickleby* Vincent Crummles's company includes an "elderly gentleman . . . who played the irascible old men—those funny fellows who have nephews in the army, and perpetually run about with thick sticks to compel them to marry heiresses" (23: 285), and in *Great Expectations* Pip sees Wopsle perform in various roles, including that of an enchanter assisting young lovers that suffer "on account of the parental brutality of an ignorant farmer who opposed the choice of his daughter's heart" (47: 287).

For Dickens, this theme—of parental interference or estrangement resulting from defiance of such intrusion—exercises an unusual fascination. Ross H. Dabney has perceptively examined Dickens's obsessive concern in many of his novels with mercenary marriage as a source of overwhelming distress for a child and has observed that for Dickens this kind of wedlock emerges as "a kind of central figure of evil" (30). Considering forced marriages, Dabney cogently maintains, "What Dickens evidently dislikes and fears in the relationship between parents and children is the fact of power, the near-absolute authority of one person over another's life" (158). Dabney examines a number of the examples that I wish to adduce, but we should notice that while a mercenary goal is, for Dickens, the most frequent reason for intrusion by a parent or surrogate, such a motive is not the only one.

Even in Dickens's first book, *Sketches by Boz*, we find instances of this theme of interference in marital choice. In "The Boarding-House. Chapter I" Mr. Simpson is disinherited for marrying without his father's approval (337). In "Sentiment" Mr. Cornelius Brook Dingwall, Esq., M.P., tries to end his daughter Lavinia's interest in "a person much her inferior in life" (378) by sending her to a finishing school, but finds the plan thwarted when the suitor appears by chance at a ball at the school and persuades Lavinia to elope. The adventure recounted in "The Great Winglebury Duel" begins when Alexander Trott is commanded by his father to marry Emily Brown (468); and "A Passage in the Life of Mr. Watkins Tottle" includes a report of a young couple who marry against their fathers' wishes and are made to undergo great suffering when the husband is disinherited by his own father and arrested at the secret instigation of his father-in-law (518).

Although *Pickwick Papers* is devoted to a protagonist who is an elderly bachelor, we again see the situation of family intrusion in marital choice emerge frequently. A hint appears in the first monthly number when Mr. Jingle, asked about his amatory "conquests" in Spain, refers to the death of Donna Christina as a result of the jealousy of her father, who subsequently commits suicide (2: 81). In "A Madman's Manuscript," appearing in Chapter 11, part of the fourth monthly installment, the mad narrator gleefully describes the destruction of his bride, the daughter of an "old white-headed father" and the sister of "three proud overbearing brothers," relations who compelled her to marry for wealth, even though she loved another, a "dark-eyed boy" (11: 221). In the sixth monthly number, another interpolated tale, "The Parish Clerk: A Tale of True Love," recounts how wealthy old Lobbs, the father of pretty Maria, a man disposed to be possessive of his daughter, is induced to accept her engagement to her cousin, a suitor of whom he had previously disapproved (17: 310–16). Still another inserted story, "The Old Man's Tale about the Queer Client," reveals the revenge of an imprisoned debtor, George Heyling, who has been left to suffer and watch his wife and child die because of his own father's refusal of help and the hostility of his father-in-law, who had him arrested (21: 371). That the behavior of the two fathers reflects their unexplained disapproval of their children's marriage certainly seems probable, even though this point is not made explicitly. One other interpolated tale, "The True Legend of Prince Bladud," considers the tragic problems arising when the father of the prince attempts to choose a bride for his son, who has "privately contracted himself" to another woman (36: 598), while the last of these inserted narratives, "The Story of the Bagman's Uncle," tells of the prevention of a forced marriage, although the promoters of this marriage do not seem to be the lady's parents.

Although all of these examples from the interpolated tales are extremely brief and lacking in detail, two other cases in *Pickwick Papers* involving this theme of interference are developed in a much fuller way: first, the attempt of Ben Allen, who considers himself the "natural protector and guardian" of his sister Arabella (38: 626), to induce her to marry his friend Bob Sawyer, despite her interest in Mr. Winkle; second, the anger of the latter's father on learning that his son has married without first obtaining parental consent. Fortunately, Mr. Pickwick succeeds in persuading Ben to accept his sister's marriage, but, at first, the elder Mr. Winkle seems unwilling to grant approval to his son's bride, despite Pickwick's pleas (50: 805–08), and there is the real danger that he will withhold the financial support on which his son depends and not provide the "worldly advantages" that otherwise would have been given (56: 889). In the novel's penultimate chapter, however, Winkle's father interviews Arabella without divulging his identity and then expresses enthusiastic acceptance (56: 888–91). Pickwick, despite his initial lack of success while speaking with the elder Winkle, has acted as a benevolent father, an enabler who offers financial help to the young couple (53: 837), rather than a denier, and this positive role is emphasized by his remark that he is "old enough to be the father" of both Arabella and young Winkle (39: 643) and the observation by the lawyer Perker that Winkle's father "had good right and title to consider Mr Pickwick as in some degree the guardian and adviser of his son" (47: 759). Because of the dominant comic tone of *Pickwick Papers*, harmful parental interference or estrangement is avoided, except in some of the interpolated tales, but the threat that intrusion or disinheritance may harm Arabella and Nathaniel Winkle is found in seven of the last ten numbers, and, of course, we observe a case of benevolent intervention by a surrogate parent early in the narrative when Mr. Wardle halts the elopement of his sister Rachael with Mr. Jingle.

In other Dickens novels, this motif of problems caused by intervention by parents or their surrogates in marital choice appears repeatedly. In *Barnaby Rudge* Sir John Chester and his enemy Geoffrey Haredale oppose the love of the former's son Edward and the latter's niece and ward Emma, and Sir John remarks that his own brother came to hold "low and disobedient sentiments," presumably regarding the choice of a mate, and was therefore disinherited by their father, "led a miserable life . . . and died early" (32: 312). In *Dombey and Son* Mrs. Skewton has no compunctions about inducing her daughter Edith to marry Mr. Dombey for his wealth. In *David*

Copperfield we learn that Wickfield's wife died prematurely because of anguish over the estrangement from her father caused by her marriage, while Spenlow objects to David's wooing of Dora. In *Little Dorrit* Gilbert Clennam chose a wife for his nephew, Arthur Clennam's father, and so prevented him from marrying the young woman who gave birth to Arthur, and, much later, this prescribed wife, who assumed the role of mother to Arthur, joined with Mr. Casby, the father of Flora, to keep the young people from marrying. In the same novel, a minor detail reveals that one legendary explanation of the name "Bleeding Heart Yard" describes the sad death of "a young lady . . . closely imprisoned in her chamber by a cruel father for remaining true to her own true love, and refusing to marry the suitor he chose for her" (1: 12: 176), and we learn that Mrs. Merdle pays Fanny Dorrit to discourage the attentions of the former's son, Edmund Sparkler. In *Our Mutual Friend* the fathers of both male protagonists, John Harmon and Eugene Wrayburn, seek to select wives for their sons, while Harmon's older sister was disowned by their father for not accepting the husband he designated for her (1: 2: 24). And in *The Mystery of Edwin Drood* the engagement of Edwin Drood and Rosa Bud has been arranged by their respective fathers.

Although this theme was an extremely common one in the nineteenth century, Dickens's interest in it seems unusually strong, and we may wonder if he was in any way responding to personal experience, since there is a tradition in Dickens biography asserting that Maria Beadnell's parents objected to his courtship of their daughter. But the evidence for this belief appears questionable. Some letters from Dickens to Henry William Kolle, who eventually married Maria Beadnell's sister Anne, indicate that this young man at times delivered secret letters from Dickens to Maria, but, as Michael Slater remarks, while "this clandestine correspondence" was perhaps a sign that Maria's parents disapproved of Dickens's courtship of their daughter, it may, on the other hand, "have been only a whim of Maria's" (*Dickens and Women* 51). Although the story that the Beadnells sent Maria away to finishing school in Paris to separate her from Dickens is mentioned by J. W. T. Ley in his edition of Forster's biography (1: 3: 54[n. 69]), by Edgar Johnson (1: 60, 72), and by Madeline House and Graham Storey (PL 1: 16 [n. 2]), Slater states that there is no evidence of Maria's being at school in Paris "during 1831/2 but we do know that she was there much earlier, in April 1830" (*Dickens and Women* 51). Dickens himself, however, in a letter to Maria, then Mrs. Winter, in 1855, refers to his having felt his "whole Being blighted, by the Angel of my soul being sent there [to Paris] to finish her education" (PL 7: 534 [10 Feb. 1855]). Of course, a young man refused by a woman may seek comfort in the belief that her parents, rather than the beloved one herself, decided against him. Nevertheless, if the Beadnells did interfere, Dickens appears to have restrained himself from displaying any feelings of resentment, for, as both Fred Kaplan and Slater notice, after the end of the courtship he maintained a cordial correspondence with Mr. Beadnell (Kaplan 562 [n. 30]; Slater, *Dickens and Women* 61). Moreover, Dickens's letters to Maria blame the young woman herself for the end of their relationship, since he refers to her "heartless indifference," her "kindness and encouragement one day and a total change of conduct the next," and her "*unkind* words and *cold* looks" (PL 1: 17 [18 Mar. [1833]], 24 [16 May 1833]). Finally, in a letter sent on August 2, 1845, to Thomas Powell, with whom he once was friendly, Dickens mentions an early romantic attachment of his own lasting "six or seven long years"—surely a reference to the courtship of Maria and an exaggeration of its length—and comments, "If anyone had interfered with my very small Cupid, I don't know what absurdity I might have committed in assertion of his proper liberty; but having plenty of rope he hanged himself, beyond all chance of restoration" (PL 4: 346). If Dickens did think that the Beadnells had interrupted his wooing, this letter maintains the contrary.[4]

Nevertheless, Dickens's strong interest in the theme of parental intrusion in marital choice may be attributable to factors other than the influence of Shakespeare and nineteenth-century melodrama. As Northrop Frye, among many critics, has observed, a situation in which a father or father-surrogate frustrates the amatory desires of a young man by either prohibiting a desired alliance or ordering an unwanted one is "a formula" derived from the "plot structure of Greek New Comedy, as transmitted by Plautus and Terence" (163). Edwin M. Eigner has interestingly examined Dickens's response to pantomime, a form derived from New Comedy and including Pantaloon, the "mischievous old lecher, who represents patriarchal authority and the corrupt hierarchy" (*The Dickens Pantomime* 69). Writing long before Frye and Eigner, the psychoanalyst Ludwig Jekels saw comedy as basically an "inversion" of tragedy: "*the feeling of guilt which, in tragedy, rests upon the son, appears in comedy displaced on the father*" (97). For Jekels, both tragedy and comedy present "the Oedipus situation" (102), but in comedy we find an "infantile phantasy of the father as the disturber of love," a forbidder (103). This image, however, is, in Jekels's opinion, "nothing but a projection of the son's own guilty wish to disturb the love of the parents" (103). Certainly, the father's forbidding a son to espouse a woman of his own choice and / or ordering an undesired marriage may be regarded as a version of the Oedipal conflict. Anny Sadrin, in a study that sees "the interrelation of parentage and inheritance" as "central to most" of Dickens's novels (4), suggests that each of these "inheritance plots" is a tale of a character who is both "piously filial and . . . parricidal," "part Oedipus, part Telemachus," "a guilt-ridden" figure torn between "his loyalty and his defiance" (150).

The Oedipus complex, however, seems reflected not only in the theme of parental interference, but also in two other features that commentators on Freud's studies have noticed: first, the ambivalence felt towards both father and mother (Green 32, 187; Rudnytsky 258–59), and, second, the fusion of love and death—a linking "that inheres in the original act of incest" and is seen in the "confounding of the opposites of death and sexuality [that] pervades *Antigone*" (Rudnytsky 281). These two features—ambivalence towards each parent (reflected in decomposition, the balancing of good parents or surrogates with bad ones) and the fusion of love and death—figure prominently in many of Dickens's novels, especially *Oliver* and *Nickleby*.

In the former novel, the protagonist is subject to the power of such bad "fathers" as Fagin and Bill Sikes, the latter being mistaken for Oliver's father by a man with a cart (21: 147), while the boy eventually is adopted by a good "father," Mr. Brownlow, who is called the "old gentleman" when we first meet him (10: 72), an epithet inviting comparison and contrast with Fagin, whom the Dodger first described as "a 'spectable old genelman" (8: 63). The novel, moreover, presents many "mothers" for Oliver: Agnes Fleming, whom the boy has dreamed of, believing that she had a "sweet and happy" face (12: 82), may be considered a good mother, yet one who, in a sense, betrayed Oliver by dying; Nancy, who poses as an elder sister to kidnap Oliver, is initially a bad mother-surrogate, but later becomes a benevolent, truly maternal protector, shielding the youngster from Fagin and then giving Rose Maylie and Brownlow information of crucial value in helping the child regain his identity;[5] Mrs. Mann, the name obviously signifying the absence of female nurturing qualities, is the bad "mother" to whom Oliver is "farmed" out after his birth, while her opposites are Mrs. Bedwin, Brownlow's kindly housekeeper, and Mrs. Maylie. Another bad "parent" who acts unkindly to Oliver is Mrs. Sowerberry, the undertaker's shrewish spouse; and the wife of Edwin Leeford, Oliver's father, although she never meets the boy, serves as his wicked stepmother, since she destroys a will that would have assisted him and conceals a letter that would have helped his mother, Agnes Fleming.[6]

In *Nicholas Nickleby* the main villain, Ralph Nickleby, and his cohort Squeers serve as bad "fathers" to both Smike and Nicholas, while Mr. Crummles may be regarded as a well-meaning parent. The Cheeryble brothers virtually adopt Nicholas and are, of course, exemplars of generosity, while Walter Bray, whose daughter Nicholas seeks to marry, is utterly reprehensible. As a mother, Mrs. Nickleby is ludicrously inadequate, failing to see the danger posed to Kate by Sir Mulberry Hawk and offering Nicholas no sensible advice. The actual mother of Smike is kept from him, presumably because of Ralph's desire to conceal the marriage, and this woman, by eloping, deserts not only Ralph but her son, while Mrs. Squeers, whom her husband calls "a mother" to the boys at the school (4: 45), is another wicked stepmother figure. Only Mrs. Crummles may be seen as a positive maternal surrogate for Smike or Nicholas, and her role is extremely limited. The more prominent evil surrogate parents in each book face retribution: three die by being hanged—Fagin in an execution, Sikes in an accident, and Ralph Nickleby in a suicide—while Bumble is disgraced and Squeers is transported.

In a valuable discussion of Alberto Cavalcanti's 1947 film adaptation of *Nicholas Nickleby*, Sylvia Manning points out that in the motion picture Ralph himself, not Arthur Gride, seeks to marry Madeline Bray and becomes "the sexual marauder" (54). Manning sees the film as therefore offering "a more thorough inversion of the Oedipal struggle," since "the father (uncle) . . . threatens to take the son's rightful bride" (54).

Also evident in both *Oliver Twist* and *Nicholas Nickleby* are various instances of links between sexuality and death. For example, we have already referred to the death of Brownlow's fiancée on the morning of the marriage day, and to the premature death of Edwin Leeford, Oliver's father, which prevented him from fulfilling his hope of marrying Agnes Fleming. In addition, the marriage of Rose and Harry Maylie is preceded by the brutal murder of Nancy, and Keith Hollingsworth believes that Rose has been "allowed" by Dickens "to recover" from her nearly fatal illness because "Nancy dies in her place" (123). Interestingly, both women may be seen as Oliver's "sisters": Nancy, as we have just observed, poses as his sister in abducting him, and Oliver himself, at the end of the novel, affirms that he will regard Rose not as his aunt but as his "sister" (51: 348). The wedding of Harry Maylie and Rose also seems tied to the death, more than a dozen years before, of Agnes Fleming, since Rose's acceptance of Harry comes only several pages after the revelation that Agnes undertook her final journey in an effort "to die near the grave of the father" of Oliver (51: 346). Moreover, in the opening paragraph of Chapter 17 in *Oliver Twist* the narrator notices the frequency of such juxtapositions when he refers to the theatrical "custom . . . in all good murderous melodramas" of presenting "the tragic and the comic scenes, in as regular alternation, as the layers of red and white in a side of streaky, well-cured bacon," and then later comments, "The transitions in real life from well-spread boards to death-beds, and from mourning weeds to holiday garments, are not a whit less startling" (17: 117–18).

In *Nicholas Nickleby*, besides the Crummles troupe's performance of *Romeo and Juliet*, a play in which the Capulets' "wedding cheer" is turned—first, supposedly, and then, actually—into "a sad burial feast" (4.5.87), we find Ralph stating, just prior to Gride's planned wedding with Madeline, "One would think that there was a funeral going on here, and not a wedding" (54: 669), words that ominously foreshadow Walter Bray's sudden death, a demise that prevents his daughter's marriage. A few pages later, Bray tells of a prophetic dream in which he prepares to lead Madeline to her wedding with Gride, but instead falls into a grave (54: 671).[7]

Still another Oedipal feature may be seen in Dickens's fascination in many of his novels with relationships hinting at brother-sister incest. As Harry Stone observes, the fact that Dickens's own sister Fanny served for a time as a mother-substitute may have stimulated his obsession with the sister-wife figure ("The Love Pattern" 5–7). Stone writes, "Rose Fleming, the foster-sister of Oliver, and his aunt, as it turns out, marries Harry Maylie, whose foster-sister—to compound the pattern—is the very same Rose; Kate Nickleby, the sister of Nicholas, marries Frank Cheeryble" ("The Love Pattern" 10). What Stone has in mind here is that the Cheeryble brothers have virtually adopted Nicholas, with Kate therefore indirectly gaining the status of a foster-daughter of theirs, while their nephew Frank, as Nicholas remarks, is regarded by them "as a son" (55: 686). We may also add that in both *Oliver* and *Nickleby* there are further convolutions of this incest motif. Harry Maylie can be seen as a surrogate for Oliver in expressing romantic desire for Rose, for the boy, who, at the age of twelve (37: 245), is nearing puberty, is asked by Harry to observe Rose (and Mrs. Maylie) and secretly to write reports to be sent "once a fortnight" to Harry (36: 238). In a sense, Oliver and Harry are to be each other's representatives, and, as we have noticed before, when Oliver discovers that Rose is his aunt, he insists on claiming her as his "sister." Similarly, in *Nickleby* Nicholas himself marries Madeline Bray, whom the Cheeryble twins wish to establish, in Nicholas's words, "as their own child" (61: 743), for she is the daughter of the woman who once rejected Charles Cheeryble. In other words, Nicholas becomes the husband of the surrogate daughter of his two surrogate fathers, and their other surrogate son marries Nicholas's sister. Furthermore, the virtual interchangeability of Nicholas and Frank—and of Kate and Madeline—is suggested by the parallelism between the incident in which Nicholas, having overheard Sir Mulberry Hawk speak disrespectfully of Kate, physically chastises the aristocrat (32: 394–400) and the later scene in which Frank, after hearing Madeline referred to in an irreverent way, kicks the clerk from the register-office (43: 524–28). All of these cases of veiled brother-sister incest in *Oliver* and *Nickleby* seem closely related to the Oedipal motif of the son's desire for his mother, for whom his sister may be a substitute.

Finally, the Oedipal story is also brought to mind by the fact that in both *Oliver* and *Nickleby* important secrets are brought to light through two strange, unattractive, elderly, sphinx-like women: Old Sally, who divulges on her deathbed the theft of Agnes Fleming's locket, which held proofs of Oliver's identity, and Peg Sliderskew, whose theft from Gride of a wrongfully obtained deed leaving a bequest to Madeline leads to Ralph's enlisting Squeers to acquire the document, a scheme that arouses the suspicion of Newman Noggs, who, with the assistance of Frank Cheeryble, eventually obtains the secret paper (57: 707–10).

The emphasis in *Oliver Twist* and *Nicholas Nickleby* on the suffering of Oliver and Smike serves to warn us in a strong way about the harm that may be caused by familial interference in marriage decisions. By intruding in these matters, parents, the source of life, ironically transform themselves into destroyers. In the cases of both Edwin Leeford and Ralph Nickleby such intervention leads to the desperate unhappiness of the young couple and to sexual misbehavior. Leeford's wife, Brownlow asserts, was "wholly given up to continental frivolities" and "had utterly forgotten the young husband ten good years her junior" (49: 326), and Leeford himself has an affair with Agnes Fleming. Ralph Nickleby, because of his greed, would not make his marriage public and evidently denied his wife her conjugal rights and access to their child, leading her to elope with another man (60: 738). For these misdeeds, Dickens imposes a punishment of premature death: Edwin Leeford succumbs to illness (49: 327), as does his wife (51: 344–45), while both Agnes and her surrogate, Nancy, also die young. In *Nickleby*, Ralph's wife dies "not long after" eloping (60: 738), while Ralph himself eventually commits suicide.

As we have noticed, emphasis on the lamentable consequences of parental hostility to a marriage is also seen frequently elsewhere in the Dickens canon. On the other hand, benevolent opposition to the marital desires of a couple is rare, although found in the previously mentioned account in *Pickwick Papers* of Wardle's stopping his sister's elopement with Jingle and in Twemlow's intervening in a parental way to keep Georgiana Podsnap from being matched with the odious Fledgeby in *Our Mutual Friend*. Interestingly, in *Little Dorrit* we find a case of attempted interference that unfortunately is unsuccessful, for Daniel Doyce reveals that Mr. Meagles "has twice taken his daughter [Pet] abroad in the hope of separating her from Mr Gowan" (1: 17: 253). In 1860 Dickens himself tried in vain to dissuade his daughter Kate from marrying Charles Collins, Wilkie Collins's brother, and he also disapproved of his son Charley's marriage in 1861 to Bessie Evans, from whose father, Frederick Evans, Dickens was estranged (Johnson 2: 960, 997; Kaplan 419–20, 399; Ackroyd 874, 825).

Significantly, in *Nickleby* the Cheeryble brothers are "good" parental surrogates who assist the marital desires of their "children," even when the latter are willing to suppress these wishes. Just as Nicholas is ready to sacrifice his amatory interest in Madeline, so his sister Kate initially rejects the proposal of Frank Cheeryble, both actions being intended to show deference to the Cheeryble twins (61: 743–48). The latter, however, are eager to bless and further each match. Indeed, the brothers in this way anticipate a benefactor like John Jarndyce in *Bleak House*.

Dickens seeks in both *Oliver Twist* and *Nicholas Nickleby* to affirm the importance and inescapability of heredity and simultaneously to suggest, paradoxically, that the hold of the past can be broken. For Oliver, the physical appearance of his face represents his heritage from both his mother and father, for, as we remarked much earlier, he not only looks like Agnes Fleming, his mother, who is the subject of the portrait in Brownlow's home, but he also resembles his father, Edwin Leeford, a similarity that led to the boy's being

recognized by Monks. Similarly, in *Nicholas Nickleby* Dickens introduces the motif of inheritance of facial resemblance. Ralph Nickleby,
after looking at his distressed niece, Kate, finds that "the face of his
dead brother seemed present before him" (19: 240). Afterwards, in
the climactic scene in which Nicholas and Kate try to interrupt the
wedding of Madeline Bray and Arthur Gride, the narrator comments on the brother and sister, "a close likeness between them was
apparent," and also notices "some indefinable resemblance in the
face of Ralph to both" (54: 672). In the very next chapter, we learn
that Madeline finds "the image of Nicholas so constantly recurring
in the features of his sister that she could scarcely separate the two"
(55: 681).

While facial resemblance serves to represent the power of heredity, the idea that inheritance is not overridingly important is suggested by the use in both novels of the device of bequests that prove
superfluous to the happiness of the central characters. Although
Edwin Leeford's will was destroyed by his wife (51:344), her son,
who has taken the name Monks, is illegally coerced into revealing
its terms by Brownlow's threat of disingenuously implicating him
in the murder of Nancy. In addition, Oliver's dissolute half-brother
agrees to abide by the terms of the destroyed will, but much of
the property has been squandered, and Oliver "joyfully" accepts
Brownlow's suggestion that the remainder of the estate, approximately six thousand pounds, be shared with Monks. But Oliver
does not need this inheritance, since he is to be formally "adopted"
as the wealthy Brownlow's "own son" (53: 357). In *Nicholas Nickleby*
Madeline and Nicholas do eventually gain the twelve-thousand-
pound bequest to the former from her maternal grandfather, an
inheritance bestowed in a will that had been illegally concealed by
Arthur Gride (63: 757–58), but while this "money which Nicholas
acquired in right of his wife" is invested in the Cheerybles' firm and
leads to Nicholas's eventually joining Frank and the twin brothers as
a partner (65: 774), the narrator does not suggest that this wealth
was needed for the happiness of Madeline and Nicholas, since both
have become, in effect, adopted children of the Cheerybles. Indeed,
although the novel indicates that money is desirable, Kate and Nicholas are determined not to exercise their legal right to claim the ill-
gained wealth of Ralph, their deceased uncle, and his riches are
"swept at last into the coffers of the state" (65: 775), a government
that seems undeserving, since it certainly has done little to control
the rapacity and cruelty of men like Ralph and Squeers.

In *Oliver Twist* and *Nicholas Nickleby*, while the sins of a father and of a father-in-law's surrogate harm one generation—that of Edwin Leeford and Ralph Nickleby—and also their children—Oliver and Smike, respectively—this younger generation manages in some way to overcome the damage: Oliver is adopted by Brownlow, a man who might under other circumstances have been his uncle, while Rose, the aunt whom Oliver regards as his "own dear sister" (51: 348), finds Harry Maylie willing to defy attempts at interference by his relations; although Smike dies, his first cousin Nicholas may be seen as a surrogate who triumphs because of his own initiative in trying to halt Madeline's forced marriage, the timely demise of Walter Bray, and the assistance of the Cheeryble brothers.[8] Moreover, there is also cause for optimism in the way in which each story is disclosed. In each narrative we find the fragmentary, gradual, clouded revelation of secrets that were deeply hidden for many, many years: present problems can be traced back to a very distant past. In *Oliver Twist* Edwin Leeford's forced marriage took place twenty-six years before the end of the story (49: 327), and Oliver was born a little more than twelve years prior to the narrative's conclusion (37: 245; 49: 327). In *Nicholas Nickleby* Ralph's marriage took place about twenty-five years before the novel's close (60: 737), and Smike was abducted and imprisoned in Dotheboys Hall approximately fourteen years prior to Brooker's confession (60: 739). There may, of course, be significance in the fact that Dickens composed these two books from his twenty-fourth to his twenty-fifth years, a time twelve to fifteen years after his blacking-house captivity, an interval of the same duration as those just mentioned in *Oliver* and *Nickleby*. In both novels, the long-concealed wrongs of the past come to light. Despite the clever attempts of the malefactors to conceal their misdeeds and despite the obscurity added by the passage of time, the secrets are eventually discovered, through chance and the efforts of Nancy and Noggs, both of whom are responding to goodness, Nancy to that of Oliver, "the persecuted child" (49: 330), and Noggs to that of Nicholas's father, who once performed for him an act of "kindness when there was no hope of return" (7: 93).

Clearly, both of these novels imply that providence will ultimately thwart the wicked, and both books seem to endorse the confidence expressed by Hamlet: "[Foul] deeds will rise, / Though all the earth o'erwhelm them, to men's eyes" (1.2.256–57). The mixture of happiness and sorrow which the narrator of *Oliver* describes

in recounting the discovery by Oliver and Rose of their true relationship remains, since these two novels conclude, respectively, with
references to Agnes's memorial tablet in a church and to Smike's
grave. At the same time, *Oliver* includes a reminder of divine forgiveness that is available to those who, like Agnes Fleming, are
"weak and erring" (53: 360), and *Nickleby* emphasizes the loving
remembrance of Smike by the children of Nicholas and Kate. Then,
too, each of these two novels stresses the importance of an observer's perspective, the beholder's power to select in a way that can
impose either a positive or a negative significance on life. In the final
chapter of Dickens's preceding book, *Pickwick Papers*, the narrator
observes, "There are dark shadows on the earth, but its lights are
stronger in the contrast. Some men, like bats or owls, have better
eyes for the darkness than for the light" (57: 896). This idea is repeated in *Oliver Twist*: "Men who look on nature, and their fellow-
men, and cry that all is dark and gloomy, are in the right; but the
sombre colours are reflections from their own jaundiced eyes and
hearts" (34: 229).[9] In *Nicholas Nickleby* a "merry-faced gentleman"
responds to the interpolated tale of "The Five Sisters of York," a
sad narration, with the words, "There are shades in all good pictures, but there are lights too, if we choose to contemplate them"
(6: 77), and in the tale presented immediately after, "The Baron of
Grogzwig," the title-character, after deciding not to commit suicide,
asserts, "I'll brood over miseries no longer, but put a good face on
the matter, and try the fresh air and the bears again" (6: 85). In
Oliver and *Nickleby* the sins of the grandfathers cause great harm,
but the guilty secrets are eventually disclosed, and in this revelation,
as well as in the goodness of the surviving generations and of their
providentially found benefactors, rests hope for a happy, blessed
future.

Nicholas Nickleby in many respects retells the story presented in
Oliver Twist, but the later novel, although often lighter in tone because of its attention to figures like Mrs. Nickleby and the Crummles
troupe, includes details with implications that are darker than the
analogous material in the earlier book. Smike's errant father, Ralph
Nickleby, is more culpable than Edwin Leeford, Oliver's father,
since the former was not forced into an early, unwanted marriage.
Moreover, Ralph kept his son as a hidden prisoner in a garret, while
Leeford, prior to his untimely death, sought to provide for his yet
unborn child. The mother of Smike deserts not only Ralph, but her
young child as well. On the other hand, Agnes Fleming is far less

blameworthy, for we assume that she would certainly have nurtured Oliver had she lived. Although *Nicholas Nickleby* contains no setting as bleak as Jacob's Island and no event as horrifying as the murder of Nancy, and although Nicholas himself suffers no hardship quite like those imposed upon Oliver, the cruelty of Squeers may be seen as more gratuitous than Fagin's harshness. Unlike Oliver, Smike is permanently harmed by the deprivations suffered in childhood, and his death affects us more strongly than the demise in *Oliver Twist* of the protagonist's surrogate, little Dick, a figure who remains undeveloped. Nevertheless, in both books we find not only the motifs of neglected, abused children and guilty parents, but also the comforting figures of altruistic and benevolent parental surrogates who help to guide events to pleasing outcomes.

Notes

1. For Dickens's literary activities during these early years, see pp. xvii–xxiv in Kathleen Tillotson's introduction to her edition of *Oliver Twist*. Dickens began *Pickwick Papers* in February 1836 (PL 1: 132, to Messrs. Chapman and Hall [18 Feb. 1836]), started *Oliver* in January 1837 (PL 1: 223–24, to Richard Bentley [?18 Jan. 1837]), completed *Pickwick* in October 1837 (PL 1: 318–19, to John Forster [?12 Oct. 1837]), began *Nickleby* in February 1838 (PL 1: 377, to Forster [?21 Feb. 1838]), and finished *Oliver* the following October (PL 1: 449–50, to Mrs. Charles Dickens, 5 Nov. [1838]), so that the entire narrative could be published in a three-volume edition in November, prior to the conclusion of the serialization in *Bentley's Miscellany* in April 1839. The writing of *Nickleby* was concluded in September 1839 (PL 1: 581–82, to Forster [18 Sept. 1839]). Tracy refers to "the extraordinary pressures" on Dickens during the composition of *Oliver Twist* (7).
2. Herst points out that Pickwick, Oliver, and Nicholas all "ended their adventures by withdrawing to a country refuge, their experiences permanently rewarded by a pastoral idyll" (82).
3. Caserio aptly comments, "The plot Ralph makes up as a fiction to hurt Nicholas turns out to be the plot of his [Ralph's] real life" (77), but Caserio is incorrect in attributing the lie about Smike's death to Ralph's "own estranged wife" (77) rather than to Brooker, the actual deceiver.
4. Pool reminds us, "Until 1823 [in England], a man or woman under the age of twenty-one could not marry without parental permission" (180). As Lawrence Stone observes, however, "There can be no doubt that public opinion in landed and bourgeois circles in the late eighteenth century was turning against parental dictation of a marriage partner" (289).

5. The name "Nancy" may be a diminutive form of the Middle English *Annis* or *Agnes*. This point was called to my attention by my student Samuel J. Noël, in a paper written in April 1994 for an undergraduate course in Dickens at Queens College, CUNY. Regina Barreca observes, "the two women who are sexually active in this novel—Nancy and Agnes—die horrible, lonely deaths" (93). Although Kathleen Tillotson (Introduction xxxv) accurately states that Nancy's "emergence as Oliver's defender" in ch. 16 is not anticipated in the "previous chapters in which she appears," we do find some preparation for this transformation very early in ch. 16 itself, well before she intervenes to protect the boy. When Nancy, with Sikes and Oliver, passes Newgate, where Bill's and her acquaintances await execution, her extremely intense reaction seems to signal an epiphany, a realization of the fate to which she is helping to consign the boy: "Oliver felt her hand tremble; and, looking up in her face as they passed a gas-lamp, saw that it had turned a deadly white" (16: 110).

6. Dabney notices that Edwin Leeford's wife in *Oliver* and Mrs. Clennam in *Little Dorrit*, two "wives forced on" their husbands, "fulfil remarkably similar roles, even to the suppression of wills" (98). Sadrin considers resemblances between the fathers of Oliver and Arthur Clennam (74).

7. The marriage-funeral combination presented in *Romeo and Juliet* also appears in such other Shakespearean plays as *Much Ado About Nothing*, *Hamlet*, *Othello*, *King Lear*, and *Antony and Cleopatra*. Webber comments perceptively on "the funeral-feast imagery" as an example of the juxtaposition of the tragic and the comic, a pairing found throughout *Hamlet* and other works in Shakespeare's canon (94). Among the many discussions of the linking of love and death in *Romeo and Juliet*, see those by M. B. Smith (83–86) and Mack (80–81). Like Shakespeare, Dickens also shows a great predilection for the marriage-funeral juxtaposition. We may note, besides the cases from *Oliver* and *Nickleby* mentioned in my discussion, several examples among many: in *Pickwick Papers* the narrator of "A Madman's Manuscript" states that the woman forced to marry him "would rather have been placed, stiff and cold in a dull leaden coffin, than borne an envied bride to my rich, glittering house" (11: 221); in *David Copperfield* Traddles, after mentioning that the family of his beloved Sophy selfishly wishes to keep her, expresses his fear that when he and she finally do marry the event "will be more like a funeral, than a wedding" (41: 658); and in *Our Mutual Friend* Fanny Cleaver, alias Jenny Wren, tells Mr. Riah that the clergyman officiating at her father's funeral gave her an idea for a doll, but that her creation would be presiding at a wedding, not a burial (4: 9: 716), and Bradley Headstone later falls into a fit upon learning that the Reverend Mr. Milvey is going to assist Lizzie Hexam not with a funeral but with her marriage (4: 11: 730).

8. Slater cogently suggests, in the introduction to his edition of *Nickleby*, that Nicholas is, "to some extent, an idealized portrait of the artist" (26). The name that Nicholas uses as a pseudonym with Crummles's company—"Johnson" (23: 281))—may be seen as supporting Slater's proposal, since Dickens himself, the son of John Dickens, was John's son. Of course, the pseudonym "Johnson" is first given to Nicholas by Newman Noggs, in introducing him to the Kenwigs family (16: 199). Gager observes, "Clearly, there is a bit of wish-fulfilment in Dickens's portrayal of Nicholas Nickleby as resident 'author and stage-player' to the Crummles company" (98). (As Gager indicates, the expression in quotation marks is used by Dickens to refer to Shakespeare in *Little Dorrit* [1: 12].)

9. Paroissien ("Literature's 'Eternal Duties' " 29 and 49 [n. 11]) notes the likeness between the aforementioned passages in *Oliver* and *Pickwick*, as well as the similarity to the remark in *Nickleby* that "youth is not prone to contemplate the darkest side of a picture it can shift at will" (53: 653) and the parallel comment in a speech that Dickens delivered in Boston on February 1, 1842. We might add still another example from these early years in Dickens's career: the narrator in *Barnaby Rudge* apostrophizes "men of gloom and austerity" and tells them that in "the Everlasting Book" the "pictures are not in black and sombre hues, but in bright and glowing tints," while the music "is not in sighs and groans, but songs and cheerful sounds" (25: 249).

Chapter 3

A Christmas Carol: Paradox, Puzzle, Exemplum

In *A Christmas Carol*, Dickens provides, besides the "two Scrooges" (one sinful, one redeemed) considered in Edmund Wilson's classic essay, two Tiny Tims—a victim and a survivor—and two radically different narratives: a fairy tale recounting a miracle in which a "dead" old man becomes a living "baby" (5: 128) and a realistic story revealing how diverse stimuli can powerfully affect memory and imagination, leading to epiphany and reform. At tale's end, an exuberant old Scrooge eagerly grasps his new chances at life, at family (in becoming "a second father" [5: 134] to Tim), and at community (in joining the festive celebration at the home of his nephew Fred). But we must remain aware that although Scrooge may be elated, he is also belated, for, if we judge by his new values, much of his life has been misspent and lost.

Herman Melville, writing in 1851 to his friend Nathaniel Hawthorne, despondently thought of his own literary career and speculated, "Though I wrote the Gospels in this century, I should die in the gutter" (192). While Dickens, who earned more from his writings than any predecessor, was concerned about providing for his many dependents, he did not worry about landing in the gutter and managed to compose not only a children's version of the Gospels but also—in the *Carol*—a gospel that has proved truly ecumenical.

The miracles attributed to Jesus in the Gospels often involve three kinds of supernatural feats that recall acts performed by the prophets Elijah and Elisha: providing food for a multitude out of limited provisions, curing illness that has persisted despite all prior attempts at remedy, and resuscitating someone who has been declared dead. In Dickens's *Carol*, we find variants of all three types of wondrous deeds, and we must speculate about the extent to which these are attributable to divine power. Scrooge does not provide an inexhaustible supply of loaves and fishes to a multitude, but he does replace the Cratchit family's meager Christmas meal with a prize turkey. While sending such a gift is not supernatural, his reformation that precedes it may be. Tiny Tim's illness seems to disappear soon after Scrooge's change of heart, and, of course, the two deaths of which we have seen the aftermaths in Stave Four—the demises of Tim and Scrooge himself—turn out not to have occurred. Furthermore, the names of the two most memorable characters, Ebenezer Scrooge and Tiny Tim, seem intended to make us focus on some of the story's major religious and moral themes.

In 1 Timothy 6: 10, the apostle Paul exclaims, "the love of money is the root of all evil." The folly of this pursuit of riches is suggested by the earlier affirmation by Paul, "we brought nothing into *this* world, *and it is* certain we can carry nothing out" (6: 7). Timothy is told, "Charge them that are rich in this world, that they be not highminded [haughty], nor trust in uncertain riches" (6: 17). Instead, the wealthy are to be instructed to "do good, that they be rich in good works, ready to distribute, willing to communicate; Laying up in store for themselves a good foundation against the time to come, that they may lay hold on eternal life" (6: 18–19). In Dickens's story, his Timothy knows these lessons instinctively, but they must be learned by Scrooge.[1]

"Ebenezer," the first name of Scrooge, is also significant. In 1 Samuel 7: 10, the Israelites are approached by a hostile horde of Philistines, but "the Lord thundered with a great thunder on that day upon the Philistines, and discomfited them." After the Israelites pursue the Philistines and smite them, "Samuel took a stone, and set *it* between Mizpah and Shen, and called the name of it Ebenezer, saying, Hitherto hath the Lord helped us" (7: 12). Certainly, many of us are likely to conclude that Scrooge receives divine assistance in achieving his reformation, and since the name "Ebenezer" literally means "stone of help," we may notice, too, that this aptly describes the role of the changed Scrooge in relation to the needy of London in general and to the Cratchit family in particular.[2]

We witness Scrooge seeing his life from the perspectives of the past, the present, and the future, and from the viewpoints of Belle (his former fiancée) and her husband, Scrooge's nephew Fred and Fred's wife and friends, the Cratchits, a charwoman, a laundress, an undertaker, and a couple in debt to Scrooge. The narrator, too, acts as a guide, his frequently facetious tone in the story providing reassurance that all will end well. For example, after learning that Scrooge can see through the torso of Marley's Ghost, we are told, "Scrooge had often heard it said that Marley had no bowels, but he had never believed it until now" (1: 57), a comment so absurd as to dispel at least temporarily all of our fear.[3]

The main power of the *Carol* seems derived from paradoxes: the different types of ghosts (Marley and the spectres flying through the night air at the end of Stave One, as well as the three Spirits of Christmases Past, Present, and Yet to Come) are actual, according to the teller, but they also seem unreal. Although the narrator assures us that "Scrooge had as little of what is called fancy about him as any man in the City of London" (1: 54), we learn later that his earlier childish self reveled in fantasy. The negative change that overtook the young man Scrooge is left unexplained but may seem comprehensible when we recall the prevalent business ethos of mid-Victorian England. The story is certainly religious with its focus on Christmas and the emphasis on Tim's visit to the church, but at the same time it seems not religious, for it is, paradoxically, a secular gospel. The early remarks of Scrooge's nephew about the holiday illustrate this point:

> But I am sure I have always thought of Christmas time . . . —apart from the veneration due to its sacred name and origin, if anything belonging to it can be apart from that—as a good time: a kind, forgiving, charitable, pleasant time: the only time I know of, in the long calendar of the year, when men and women seem by one consent to open their shut-up hearts freely, and to think of people below them as if they really were fellow-passengers to the grave, and not another race of creatures bound on other journeys.   (1: 49)

Except for the brief reference to "its sacred name and origin," the main sentiment of the comment seems virtually indistinguishable from a statement by Bertrand Russell, a professed atheist, in the penultimate paragraph of his essay "A Free Man's Worship," first published in 1903. After asserting that all human beings are "united . . . by the tie of a common doom," Russell urges us to help "our comrades": "Be it ours to shed sunshine on their path, to lighten their sorrows by the balm of sympathy, to give them the pure joy of a never-tiring affection, to strengthen failing courage, to instil faith in hours of despair" (56).

Other paradoxes also mark Dickens's *Carol*: the ghosts are frightening but ultimately comforting to Scrooge; the story is disturbing but funny; Scrooge wastes his life but he finds it, for he is like the figure of Mary Magdalene, another reformed sinner, inescapably a character about whom we feel ambivalent, depending on whether we emphasize the sins or the subsequent reformation; his late repentance is plausible but also miraculous; a reader of, or listener to, the tale weeps and also laughs. The result of all these antithetical features is, of course, to provide us with not one but multiple *Carols*, for Dickens's text invites us to emphasize elements that we may select so that each of us can compose a narrative suiting his or her own individual mood.

Even the full title of Dickens's "Ghostly little book" (41 [Preface, December 1843]) appears designed to puzzle us: *A Christmas Carol. In Prose. Being a Ghost Story of Christmas*. Although carols are customarily linked with Christmas, a carol ordinarily is in verse, not prose,[4] and it is usually joyous, a celebration of birth, while ghost stories are linked with death and are often unpredictable. Moreover, as Morton Dauwen Zabel observes, while "Ghosts and Christmas have traditionally gone hand in hand in European tale-telling," the "conjunction . . . is . . . an incongruous one" (17). Although Zabel does not develop this last point, we may assume that he refers to the fact that the fear evoked by the idea of ghosts contrasts with the sense of Christmas as an auspicious and benevolent time. We recall the words of Marcellus in the opening scene of *Hamlet*:

> Some say that ever 'gainst that season comes
> Wherein our Saviour's birth is celebrated,
> This bird of dawning singeth all night long,
> And then they say no spirit dare stir abroad . . .
> (1.1.158–61)

But the *Carol*, even though the fourth paragraph in its opening stave refers to this initial scene in Shakespeare's play, presents a Christmas season replete with diverse types of ghosts and is concerned largely with death, both spiritual and physical.

James Boswell reports Samuel Johnson's criterion for ascertaining the credibility of apparitions: "I make a distinction between what a man may experience by the mere strength of his imagination, and what imagination cannot possibly produce" (287).[5] According to

Boswell, Johnson repeated this idea, offered in June 1763, nearly eighteen years later, in April 1781 (1137). Applying it to the ghosts in the *Carol* seems a useful approach.

Stave One of Dickens's tale opens with the declaration, "Marley was dead," and repeats this assertion four times in the initial four paragraphs, for, as the narrator explains, "This must be distinctly understood or nothing wonderful can come of the story I am going to relate" (1: 45). The effectiveness of the narrative, we are told, depends on our belief that the first apparition to reveal itself to Scrooge is actually the ghost of his partner, Jacob Marley. But if death and ghosts are ominous subjects, the tone—marked by whimsicality and leisurely redundance—offers reassurance, a lack of urgency or threat, a levity achieved by details like the reference to King Hamlet's "son's weak mind" (1: 46). In a sense, too, the existence of a ghost offers, as Julia Briggs observes, "comforting proof" of "something beyond" this world (24).

Scrooge has retained his deceased partner's name linked with his own "above the warehouse door" and actually "answered to both names: it was all the same to him" (1: 46), a tacit acknowledgment that he himself is spiritually dead. But, again, the seriousness of such a state appears negated by the narrator's lively enjoyment of the language used in the ensuing description of Scrooge: "a squeezing, clutching, covetous old sinner!"—"Hard and sharp as flint" (1: 46). We have no difficulty accepting the claim that Scrooge is completely estranged and alienated from his fellow human beings.

The story's events begin with the best-known formulaic opening for fairy tales, "once upon a time" (1: 47). Having previously been told that Scrooge "carried his own low temperature always about with him" (1: 46), we are informed that the weather outside is "cold, bleak, biting," a foggy, dark Christmas Eve (1: 47). When Scrooge's nephew intrudes on the old man and his clerk with a cheerful holiday greeting, the irritated Scrooge exclaims "Humbug!" and offers the wish that "every idiot who goes about with 'Merry Christmas,' on his lips, . . . be boiled with his own pudding and buried with a stake of holly through his heart" (1: 48), so excessive a statement that it is almost certain to evoke from readers laughter rather than alarm or annoyance. Indeed, Scrooge's wit leads G. K. Chesterton to comment whimsically, "There is a heartiness in his inhospitable statements that is akin to humour and there to humanity; he is only a crusty old bachelor, and had (I strongly suspect) given away turkeys secretly all his life" (120–21). Such a view, however, is probably not meant to be taken seriously, for it is not supported by any detail in the text and would rob the story of its power and point. The unredeemed Scrooge allows us release of any suppressed anti-social feelings we may have, but then his subsequent reformation comfortingly repudiates such sentiments.

When Fred, after extolling Christmas as a "charitable, pleasant time" (1: 49), hears his uncle fiercely reject a dinner invitation, the young man asks, "Why?" The uncle's reply seems a non sequitur, a discordant, out-of-context query, "Why did you get married?" (1: 49), a response suggesting that in some strange way Fred's getting married has offended Scrooge, even though the nephew soon retorts that Scrooge never accepted invitations prior to the marriage.

As Fred leaves, two gentlemen collecting for the poor enter, and Scrooge, in rejecting their solicitation, reveals that this Christmas Eve is the seventh anniversary of Jacob Marley's death. After chasing away a boy singing carols, Scrooge grudgingly gives Bob Cratchit Christmas Day as a holiday and then eats alone "in his usual melancholy tavern" (1: 53–54), before going home to "chambers which had once belonged to his deceased partner," Marley (1: 54).

All of the aforementioned events—only about a tenth of the tale—serve as a prologue to the rest of Dickens's *Carol*, a narrative presenting two main miracles: one involves the fusion—or confusion—of time, as the visits promised for three successive evenings are eventually revealed to have occurred within one, while the other concerns the transformation of the cold, deadened, harsh Scrooge, a malefactor, into a benefactor, a warm, vital, affectionate human being.[6] The story implies that moral improvement brings increased happiness, which in turn leads to greater reform and added joy. Scrooge benefits from the tutelage of four supernatural teachers—the ghost of Jacob Marley and the Spirits of Christmases Past, Present, and Yet To Come, three personifications of the holiday as it was, as it is, and as it will be experienced.

As Dickens presents his story, we are led to wonder about the previously mentioned test proposed by Samuel Johnson in determining the credibility of ghost stories. We may ask if the reform of Scrooge is a natural occurrence prompted by his advancing age and by visits on Christmas Eve of Fred, the two gentlemen collecting for the poor, and the boy singing carols, as well as by Scrooge's awareness that this evening that commemorates a birth is also the anniversary of the death of his partner, only friend, and alter ego, Jacob Marley. Indeed, all of the remaining events in the first two staves of the *Carol* could readily be seen as imaginings prompted in Scrooge by his experiences earlier in the evening. His being asked if he is Marley on the anniversary of the latter's death and then going home to this late partner's former residence certainly would evoke thoughts of Marley. When Scrooge, escorted by the Spirit of Christmas Past, sees himself as a schoolboy, he regrets his previous churlish rebuff of the boy singing carols: just as the sight of a boyish self reminds Scrooge of the other boy, so the reverse process is a strong possibility—the recollection of the boy singing reminds Scrooge of his own younger self, who in turn reminds him of the boy singing. Similarly, since Scrooge and the Ghost of Christmas Past, after seeing Scrooge's sister Fan, begin to talk of her son, Fred, we realize that Scrooge's recollection of his nephew may have inspired remembrance of the young man's mother, Fan. Scrooge's earlier exchange with his clerk, Bob Cratchit, perhaps stimulates the thought of employer-employee relations and leads Scrooge to recall his first employer, the generous Mr. Fezziwig. Even the scene of Belle with her family, a vision that disturbs Scrooge much more strongly than any of the other sights shown by the Spirit of Christmas Past, could be attributed to the earlier conversation with Fred about the young man's marriage, for the excessive reaction to Fred's having taken a bride may reflect the uncle's regret over his own decision decades before to allow Belle to release him from their engagement. As her name suggests, Scrooge allows beauty to depart from his life. When Belle's husband, in the final vision shown by this Spirit, reports having passed by the office window of Scrooge and observed him, we may assume that the husband was himself noticed by Scrooge. In other words, if we try to apply Johnson's criterion for credibility to the events in Staves One and Two, we may decide that Scrooge sees and hears nothing that he could not have recalled or else imagined.

Even though the narrator, as we have noticed, states that Scrooge possessed "little . . . fancy" (1: 54), the schoolboy Scrooge was evidently a child who delighted in imagining characters like Ali Baba and Robinson Crusoe (2: 72–73). When the spirit of Marley appears, we learn that Scrooge "remembered to have heard that ghosts in haunted houses were described as dragging chains" (1: 57)—in other words, Scrooge has previously acquired information about ghosts. In Stave Two, moreover, Scrooge wonders whether Marley's appearance "was all a dream" (2: 67), a sign that Scrooge regards himself as a person who at times has vivid dreams.

Even the two visitors in Staves Three and Four—the Spirits of Christmas Present and of Christmas Yet To Come—reveal to Scrooge no facts that he could not have inferred from his prior knowledge, no details that meet Dr. Johnson's test of being unknowable except "by supernatural means." All of the scenes observed could be the result of extrapolation from earlier awareness: if the schoolboy Scrooge used to greet imaginary visitors like Ali Baba, the adult Scrooge could, we assume, invent apparitions and spirits. To all of the lessons Scrooge derives from the wild adventures of what turns out to have been one night, we could respond with Horatio's lines, "There needs no ghost, my lord, come from the grave / To tell us this" (1.5.125–26).

Nevertheless, Dickens includes in the *Carol* features that may make us reluctant to categorize the events recounted as simply the dreamwork of a lonely, aging, embittered man. In *Hamlet* Shakespeare seeks to induce the audience to accept the Ghost by having Horatio first express complete skepticism and then be led immediately to believe by his own sensory experience. Similarly, Dickens has Scrooge himself initially doubt his own senses and recall that "a slight disorder of the stomach makes them cheats" (1: 59). But Scrooge's attempt to dismiss Marley's ghost with some jocular wordplay, "There's more of gravy than of grave about you, whatever you are" (1: 59), quickly fails when the apparition raises "a fearful cry," rattles its chains, and, "taking off the bandage round its head," lets "its lower jaw" drop "down upon its breast" (1: 60). Not only does Scrooge become wholly convinced about the reality of this ghost, but the narrator describes the events in a straightforward, accepting manner, despite an ironic reference to the apparition's "dull conversation" (1: 65). Moreover, in subsequent parts of the story this teller evidently affirms the reality of the supernatural apparitions, for he uses without hesitation the terms "Ghost," "Spirit," and "Phantom." Although John Leech's illustrations accompanying the text allow us to see for ourselves Marley's Ghost, the other apparitions that Scrooge sees through his window at the end of Stave One, and both the Spirit of Christmas Present and the Spirit of Christmas Yet To Come, these drawings cannot be taken as definite signs that Dickens intended us to accept the reality of the ghosts. For in *The Chimes* Leech's illustration "Richard and Margaret" shows a degraded Richard coming to visit a forlorn Meg (*Christmas Books* 1: 218–19), and this is a scene that we later learn was only dreamed by Trotty Veck. Nevertheless, Leech's drawings of the spirits in the *Carol* may have the effect of swaying us to suspend our disbelief.

The *Carol* includes two basic types of ghosts. First, we encounter the conventional apparition, a transparent creature bearing the likeness of a human being who is dead. Besides Marley's ghost, Scrooge sees many phantoms moving through the night sky when he goes to the open window out of which Marley's spirit has gone. All of these figures, like Marley's ghost, wear chains. One of them, recognized by Scrooge as the apparition of a person with whom he "had been quite familiar," is described as an "old ghost, in a white waistcoat, with a monstrous iron safe attached to its ankle, who cried piteously at being unable to assist a wretched woman with an infant, whom it saw below upon a door-step" (1: 65). We may wonder if this ghost has any connection with a character in *Oliver Twist*, a hard-hearted member of the workhouse board—a "gentleman in a white waistcoat"—who twice predicts Oliver's execution on the gallows and whose demise is reported by Bumble late in the novel (even though the member of the workhouse board evidently lives in Oliver's natal town, not in Scrooge's London).

The second variety of apparition is represented by the Spirits of Christmas Past, Christmas Present, and Christmas Yet To Come, each an allegorical personification (H. Stone, *Dickens and the Invisible World* 122) that conducts Scrooge on a voyeuristic journey. Appropriately, the first seems to stress the paradox of memory: old but young, wintry but summery, vague but clear. The past evokes from Scrooge emotion, which is needed for change: in particular, it summons the self-pity needed to awaken the old man's ability to feel compassion for others (Gold 150). In this part of the *Carol*, the narrator presents puzzles which are not solved. We learn that Scrooge's father, a malevolent parent, suddenly becomes "much kinder" just prior to one Christmas (2: 73), but no motive is mentioned for either the past hostility to the young son or the new benevolence. Ebenezer, once an imaginative, sensitive boy, and later a joyous young apprentice who becomes the fiancé of a beautiful, appealing woman, turns into a hardened, money-worshipping person who allows Belle to release him from the engagement. When Scrooge tells her that his new values derive from his increased knowledge of the world's desires (2: 79–81), the explanation seems too general to be adequate. Harry Stone surmises that Scrooge "chooses money over love" because he "seeks through power and aggrandizement to gird himself against the vulnerability that had scarred his childhood" (*Dickens and the Invisible World* 124), but the earlier depiction of Scrooge as a young apprentice suggests that he had overcome any ill effects of his childhood hardships.

Although Scrooge initially resists the invitation of the Spirit of Christmas Past to go forth and although he later "seize[s] the extinguisher-cap" and "presse[s] it down" upon the apparition's head

in an attempt to be released from memory's pains (2: 84), he displays
an entirely different mood in greeting the next Spirit, that of Christmas Present: "I went forth last night on compulsion, and I learnt a
lesson which is working now. To-night, if you have aught to teach
me, let me profit by it" (3: 87). Except for the view of Belle with her
family, the sights shown by the Spirit of Christmas Past appear to
come from Scrooge's memory. The scene of Belle interacting with
her children and husband may represent Scrooge's inference from
what he has been told by others. Similarly, all the incidents shown
by the Spirit of Christmas Present, a green giant who can adjust his
size, appear derived from Scrooge's imagination as it works with
past observations and hearsay information, since Scrooge himself
has evidently never attended one of Fred's Christmas celebrations
nor has he ever visited the Cratchits' household. Besides showing
events presently occurring, this Spirit can speak of the possible or
even probable future, for he offers a tentative but decidedly negative
response when Scrooge urgently requests, "tell me if Tiny Tim will
live" (3: 97). Although the answer seems pessimistic—" 'If these
shadows remain unaltered by the Future, none other of my race,'
returned the Ghost, 'will find him here' " (3: 97)—it actually offers
hope, since the "If" suggests an alternative possibility.[7] Showing
signs of aging, the Spirit finally focuses Scrooge's attention on two
children markedly different from Tiny Tim, a "ragged, scowling,
wolfish" boy and girl, who allegorically depict Ignorance and Want.

The third apparition, the "mysterious presence" (4: 110) called
the Spirit of Christmas Yet To Come, is frightening to Scrooge, but
he eagerly desires its help. As Scrooge surmises, the ominous phantom offers predictions that should be seen only as possibilities—
"shadows of things that May be" (4: 124)—rather than as certainties.
Because of this qualification, Dickens can offer two entirely different
conclusions to the story of Scrooge, as well as alternate outcomes
to the tale of Tiny Tim. The device allows the *Carol* to evoke first
a blend of pathos and fear and then a feeling of comfort, relief,
and joy.

To make Scrooge's redemption more acceptable, Dickens takes
care not to allow us to witness the old man ever doing serious
harm to anyone. We hear Mrs. Cratchit's remarks about Scrooge's
stinginess and hardness (3: 47–48), but these complaints are relatively mild. In fact, the closest we come to hearing about Scrooge's
really hurting anyone is the scene in which a husband and wife
who owe a heavy debt to him have their hearts made "lighter" by
news of his death (4: 120). Although we may assume that in prior

times Scrooge caused the ruin of creditors like these, details about such matters are omitted. We find no reference to imprisonment for debt or to dispossession or to extreme deprivation or to suicide. Even though Scrooge's parsimony has limited the material wealth of the Cratchits, they seem to be surviving, except perhaps for Tim, whose frailty does not really appear to be attributable to poverty. If we recall the scene in *Oliver Twist* in which Sowerberry arrives at the house of a pauper whose wife has just expired, presumably from malnutrition (5: 47–48), or even the earlier meeting between Bumble and Sowerberry in which they discuss the death from exposure of an impoverished tradesman (4: 38), we can better recognize Dickens's great restraint in the *Carol*.

Because each of the visits from the three allegorical Spirits that serve as teachers to Scrooge begins and ends with him in bed, we readily wonder about whether the events are all a dream. After all, such a revelation is the simplest way for an author to retract some of the events of his tale, and this is the central device of Dickens's next Christmas book, *The Chimes*, in which Trotty Veck happily awakens from a nightmare. In the *Carol*, however, the narrator himself, as we have noticed, seems to accept the reality of the supernatural apparitions by employing terms like "Ghost," "Spirit," and "Phantom." But Dickens also has this same narrator undermine credulity about ghosts by remarking that the Ghost of Christmas Past was standing as close to Scrooge "as I am now to you, and I am standing in the spirit at your elbow" (2: 68), and the narrator cannot resist joking in the last paragraph of his narrative when he observes that Scrooge from this time forth lived his life "upon the Total Abstinence Principle," since he "had no further intercourse with Spirits" (5: 134). Moreover, whether the apparitions are actual or not is far less significant than the assurance from the narrator that Scrooge, who had pledged to reform, "was better than his word" (5: 133).

The story of Scrooge is not really figurative and therefore cannot be called a parable like that of the lost sheep (or, in Scrooge's case, bellwether) or that of the prodigal son (or, in the case of Scrooge, an older figure who is a miser wasteful of life, a prodigal "father"). But the tale is clearly an exemplum: the account of Scrooge demonstrates that there is hope for anyone, even an extreme sinner nearing the end of his earthly pilgrimage. The reversal of the deaths of Tiny Tim and Scrooge seems clearly attributable to the penitence and reformation of the latter.

Indeed, the conversion of Scrooge leads to a whole series of reversals. The rude refusal of Fred's invitation is balanced by Scrooge's eager request to participate in his nephew's party; the rebuff of the two gentlemen collecting for the poor turns into an offer of a voluntary gift of surprising magnitude; the harshness to the boy singing carols is replaced by generosity to the boy sent for the prize turkey; cruelty to Cratchit is transformed into kindly concern. A friendless, lonely man becomes loving and beloved. Most important, as in the Gospels, death is changed to life, as we are shown that even an elderly reprobate like Scrooge can work miracles.

Doubting the durability of this redemption, Edmund Wilson declares, "Unquestionably he [Scrooge] would have relapsed when the merriment was over . . . into moroseness, vindictiveness, suspicion. He would . . . reveal himself as the victim of a manic-depressive cycle" (64). But this claim subverts Dickens's clear desire to describe a case of unexpected and perhaps miraculous conversion. Moreover, Wilson's proposal directly contradicts the narrator's assurance in the story's final paragraph: following the reformation of Scrooge, "it was always said of him, that he knew how to keep Christmas well, if any man alive possessed the knowledge" (5: 134).

Other puzzles, however, remain. Does Scrooge's generosity at the end compensate for all his prior misdeeds over many years? The message of the Gospels would indicate that it does, especially when we think of the parable of the laborers in the vineyard, of whom some complain about the same reward being given to all, even those that were hired at near the eleventh hour: "So the last shall be first" (Matthew 20: 16). Why does Marley's Ghost wait a full seven years before coming to warn his former partner, a delay far longer than the three months that pass before the ghost of King Hamlet appears on the battlements? The spirit of Marley affirms that in the past it has frequently "sat invisible" beside Scrooge and "may not tell" why this time it has been allowed to make itself apparent (1: 63). In other words, "There are more things in heaven and earth, Horatio, / Than are dreamt of in your philosophy." Marley's Ghost, like that of King Hamlet, is a "perturbed spirit," but Scrooge's night visitor comes to call not for revenge but for repentance and reform. In Luke 16:27–31 Jesus tells of a rich man in hell who asks that a warning be delivered to his five brothers by "one . . . from the dead," only to be told by Abraham, "If they hear not Moses and the prophets, neither will they be persuaded, though one rose from the dead." Scrooge, however, does benefit from the words of a revenant, Marley's apparition.

In effect, the *Carol* contradicts Lady Macbeth's statement to her husband, "what's done, is done" (3.2.12), as well as her later words during the sleepwalking scene, "What's done cannot be undone" (5.1.68), for Scrooge finds he still has time to change his behavior. And Dickens gives himself an opportunity to depict in two entirely different ways the fates of Tim and Scrooge. Dickens's penchant for doubling leads him to discover how to present two different tales at the same time and thereby display a pleasing duplicity as a teller. With Dickens's help, Scrooge can "sponge away" not only his name on the gravestone (4: 126), but also the pathos-filled death of Tiny Tim. As Kathleen Tillotson observes, Dickens's Christmas books present *"alternative futures"* ("The Middle Years" 18). In *The Haunted Man*, Dickens's last Christmas book, Redlaw must choose between his dark self, on the one hand, a self represented by the Phantom who, by brooding on wrongs suffered and sorrows endured, leads him to forget the ties that bind him to humankind, and his benevolent self, on the other hand (*Christmas Books* 2: 243–353). In the *Carol*, too, Dickens anticipates the extreme antithetical options, the contrasting potential selves, later faced by Stevenson's Jekyll and Wilde's Dorian Gray, but helps Scrooge to avoid the dire fates of these characters. For Scrooge, death need not be the wages of sin, for time is manipulated so that he can repent, and, ironically, his painful, tormented past leads him to a happy, generous future. Moreover, the exemplum depends on our acceptance of one further paradox and puzzle: Jacob Marley, an avaricious, cruel man who went unredeemed to his grave, becomes miraculously—and unselfishly—the agent of grace for his partner. Perhaps prompted by remorse over his own "life's opportunity [of being helpful to his fellow creatures] misused" (1: 62), Marley has been able to gain for Scrooge a "chance and hope" (1: 63). Early in the tale, Scrooge thinks that his own avaricious behavior is based upon reason. His conversion, however, is based on extreme emotion: pity for his own younger self and for Tim, fear concerning the future facing Tim and also himself. From these feelings arises a sense of caritas that brings joy and redemption.

When Scrooge begs Marley's Ghost, "Speak comfort to me," the reply is, "I have none to give. It comes from other regions, Ebenezer Scrooge, and is conveyed by other ministers, to other kinds of men" (1: 61). Basically, however, *A Christmas Carol* itself offers comfort, for it provides an appealing myth of empowerment, a story suggesting that the most extreme of miracles—reviving others and oneself from death—is within the reach of all human beings, even so grotesque a sinner as Scrooge, and that as long as a person is alive, there remains hope.

Notes

1. Vogel sees Tim as a "sprig of Timothy, the youthful disciple of St. Paul, the frail and unwell follower whom Paul called his child and son in Christ [1 Timothy 1: 2]" (70).

2. A differing suggestion is offered by Vogel, who, after remarking, "*Ebenezer* is the name of a stone set by Samuel," states, "stony-hearted Ebenezer Scrooge lives up to his name" (70). Patten observes that the name "Ebenezer" is "associated in the Preface to *Pickwick* with the narrow dissenting Ebenezer Chapel which has just enough religion to make people hate, and not enough to make them love, one another" (183).

3. Davies, who emphasizes the tendency of the narrator to distance himself "from the tale's events" (80), states that this teller "is all too willing to substitute for humane involvement a *bonhomie* that on occasion can be brutal" (81). But the narrator's harsh wit, as well as the gentler humor that is also present, would be highly inappropriate if the tale moved to a sad or tragic close.

4. Patten, however, maintains, "Carols were not prominent in the early nineteenth century . . . and the term came to be applied to prose as well as verse on Christmas subjects" (190).

5. Tatar refers to this test in beginning her discussion of the uncanny (167).

6. Patten refers to "the immensity of the transformation that does take place" in Scrooge (164) and also asserts that time is the story's "central concern" (166). Walder suggests, "a miracle . . . does occur, in Scrooge's change of heart" (121).

7. While the Ghost purportedly is showing Scrooge events from the present, two of the scenes witnessed never occur: the Cratchits' Christmas dinner at which they are seen eating a goose (3: 95–96) is the meal that they would have had if Scrooge had not reformed and sent them a prize turkey, and the party given by Fred and his wife (3: 101–07) has not yet taken place. Both the Spirit of Christmas Present and the narrator seem trustworthy, but both deceive us—paradoxically, however, deception, which is often a type of aggression, here is benevolent and pleasing.

Chapter 4

David Copperfield: "In More Senses Than One"

From the opening clause, *David Copperfield* raises the question of perception—"Whether I shall turn out to be the hero of my own life"—and perception, of course, depends largely on perspective. Especially during the initial six monthly numbers, which contain the first eighteen chapters, Dickens emphasizes the contrasts between the point of view of the protagonist in childish and youthful days and the direct or implied judgments of the same protagonist as a narrator whose diction, syntax, whimsicality, and indirectness indicate maturity. Indeed, we often find not just two, but three narratorial perspectives: that of David as he experienced his earlier life, the retrospective view as he recalls the characters and events many years later, often with an intensity and a vividness that make them seem present ("At this minute I see him [Murdstone] turn round in the garden" [2: 24]), and the hypothetical response that he believes he would have had in the past had he possessed foreknowledge of the future. An example of the last of these appears when David, after describing the child Emily's dangerous dash out onto a pier, comments,

> There has been a time since when I have wondered whether,
> if the life before her could have been revealed to me at a glance,
> and so revealed as that a child could fully comprehend it, and if

her preservation could have depended on a motion of my hand,
I ought to have held it up to save her.   (3: 39)

Certainly, we are kept aware that subsequent experiences color
memories: "my later understanding comes, I am sensible, to my aid
here" (2: 23).

Perspective as a theme, however, also enters the novel in many
other ways. For example, extremely different reactions regarding
Emily's elopement are expressed by Ham, Mr. Peggotty, Minnie
Joram (Mr. Omer's daughter), Rosa Dartle, Miss Mowcher, Aunt
Betsey, and Martha Endell. Although Ham prays that Emily may die
"sooner than . . . come to ruin and disgrace!" (31: 382), Mr. Peggotty
declares, "remember that the last words I left for her was, 'My
unchanged love is with my darling child, and I forgive her!' " (32:
400). Minnie Joram sobs, "What will become of her! Oh, how could
she be so cruel, to herself and him!" (32: 389), the "him" here referring either to Mr. Peggotty or to Ham, but the enraged Rosa Dartle
exclaims, "I would have her branded on the face, drest in rags, and
cast out in the streets to starve" (32: 399). While Miss Mowcher
refers to Emily as "the poor unfortunate girl" (32: 392), "the poor
betrayed girl" (32: 393), Aunt Betsey later asserts, "She should have
thought of that, before she caused so much misery!'(35: 425). Subsequently, the fallen Martha Endell, to whom Emily had shown kindness, cries, "I would have died to have brought back her good
name!" (47: 576).

The idea of perspective is also emphasized when David tells of
leaving Dr. Strong's school and feeling confused by "the opening
prospect," for at the time life seemed "more like a great fairy story . . . than anything else" (19: 235). To help David choose a voca-
tion, Aunt Betsey suggests that he consider the problem "from a
new point of view, and not as a schoolboy" (19: 235) and recom-
mends "a little journey" (19: 236) as a way of achieving this new
approach. Indeed, the idea of viewpoints appears to have been very
much in Dickens's thoughts at this time: in a letter to Forster in
April 1849, during the composition of the second installment of
David Copperfield, Dickens reports that he is "lumbering on like a
stage-waggon. . . . the long Copperfieldian perspective looks snowy
and thick, this fine morning" (PL 5: 526 [?19 April 1849]).

Perspective, of course, is highly subjective, determined not only
by our place in time—past tense or present—but also by the position
in an individual's life—childhood, youth, maturity, old age. Moreover, the mood of the observer shapes responses: Mrs. Heep reminds David that she looks on her son with "a mother's eye" (39:

481); in a letter to Traddles, Mrs. Micawber asserts that the "quick eye of affection" has enabled her to be especially aware of her husband's newly aberrant behavior (49: 593); after the deaths of Dora and Steerforth, the narrator states that he cannot adequately "retrace, one by one, all the weary phases of distress of mind through which . . . [he] passed" (58: 685).

In exploring the themes of perception and perspective, Dickens makes highly effective use of three narrative techniques—foreshadowing, remarks that explicitly call attention to change in various characters, and guidance provided by equivocal chapter-titles. Although these literary devices are also employed skillfully in other novels by Dickens, they seem particularly significant in this book.

As a narrator, David employs foreshadowing with varying degrees of directness. In Chapter 2, for example, he abruptly refers to the premature death of his mother by suddenly posing a series of questions:

> Can I say of her face—altered as I have reason to remember it, perished as I know it is—that it is gone, when here it comes before me at this instant . . . ? Can I say of her innocent and girlish beauty, that it faded, and was no more, when its breath falls on my cheek now, as it fell that night? (2: 29)

We are made to realize that this narrator already knows the outcomes of events that are unknown to us. The device makes us anticipate and be more attentive to details in the story that may lead to what has been prefigured, and this technique also prepares us for events that will cause distress, since we can best respond to these if we are on guard.

Nearly all of the foreshadowings in the novel seem to refer to unhappy events. I have previously noticed the indication by David that Emily will meet a fate that will later make him wonder whether an early death would have been desirable for her (3: 39), a veiled reference to her seduction by Steerforth. In addition, after mentioning that he told Steerforth about visiting Mr. Mell's mother and her companion in the almhouse, David also observes that "the visit had its unforeseen consequences; and of a serious sort, too, in their way" (7: 87). We may be likely to anticipate—correctly—that these consequences will involve Steerforth's using the information to denigrate Mr. Mell, whom the older boy had frequently "treated . . . with systematic disparagement" (7: 86). But in the same chapter another foreshadowing is left obscure when David assures us only that there were "many reasons" for the survival of the "impression" made on him by the visit of Ham and Mr. Peggotty to Salem House (7: 93), a visit during which Steerforth meets them and is invited to see their boat-home should he ever go to Suffolk (7: 95–96). Of course, this invitation later leads to Steerforth's meeting Emily.

In the next chapter we find two more foreshadowings of the death of Clara Copperfield Murdstone, the first being a reference to a happy evening David spends with his mother as being "the last of its race" (8: 105), and the second, a more explicit statement after the boy bids her farewell: "So I lost her" (8: 110).

Although the narrator does anticipate the beneficent role Agnes is to play subsequently in his life—"The influence for all good, which she came to exercise over me at a later time, begins already to descend upon my breast" (16: 201)—other important foreshadowings prepare us for the rift between Dr. Strong and Annie (16: 214); Littimer's part in Steerforth's seduction of Emily (21: 257); David's eventual recognition of Steerforth's insincerity and duplicity (21: 265); Rosa's capacity for fury, which the narrator "had reason to remember . . . thereafter, when all the irremediable past was rendered plain" (29: 368), an indirect pointing to the enraged denunciation of Emily late in the novel, just before her rescue by her uncle; the dissolution of the friendship between David and Steerforth (29: 370); "the inexorable end" of Ham's state of being "kiender muddled" (32: 387); the death of Dora (44: 544; 48: 590); the "stormy sea" that would rise to the feet of Mrs. Steerforth and Rosa Dartle (46: 568), a figurative remark that gains power when we recognize its anticipation of the actual tempest that kills Steerforth; and the ominous announcement of the narrator that he is approaching "an event . . . so indelible, so awful, so bound by an infinite variety of ties to all that has preceded it, in these pages," that he has "seen it growing larger and larger" as he "advanced, like a great tower in a plain, and throwing its fore-cast shadow even on the incidents" of his "childish days" (55: 660)—a preparation for the climactic storm that destroys Ham and Steerforth. The image of "a great tower in a plain"—employed here to prepare for a prospective event—may remind us of the figure used much earlier in the account of the death of the narrator's mother—"this stands like a high rock in the ocean" (9: 118), despite the contrast between "a plain" (in the reference to the disaster at sea) and "the ocean" (in thinking of the death on land).

With all of the foreshadowing passages, David directs our attention to major events in his narrative, and in this way he seeks to influence our perspective. Similarly, Dickens uses the idea of a change in a character or in David's assessment of that person to highlight the prejudices in our judgments of others. After Mrs. Seymour Hill, a model for Miss Mowcher, protested about the negative depiction of this figure (Johnson 2: 674–75; PL 5: 674–75, and 674 [n. 5]), Dickens sought to change quickly his presentation of the character and resorted to the device of having David first express surprise at her distress over the flight of Emily and then allowing Miss Mowcher to reprimand the young man for being like other "inconsiderate young people," who judge by external appearances and falsely assume that they will not see "any natural feeling" in "a little thing" like her (32: 390–91). Subsequently, the narrator reports, "I gave Miss Mowcher my hand, with a very different opinion of her from that which I had hitherto entertained" (32: 393). In similar fashion, Mr. Peggotty later assures Martha Endell that he has endured a "change" and is no longer judgmental about her fall from virtue (47: 576).

In addition, David records various changes undergone by characters when they find that modifications in circumstances have altered their perspectives towards themselves or others: Mrs. Gummidge responds to the loss of Emily by abandoning self-pity and complaint: "What a change in Mrs. Gummidge in a little time! She was another woman" (32: 388). After Uriah Heep has forced Wickfield to reveal to Dr. Strong suspicions about Annie, the latter eventually discerns her husband's discomfort, and, in turn, a change can be seen in her: "It came on slowly, like a cloud when there is no wind. . . . Gradually, an unhappy shadow fell upon her beauty, and deepened every day" (42: 524). Within the same chapter, Mrs. Micawber's letter to Traddles exclaims, "Mr. Micawber is entirely changed" (42: 526), an alteration later attributed to Micawber's guilt at having been led by Heep to engage in questionable activities. After the defeat of Uriah, Traddles reports that Mr. Wickfield, having been freed of Heep, "the incubus that had fastened upon him for so long a time, . . . is hardly the same person," for he is much improved in mental capacity (54: 653). In each of these last four cases the way in which the character regards himself or herself, as well as others, has been affected, and, as a result, the impression this person gives to others has been changed.

But perhaps the most striking way in which Dickens emphasizes the theme of varying perspectives or subjectivity is in his use of chapter-titles that can be read in more than one way. Although this device is also found in other novels by Dickens, the extensiveness of its use in *David Copperfield* is extraordinary.[1]

The title of Chapter 16, "I am a New Boy in more senses than one," calls attention to the idea of the multiple meanings that an expression may convey, since David, besides being introduced as "a new boy" (16: 198) at Dr. Strong's school—new to the teachers and the other students—also sees himself as a new person, having been adopted by Aunt Betsey and renamed "Trotwood." While Mr. Mell has referred to David as "the new boy" when taking him to Salem House (5: 69), this expression becomes far more meaningful and more positive when the narrator describes his initial days at Dr. Strong's school. Indeed, the first sentence in the final paragraph of a previous chapter reads, "Thus I began my new life, in a new name, and with everything new about me"—clothing, home, companions (14: 188). Moreover, this technique of double entendre or deliberate ambiguity is also found in a great many of the novel's other chapter-titles. In Chapter 3, "I have a Change," the word "change" refers, first, to what Clara Peggotty calls a "treat," the opportunity for David to spend a fortnight with her at her brother's boat-home in Yarmouth. This "change" is, of course, temporary. But the chapter also describes another change, a permanent alteration in David's life, for his idyllic, Eden-like existence with his mother and Clara Peggotty ends with the advent of his "new" father, Edward Murdstone, who torments the boy and seeks to separate him from his mother. While one change is pleasant, the other is decidedly nightmarish.

In the next chapter, the title "I fall into Disgrace" seems initially to refer to David's difficulty in mastering the "solemn lessons"—"very long, very numerous, very hard"—assigned him at the behest of the Murdstones (4: 51–52), but the disgrace incurred by failure to perform well at these lessons is minor compared to that resulting from the child's biting of Murdstone's hand.

In considering the equivocal chapter-titles, I will examine only those that seem decidedly ambiguous, although I realize, of course, that judgments of this kind are often subjective. For example, Valerie L. Gager regards the title of Chapter 1, "I am Born," as "dualistic' in that it "connects paternity and authorship" and "applies to both the child and the novel" (238), a possibility I find less convincing than the foregoing and succeeding cases.

Chapter 17, "Somebody turns up," provides another instance of double meaning, although we may not fully recognize this until after reading subsequent installments. Early in the chapter, Mr. Dick asks David, "who's the man that hides near the house and frightens her [Aunt Betsey]?" (17: 216). Only two numbers later, in Chapter 23, do we discover that this new character is not what David initially regards as "a delusion of Mr. Dick's" (17: 217), and not until eight monthly installments later does Aunt Betsey disclose that the man is her husband (47: 580), who had been reported dead according to the story told David as a child and recorded in Chapter 1. But in Chapter 17 Aunt Betsey's errant spouse is not the only impecunious figure who "turns up," for Micawber reappears, and the title words are very appropriate, for we were informed earlier, in Chapter 11, that "in case anything turned up" was Micawber's "favourite expression" (11: 145). The words "turns up" suggest a chance event, and the meeting with Micawber in Canterbury is certainly a coincidence: he and his family, after being rebuffed by his wife's Plymouth relatives, returned to London and subsequently departed once more to seek opportunities in the coal trade on the Medway River. Being near Canterbury, they decided to visit the area in order to see the great cathedral and also to be present because "of the great probability of something turning up in a cathedral town" (17: 226). But still a third person besides Aunt Betsey's husband and Micawber turns up, for, from Micawber's perspective, David himself is a "valued friend" who "turn[s] up" (17: 222).

In Chapter 19, "I look about me, and make a Discovery," an additional character "turns up"—Steerforth, who is a "discovery," perhaps the one signified by the title. Two other discoveries, however, are also important in this chapter, the second paragraph of which presents David's remark that he could not yet "discover" a "particular liking" for any "calling" and his speculation that he might have been attracted to the idea of going "round the world on a triumphant voyage of discovery" if he had any knowledge of navigation (19: 235). In developing discovery as a theme, Dickens has the narrator report his prior discovery that Wickfield has deteriorated because of his alcoholism and that the older man is being in some way manipulated by Heep (19: 238). But the chapter-title's use of the present tense alerts us to give more emphasis not to this past understanding, but to still another discovery made in this chapter—the realization that Wickfield is suspicious of Annie Strong and wishes to keep her apart from Agnes (19: 240–41), an awareness that leads David to comment that he left Dr. Strong's "roof with a dark cloud lowering on it" (19: 242). Following this, we find another kind of discovery when David looks around in the hotel's coffee-room and recognizes Steerforth (19: 247). The proximity of this reappearance to the concern over Annie Strong and her possible sexual

infidelity may subsequently be seen as a foreshadowing of Steerforth's role as sexual transgressor, while the place, a coffee-room,
may remind us of David's earlier victimization by the friendly
waiter in the coffee-room of the inn en route to Salem House (5:
62–65).

In addition to the five titles just considered, some fifteen others
among the novel's sixty-four chapter-titles seem to carry more than
one significant meaning. Such ambiguity in a chapter-title induces
us to consider the chapter itself in more than one way, for changes
in our response to a title affect our understanding of the chapter's
emphasis and perspective.

The title of Chapter 25, "Good and bad Angels," is anticipated in
Chapter 23 when David facetiously remarks, "The heart and hand
of the good angel Spenlow would have been always open, but for
the restraining demon Jorkins" (23: 301). After Chapter 24, in which
David describes his "first Dissipation," an incident in which Steerforth's influence leads him to become drunk and make a noisy display of himself at the theater, where he coincidentally encounters
Agnes (24: 308–09), the primary significance of Chapter 25's title
seems obvious: David calls Agnes his "good Angel," and she, in
turn, warns him against his "bad Angel," by whom, she readily
admits, she means Steerforth (25: 312). Afterwards, however, Agnes
reports that Uriah Heep has been in London and is to become the
law partner of her father (25: 313–14). Heep, soon encountered at the
dinner given by Mr. and Mrs. Waterbrook, is described as having a
"cadaverous face" (25: 316) and is clearly to be regarded as another
bad angel, for David refers to him as "some meaner quality of devil"
(25: 326). This comparison is repeated at various times—when Mrs.
Micawber, in a letter to Traddles, mentions hearing her husband
talk of having "sold himself to the D" (49: 592), when David finds
that Heep's looking at Agnes is reminiscent "of an ugly and rebel-
lious genie watching a good spirit" (52: 628), when Micawber, in
denouncing Uriah, speaks of the latter's "infernal business" (52:
631), when Micawber then refers to Heep as "one whom it were
superfluous to call Demon" (52: 636), and when Traddles describes
Heep as "the incubus that had fastened" upon Mr. Wickfield "for
so long a time" (54: 653). Moreover, in Chapter 25, "Good and bad
Angels," David has, after a separation of many years, again met
Traddles, who becomes for him another benevolent angel.

Of course, in the dialogue between David and Agnes early in the
chapter the word "angel" is employed in two different ways. When

applied to Steerforth, the term seems related to its use in Shakespeare's Sonnet 144 to refer to human beings: however, while Shakespeare's speaker uses the term "better angel" to designate the intensely loved male friend and the words "worser spirit" to indicate the female mistress, Agnes here sees the male Steerforth as a misguided and misguiding force.[2] But when David calls Agnes his "good Angel," he seems to wish not only to refer to an exemplary person but also to convey a religious association, for, much earlier, when the boy David first met Agnes, he connected her with the "tranquil brightness" once noticed in "a stained glass window in a church" (15: 194; 16: 201).

On first seeing the title of Chapter 26, "I fall into Captivity," we may think that the statement will refer mainly to David's being articled to Spenlow and Jorkins, but we quickly learn otherwise, for, upon meeting Dora, David remarks, "All was over in a moment. I was a captive and a slave" (26: 331). But the most significant ambiguity in the first half of the novel comes in the title to the climactic Chapter 31, "A greater Loss." For David and the other characters, Emily's fall from virtue is, obviously, a greater loss than the "loss" of the preceding chapter, the death of the elderly and ailing Barkis. Moreover, the chapter-title suggests not only the loss of Emily to Ham and Mr. Peggotty, but also the loss to herself of her virtue and her reputation. The adoring Ham, in asking God to "kill her . . . sooner than let her come to ruin and disgrace" (31: 382), clearly accepts the idea that for a woman to be seduced is a fate worse than death.

Here, too, however, we find that the meaning first evoked by a chapter-title is supplemented—and perhaps to an extent even superseded—by another significance when we reflect further. Stunned to learn that Steerforth has been responsible for Emily's flight, David initially is tempted to "curse" his former friend, but yields "to a better feeling" and weeps (31: 385). Not until the opening paragraph of the next chapter, however, is there a truly clear indication that for David the loss of Steerforth as an admired friend may well be even greater than the loss of Emily and of Emily's reputation: "I had never loved Steerforth better than when the ties that bound me to him were broken" (32: 385). The remaining five sentences of this initial paragraph, as well as the two sentences that constitute the following paragraph, give further emphasis to this deprivation.[3]

Chapters 35 and 36, the first two chapters in No. 12, bear the titles "Depression" and "Enthusiasm" and balance each other. In

"Depression" David finds in sequence three relatively distinct reasons for being low-spirited: first, he briefly feels "a vague unhappy
loss or want of something" (35: 426), a mood mentioned again peri-
odically (e.g., 44: 545 and 47: 587) and linked to his growing awareness that Dora, attractive and pleasant though she is, is not really
an entirely satisfying life's companion for him; second, David realizes that Aunt Betsey's greatly reduced circumstances make much
more difficult his attempt to win Dora in marriage; and, third, in
the middle of the chapter he finds an added reason for distress in
learning of Heep's growing ascendancy over Mr. Wickfield. The
significance of the chapter-title is therefore augmented and developed as the narrative unfolds. Similarly, the title of Chapter 36,
"Enthusiasm," can be seen as extending to refer not just to David's
eagerness to assume extra work assisting Dr. Strong, but also to
describe Mr. Dick's extreme pleasure when he finds that by working
as a copyist he can earn money to assist Aunt Betsey, and then to
denote Mr. Micawber's delighted anticipation of working as Heep's
clerk. The enthusiasm of all three characters pointedly contrasts
with the indifference proudly laid claim to by Jack Maldon (36: 443),
the type of indifference later displayed in *Little Dorrit* by the odious
Henry Gowan.

This pattern of titles with equivocal meanings that extend as a
chapter progresses continues with Chapter 37, "A little cold Water."
For Dora, the disillusioning news is that of David's straitened financial circumstances, while for David himself it is his realization
that Dora refuses to respond in a serious manner. Similarly, in Chapter 38, "A Dissolution of Partnership" may initially seem to refer to
the end of the secret engagement between David and Dora, but the
main meaning arises when the sudden, surprising death of Spenlow
dramatically ends his business partnership with Mr. Jorkins. A comparable effect is achieved by the title of Chapter 40, "The Wanderer." This term initially appears to denote Mr. Peggotty, who has
announced his determination to seek Emily, his niece, "through the
wureld" (31: 385), "to seek her, fur and wide" (32: 401), for David
has frequently thought of him since Emily's flight as a "solitary
figure, [a] poor pilgrim" (32: 401). Indeed, early in Chapter 40 we
are told that Mr. Peggotty has "toiled and wandered through all
varieties of weather" (40: 491) and that in his journeying through
Europe he has become a mythic person, a man whose story precedes
him (40: 493). He reveals how in spite of disappointments he "wandered on" (40: 494).

Later in this chapter, however, David notices the "haggard" Martha Endell eavesdropping on his conversation with Mr. Peggotty (40: 493–94), and we realize that she, too, is a wanderer, a "lonely figure" (40: 497), a woman who in a subsequent chapter declares that she would have been willing to have continued her present existence as a streetwalker and to "have lived to be old, in the wretched streets—and to wander about, avoided, in the dark," if this could have saved Emily (47: 576). Of course, at other times in the novel the narrator himself seems to be a wanderer: as a child in London, he "lounged" about the streets (11: 144); after the death of Dora, he stays over at the Wickfield house, where he feels "like a shipwrecked wanderer" (54: 658); and near the end of the narrative he sees himself in imagination as "a ragged way-worn boy" (62: 725), a reference to his heroic trek much earlier from London to Dover. Interestingly, Hablot Browne's illustration for Chapter 40, "The Wanderer," bears this title and includes all three candidates for the epithet: in the focal center and facing the reader is the dominating figure of Mr. Peggotty, while David, his back to us, is placed in the foreground, and a wraith-like Martha is seen peering in as she stands beside the open door (fig. 1). The text of the chapter, of course, also gives us tidings of a fourth wanderer, Emily herself.

Dickens persists in this pattern of using titles with shifting meanings. In Chapter 42, "Mischief," this word can be understood to refer to Heep's malicious revelation to Dr. Strong that Wickfield has long had suspicion of impropriety in the relationship between Annie and her cousin Jack Maldon (42: 518–20), for this information causes extreme distress in the Strongs' marriage. But at the end of the chapter we encounter another instance of mischief: Emma Micawber's letter to David tells of the rift between her husband and her, and we subsequently learn that in this marriage, too, the disharmony is attributable to Heep, who has led Micawber into actions that arouse guilt and self-loathing.

In Chapter 49, "I am involved in Mystery," Traddles and David find in a letter from Micawber several mysterious remarks: (1) the claim that his purpose in writing "is not of a pecuniary nature" (49: 591), (2) an oblique reference to Micawber's having the "latent ability . . . of wielding the thunderbolt, or directing the devouring and avenging flame" (49: 591), (3) mention of his great distress, and (4) a postscript indicating that he has not confided in Mrs. Micawber. Very soon after, however, Mrs. Micawber's letter to Traddles arouses further bafflement. Although the "mystery" created by

her letter also involves Mr. Micawber's secrecy and self-condemna-
tion, Emma Micawber is an independent source of this puzzling information.

In five of the remaining chapters, three of these offering important
climaxes, Dickens continues to use equivocal titles. In Chapter 52,
"I assist at an Explosion," the word "explosion" refers mainly to
Micawber's outburst, his passionate denunciation of Heep. Much
earlier, in Chapter 35, David has used the term "explosion" to describe Aunt Betsey's impatient and irritated order to Heep to cease
his physical twisting and writhing: "If you're a man, control your
limbs, sir!" (35: 437). Shortly before Chapter 52, Micawber announces his intention of shaking no man's hand until he has
"moved Mount Vesuvius—to eruption—on—a—the abandoned
rascal—HEEP!" (49: 599), and in a letter he subsequently refers to
his "excitement" in front of Aunt Betsey as "an explosion of a
smouldering volcano long suppressed" (49: 600). In Chapter 52,
Aunt Betsey tells Micawber, "we are ready for Mount Vesuvius, or
anything else, as you please" (52: 623), and he promises that she
will "shortly witness an eruption" (52: 623). The "explosion" in the
chapter-title, however, may also refer to the demolition of Heep's
conspiracy, his attempt to use his defalcations to gain dominance
over the self-blaming Wickfield and in this way coerce Agnes into
marriage. In anticipating the exposure, Micawber has promised to
"know nobody—and—a—say nothing—and—a—live nowhere—
until" he has "crushed—to—a—undiscoverable atoms—the—trans-
cendent and immortal hypocrite and perjurer—HEEP!" (49: 599).
In the second chapter after Micawber's impassioned denunciation,
David refers to "what Mr. Micawber called the 'final pulverisation
of Heep' " (54: 648).

While Chapter 52, "I assist at an Explosion," describes the comic
exposure and defeat of Heep through human effort, Chapter 55,
"Tempest," records the retributive and tragic destruction of another
of the novel's three main villains, Steerforth, by the power of nature.
The chapter-title obviously refers to the cataclysmic storm depicted
so vividly that for Tolstoy the scene was preeminent in all of "the
world's prose literature" (DCH 242), while Ruskin believed "there
is nothing in sea-description" with such effective use of detail (DCH
443 [headnote]). Dickens himself at times chose the storm-scene for
his public readings, for it is truly exceptional in conveying sights,
sounds, and feelings. But just as Robert Frost in his short poem
"Tree at My Window" has the speaker consider two kinds of
weather—"outer" and "inner"—so Dickens has David present both

Figure 1: The Wanderer

external and internal upheavals, for the chapter, besides dwelling on the ever-increasing tumult of wind, rain, and sea, also reveals the mounting psychic turmoil that the protagonist is experiencing. As we have already observed, in the chapter immediately preceding, David, on entering the Wickfield house, has felt "like a shipwrecked wanderer come home" (54: 658). Throughout Chapter 55, we recognize David's growing distress and unease, his dis-ease.

The title of Chapter 56, "The new Wound and the old," like the prior examples examined, may be seen in differing senses: the "wounds" are David's, the new one being Steerforth's death and the old one probably being Steerforth's past betrayal of David and their friendship in the seduction of Emily. (The possibility that the "old" wound signifies the loss of Dora and the new one the death of Steerforth seems less likely, for the death of Dora, though less recent than Steerforth's demise, is not yet "old.") Two wounds, however, a new one and an old one, have also been sustained by Rosa Dartle: the scar on her lip and the death of Steerforth. In addition, we realize that Mrs. Steerforth has suffered both an old and a new wound: estrangement from her son and then his death.

The title of Chapter 58, "Absence," provokes us to ask who is absent from whom or what, and although David's self-imposed absence from England is the obvious answer, the chapter-title, as Garrett Stewart aptly observes, "describes not only his [David's] expatriation to the Continent but the sudden vacuum at the center of his emotional life" (*Death Sentences* 79).[4]

In the novel's final installment, the double-number containing Chapters 58–64, Chapter 62 is climactic and carries a title with a double meaning, "A Light shines on my way." The light is, first, the sudden illumination that comes to David as he tries to question Agnes about her future and receives evasive replies: " 'In the course of years!' 'It is not a new one!' New thoughts and hopes were whirling through my mind, and all the colors of my life were changing" (62: 724). Expressing the "new-born hope" that he may call Agnes "something more than Sister," David is joyfully accepted by her as her future husband (62: 724). The "Light" on his "way," however, refers not just to the perception that Agnes loves him, but also to Agnes herself, who, from the first time when David as a child saw her, has been associated in his mind with the "tranquil brightness" of "a stained glass window in a church" (15: 194): "the soft light of the colored glass window in the church, seen long ago, falls on her always" (16: 201).

This pattern in the chapter-titles—the "look again" or "think again" effect—is far more noticeable in *David Copperfield* than in any of Dickens's other novels, and the device certainly emphasizes the theme of varying perspectives. Indeed, equivocation, an important device to evoke questions in *Macbeth*, one of Dickens's favorite plays, also becomes, through the use of chapter-titles, a significant element in *David Copperfield*, a novel opening with a question, whether David is to see himself as the hero of his own life. Moreover, Dickens uses not only ambiguity but also repetition to lend significance to the chapter-titles in this book.

We find, for instance, four chapters linked by titles containing the noun "retrospect": Chapter 18, "A Retrospect," reviews David's years from about twelve to seventeen, the time spent at Dr. Strong's school, after which he must seek a profession; Chapter 43, "Another Retrospect," examines his courtship of Dora and their wedding; Chapter 53, also called "Another Retrospect," records Dora's last days and her death; and Chapter 64, "A last Retrospect," reviews the characters who have not migrated to Australia. Although each of these chapters looks back at a significant time in the narrator's life, no one of them actually is retrospective from the reader's viewpoint, for each imparts new information. Indeed, each may ironically be seen as ending with a prospect for David: choosing a career after leaving Dr. Strong's school, starting married life with Dora, facing the shock of the loss of Dora, and prayerfully hoping for Agnes's spiritual and emotional support until the time of his own death.

In this use of chapter-titles to provide directions for readers but also to surprise, Dickens appears to emphasize the complexity of our responses to life. We are meant to use this increased awareness of subtlety in responding to issues besides those regarded in these titles. For example, Clara Copperfield may be self-centered and foolish, but she deserves our pity for being deceived and maltreated. Aunt Betsey is wrong to desert David's mother and later to test him without cause (since she has not really, we learn, lost all her money), but she is still to be viewed as a generous and affectionate person. The titles, which guide and redirect, also may remind us of the need to interpret and then reinterpret life, to perceive patterns and to find lessons, to determine priorities and to decide which experiences and observations should receive attention and emphasis.

By the shifts in perspective, the foreshadowings, the claims of change in characters, and the often ambiguous chapter-titles, Dickens reminds us that our responses to life as well as to art may be subjective. We must learn how to react to ambiguous situations like that described in the opening scene of *Macbeth*: "Fair is foul, and foul is fair." Nevertheless, like both Shakespeare and Dickens, we must retain our basic moral values: there is no question that we are to prefer Agnes to Heep as a guide, that Traddles proves far superior to Steerforth as a friend.

In the concluding pages of *The Achievement of Samuel Johnson*, Walter Jackson Bate writes, "to pick one's way through the large, chaotic body of man's literature, evaluating and getting anything out of it, involves first of all the use of the same qualities of mind needed to extract any point or meaning from life itself" (230–31). In much fiction, but especially in *David Copperfield*, the reading and comprehending of the text help train us to respond to the complexity found in actual life.

Notes

1. Stewart observes, "Dickens had begun even by the time of *Dombey and Son* to experiment with those condensed, suggestive chapter headings that become one of the hallmarks of his later fiction, pregnant phrases that often issue in referential twins or triplets" ("New Mortality" 457). Although Stewart suggests, "Probably the chapters of *Bleak House* are the most richly titled of all" ("New Mortality" 457), I believe that Dickens's most effective employment of chapter-titles is found in *David Copperfield*.
2. Gager remarks, "Despite Dickens's reversal of the sexes of the good and bad angels, the exchange between David and Agnes concerning Steerforth's reliability as a friend establishes a triangle of two males and one female as in Shakespeare's sonnet" (193). For Gager, the "frequent references" to this sonnet "provide the basis for at least five shifting triangles which illuminate the relationships between seven of the characters [in the novel]"—Steerforth, David, Agnes; Steerforth, David, Emily; Steerforth, David, Rosa Dartle; Uriah Heep, David, Agnes; David, Dora, Julia Mills (193–95). (These five triangles involve eight, rather than seven, characters.) Although Gager sees Heep as a bad angel, she does not suggest that Traddles is a good one.
3. Tambling comments, "The 'greater loss' . . . that DC experiences . . . is not that of Emily in comparison to Barkis, . . . but that of Steerforth" (ix-x). This point was previously called to my attention, however, by Isabel Varlotta, my student in a course in Dickens during the Spring 1994 semester at Queens College, CUNY.
4. Commenting on Chapter 59, "Return," Stewart states that here, too, "the bearings [are] again internal as well as geographical," since "David's homecoming is . . . an emotional retrieval as well as a reversed itinerary" (*Death Sentences* 79).

Chapter 5

Mudfog Revisited: Echoes and Reflections in *Bleak House*

The opening two paragraphs of *Bleak House* focus respectively on London's mud and fog: "As much mud in the streets, as if the waters had but newly retired from the face of the earth," "tens of thousands of other foot passengers have been slipping and sliding . . ., adding new deposits to the crust upon crust of mud"; "Fog everywhere," "a nether sky of fog" (1: 5). In the fifth and sixth paragraphs the mud and the fog are emphatically paired to such an extent that we may wonder if Dickens is playfully renaming the capital city "Mudfog," the appellation given to Oliver Twist's natal town in the serialization first published in *Bentley's Miscellany*.[1] Although previous commentators have noticed parallels between *Oliver Twist* and *Bleak House*,[2] any additional similarities in large patterns and in small details have not, I believe, been discussed. Indeed, the numerous resemblances suggest that in the later, much more complex novel Dickens is choosing to retell with variations his earlier story of virtue imperiled and surviving. The likenesses and the contrasts illuminate Dickens's continuing concerns, his modifications in outlook and in technique, and his overall creative processes.

Dickens finished writing *Oliver Twist* in November 1838, when a three-volume edition was issued, even though the serialization in

Bentley's Miscellany was to continue until April 1839. On February 21, 1851, Dickens wrote in a letter to his friend Mary Boyle that he felt about him "the first shadows of a new story hovering in a ghostly way" (PL 6: 298), an appropriate figurative reference to a novel dominated by revenants and specters.[3] Dickens did not, however, begin the actual writing of *Bleak House* until November 1851, thirteen years after finishing *Oliver Twist*. But during that thirteen-year span, the earlier book made claims upon his attention, for in March 1841 he composed a preface for a new edition produced by Chapman and Hall, while in 1846, after he had left this publishing house, Bradbury and Evans issued an edition in ten monthly parts and also in one volume. Three years later, installments of *Oliver Twist* began appearing in "the Cheap edition" of Dickens's works, a series that included a one-volume version issued in April 1850 with a new preface written by Dickens the month before.

In *Oliver Twist* and in *Bleak House*, each protagonist—Oliver and Esther—is the illegitimate offspring of parents from the gentility, and each child is deprived of a mother's love immediately after birth, a birth that is so difficult that the infant's survival is questionable. Until the age of nine, Oliver is given to the care of Mrs. Mann, as non-maternal as her name suggests, and afterwards he must survive life in the workhouse for a brief period of under a year, then endure a short interval as apprentice to the undertaker Sowerberry, and afterwards live for a time as a victim-in-waiting to Fagin. But Oliver, whom Dickens categorizes in an 1841 preface as representing "the principle of Good surviving through every adverse circumstance, and triumphing at last" (3), remains unscathed in nearly every respect, even in his ability to speak as though he had been educated. Indeed, he shows no sign of damage except perhaps for a completely understandable apprehensiveness that leads him to plead in a pathetic manner to Mr. Brownlow, a benefactor who has given him shelter, "Don't turn me out of doors to wander in the streets again. . . . Have mercy upon a poor boy, sir!" (14: 98).

Unlike this young boy, Esther is raised until the age of "almost fourteen" (3: 20) by her godmother, a parental surrogate harsh in ways different from Mrs. Mann's. Although Esther never lacks food or proper clothing, she is subjected to emotional and psychological mistreatment similar to that inflicted on Oliver by people like Mr. Bumble, who calls him "a naughty orphan which nobody can't love" (3: 33), and Noah Claypole, who disparages Oliver's mother as "a regular right-down bad'un" (6: 52): Esther's godmother, later revealed to be her aunt, tells the child, "It would have been far better . . . that you had never been born!" and "Your mother, Esther, is your disgrace, and you were hers" (3: 19). These remarks lead the child to feel unwanted and to resolve "to win some love" (3: 20). As Alex Zwerdling has cogently argued, the low self-esteem imposed upon Esther by her upbringing leads to such mannerisms as her protestations of humility and her repeating of words of approval addressed to her by others (430).

Oliver is falsely accused, arrested, and briefly imprisoned. Although Esther herself does not endure such experiences, George Rouncewell is, like Oliver, wrongly placed under suspicion, arrested, and sent to prison, only to be, again like Oliver, later vindicated. Moreover, George seems in some respects a surrogate for Esther, since he, like her, is a revenant who becomes reconciled with his mother, and he, too, as the former attendant or orderly of Hawdon, may be seen as the latter's child.[4] Like Oliver, Esther represents "the principle of Good": as Brian Cheadle comments, her "open anxiousness marks the efforts of goodness to survive in an unfriendly and disinherited world" (44).

As Anny Sadrin has observed (68), in each case the protagonist's striking resemblance to his or her mother is noted by someone's seeing a portrait of the mother: Brownlow sees Oliver's features in a painting of Agnes Fleming (12: 86; 49: 328), and Guppy eventually recognizes Esther's resemblance to Lady Dedlock's portrait (7: 82–83; 29: 361). While Oliver is mysteriously attracted to his mother's face in the painting, Esther is similarly drawn to the living person of her mother (17: 224–25, 228). Oliver does not discover his parentage for over twelve years, and Esther's background remains concealed from her for twenty-one years. Moreover, as Goldie Morgentgaler (40–43) and Burton M. Wheeler (53–54) have remarked, Oliver resembles not only his mother but also his father. Esther, too, perhaps bears a likeness to both parents, for George Rouncewell on first meeting her comments, "I thought I had seen you somewhere" (24: 305). Although Newsom suggests that George had known Lady Dedlock long ago at Chesney Wold and is being influenced by Esther's resemblance to her (53), various details suggest that George's departure preceded Sir Leicester's marriage. George, who is 50 (21: 264), left home some thirty-five years before, when 15 (26: 325). Since Esther was about 21 when Jarndyce employed her as Ada's companion (17: 213), and since Lady Dedlock did not marry until after Esther's birth, George was gone from Chesney Wold when she became its lady. Of course, he later discloses that he has made furtive visits to see his mother from a distance, and he may at these times also have noticed Lady Dedlock. Moreover, he apparently once bore a message from Hawdon to her *before* her marriage (63: 747). But since he still would have had few chances to see Lady Dedlock, but was very familiar with Hawdon, there seems to be at least a possibility that George, in thinking he has previously seen Esther, is unconsciously responding to a resemblance between her and her father.[5] Clearly, noticeable facial resemblances raise questions of heredity and destiny.

Each protagonist, too, is greatly assisted by a philanthropic benefactor who is a wealthy, elderly, eccentric bachelor: Mr. Brownlow and John Jarndyce. Each man has for a close friend a gruff, irascible, eccentric person—Mr. Grimwig, whose early doubts concerning Oliver prompt Brownlow to send the boy on an ill-fated errand to a bookseller, and Lawrence Boythorn, whose tumultuous behavior masks his chivalric generosity. Just as the obstreperous Grimwig plays an important role by encouraging a decision that separates Oliver from Brownlow for a time, so the loud Boythorn, by insisting that Esther and Ada accept for the former's convalescence the hospitality of his home, which is adjacent to Chesney Wold, helps to make possible Lady Dedlock's discovery of her daughter. Jarndyce's other close friend, Harold Skimpole, although like Boythorn a minor character, also greatly affects the events in the story, for he contributes to the deaths of both Jo and Richard by "selling" each—Jo to Bucket, and Carstone to Vholes, the rodent-like predator.

Grimwig's skepticism may in some ways reflect Brownlow's lack of complete faith in Oliver, while the housekeeper, Mrs. Bedwin, stands for her employer's desire to retain total confidence in the boy. Similarly, Jarndyce's contrasting two friends—Harold Skimpole and Lawrence Boythorn—represent distinctive sides of his personality: the two men are vastly different, one graceful and languorous, the other impulsive and eccentric. As Q. D. Leavis observes, Boythorn is intended to be Skimpole's "opposite" (151).[6] The first part of each surname seems significant, since Skimpole "skimps" when called upon to show true feeling, while Boythorn is *boy*ishly unrestrained and *bois*terous. The pair may be seen as extensions of Jarndyce because they display in exaggerated form qualities that he also reveals. In Skimpole's wish to be oblivious of monetary responsibilities, there is a possible reflection of Jarndyce's stance towards Chancery—simply ignoring a problem and leaving others to cope with it. Q. D. Leavis comments, "Jarndyce blinds himself to the ugly truth about Skimpole because he needs to believe it is possible to beat the system, that Skimpole has successfully opted out of it"

(150). In Boythorn's wild enthusiasm, we may see an extreme development of Jarndyce's outbursts—for example, his throwing a cake out of a carriage window when the child Esther, en route to school at Greenleaf, refuses it (3: 25); his impulsive flight from Ada's mother when she, as a very little child, attempted to thank him for a kindness (6: 58–59); his exclamation—"Look at this! For God's sake, look at this!" (15: 188)—on realizing the situation of the orphaned and impoverished children of Neckett; and his periodic retreats to the Growlery when he is " 'deceived or disappointed in—the wind, and it's Easterly' " (8: 87).

Each benefactor—Brownlow and Jarndyce—provides great assistance to the protagonist, but is unable to prevent harm from being done to others by the malevolent government institution attacked in each book. In *Oliver Twist* poor little Dick dies after maltreatment both in the establishment of Mrs. Mann, the agent of the workhouse, and in the workhouse itself. In the later novel a similarly named character—Richard or Rick Carstone—is destroyed by Chancery, which has previously caused the death of Gridley, the madness of Miss Flite, and the suffering of a great many unnamed victims. Each institution, although created to do good, has become a disturbing force of evil.

In addition to the likenesses between the illegitimate protagonists and between their benefactors, other parallels between characters can also be seen in *Oliver Twist* and *Bleak House*. At first, the main villains—the criminal Fagin and the lawyer Tulkinghorn—seem very dissimilar, but each is conniving and furtive, a scheming dealer in secrets who gains power through information and is therefore a potential extortionist: Fagin is initially referred to, by the Dodger, as "a 'spectable old genelman" (8: 63), and Tulkinghorn is first described by the anonymous narrator as "an old-fashioned old gentleman" (2: 13). Each seeks to intimidate by telling a monitory story. Fagin relates to Oliver, after the boy has been brought back by Nancy and Sikes, "the dismal and affecting history of a young lad whom . . . he had succoured under parallel circumstances, but who, proving unworthy of his confidence, and evincing a desire to communicate with the police, had unfortunately come to be hanged at the Old Bailey one morning" (18: 125). Tulkinghorn, during a gathering at Chesney Wold, tells Lady Dedlock, who is with her husband and their guests, a cautionary tale of a "townsman of this Mr. Rouncewell, a man in exactly parallel circumstances as I am told," whose daughter "attracted the notice of a great lady"—this man, according to Tulkinghorn, withdrew the young woman from the home of the great lady on discovering that the latter had "in early life" given birth to an illegitimate child fathered by her fiancé at the time, "a young rake" who was "a captain in the army" (40: 505–06). When Lady Dedlock, in the next chapter, asks the lawyer why he has told her story "to so many persons," he replies that he wished to make her aware of his knowledge of her secret (41: 508).

Moreover, Fagin and Tulkinghorn are also linked in another way. Each induces a passionate woman to wear a costume to disguise herself and deceptively gain information about or from a young boy: Nancy pretends to be a sister of Oliver to learn where he is (13: 92–94) and then to abduct him (15: 107–08), while Hortense poses as her mistress, Lady Dedlock, to trick Jo (23: 281–83). Each woman is both a pawn and a victim, and each subsequently becomes alienated from the older man who has made use of her. This alienation eventually leads to the deaths of the two villainous men, for Hortense murders Tulkinghorn, while Nancy, although she refuses to "deliver up" Fagin to justice (46: 308), confides in Rose and Brownlow, thereby setting in motion a series of events that lead to her own death and eventually to Fagin's execution. Nancy, in seeking to protect the recaptured Oliver, has threatened Fagin (16: 114–15), and Hortense, angered by the ungenerous coldness of Tulkinghorn, has defied him (43: 517–20). Just as Fagin induces Sikes to kill Nancy, so Tulkinghorn unintentionally goads Hortense to commit murder, a crime of which he himself is, ironically, the victim.

Each of the two heroines—Rose Maylie, in the earlier novel, and Esther, both protagonist and heroine in *Bleak House*—must face, as David Paroissien observes, the problem of suspected or actual illegitimacy (*Companion to* OT 215, 278–79). Moreover, each young woman survives a nearly fatal unnamed illness and recovers to the great joy of the household in which she lives. Each later marries an idealistic young man who is not deterred by seeming disadvantages in his bride: Allan Woodcourt's love for Esther leads him to disregard her illegitimacy and her loss of beauty and to abandon his mother's aspirations for him to marry a woman of high "birth" or family lineage (17: 215; 54: 752–53), while Harry Maylie, in order to gain Rose, surrenders a political career to become a parson in a remote country church (51: 349), for he does not know until the novel's conclusion that the claim of her illegitimacy (35: 235–36) is a slander (51: 347). Each man remains steadfast in his love, despite his own mother's early doubts about his choice of a bride, an opposition that is eventually overcome. Each couple eventually chooses to live away from London, in *Oliver Twist* a scene of crime and danger, in *Bleak House* the site of Chancery and its torment. Rose and Harry settle in a country village, while Esther and Woodcourt move to the Yorkshire countryside.

Both Rose and Esther display tenderness and great solicitude in attending a young boy who is ill or injured—Oliver in one case, and Jo in the other. Just as George Rouncewell may be seen as a surrogate for Esther in some respects, so, in other ways, Jo, the beneficiary of Hawdon, her father, also seems to be a substitute for her. Oliver is treated with some friendly interest by a tradesman, the undertaker Sowerberry, who is married to a shrewish wife, and Jo is shown compassion by the stationer Snagsby, who is also married to a domineering spouse.

In each narrative the erring mother of the protagonist perishes after undertaking an arduous trek on foot to the grave of the improvident lover who had fathered her only child, the issue of a birth that is illegitimate and so difficult as to be almost fatal to the infant. Agnes's death separates her from her child, while Lady Dedlock eventually discovers that her own sister's cruel deception has parted her from Esther. Although Agnes Fleming dies very early in *Oliver Twist*, the destination of her journey is not disclosed until very late in the novel (51: 346), and only in the penultimate installment of *Bleak House* (59: 711–14) do we find the account of Lady Dedlock's death near the entrance to the cemetery where Hawdon is interred.

Two minor characters—Mrs. Bedwin, Brownlow's housekeeper, and Mrs. Rouncewell, the housekeeper at Chesney Wold—are significant in being gentle, grandmotherly figures who demonstrate complete faith in the innocence, respectively, of Oliver, incorrectly thought by Grimwig and Brownlow to have absconded with the books he was asked to return to the bookseller, and of George Rouncewell, wrongly suspected by Bucket of murdering Tulkinghorn.

In addition to these numerous likenesses involving characters and their behavior, we find many other parallels concerning specific events, situations, and motifs. Each novel involves a will that is lost and disputed—in *Bleak House* a testament that benefits no one except the lawyers and in *Oliver Twist* a will that has been destroyed and becomes known only when the villainous Monks is cowed into cooperating with Brownlow.

In the early book, Nancy asks for Rose Maylie's handkerchief as a memento (46: 311), and she desperately holds up this relic, symbolic of her innocence, as she is brutally murdered (47: 316–17).

Of course, the theft by the Dodger and Charley Bates of another handkerchief from Mr. Brownlow has brought Oliver to the attention of Brownlow and also of Monks. In *Bleak House* a handkerchief that Esther leaves at a brickmaker's hovel to cover a dead infant (8: 100) is later taken by Lady Dedlock as a remembrance of her long-lost daughter (35: 439; 36: 449). When Mr. Bucket later finds this handkerchief with Esther's name on it in Lady Dedlock's room, he is led to enlist Esther's help in searching for her fugitive mother (56: 671–72). In each work, the heroine's handkerchief links two women (Rose and Nancy, Esther and Lady Dedlock) and is associated with death.

Writing about the handkerchief and Nancy's murder, Laurence Senelick has seen in *Oliver Twist* the influence of *Othello*, for there are similarities between the murders of Nancy and Desdemona, and "in both cases a handkerchief is the token of . . . misunderstanding" (97–102).[7] In *Bleak House* we find two significant references to this Shakespearean tragedy: one of the paintings in the Dedlocks' townhouse presents a scene from the play (29: 357); and, late in the novel, when the efforts of Bucket, Esther, and Woodcourt to find the fleeing Lady Dedlock are hampered by Mrs. Snagsby's absurd suspicions of her husband, the detective angrily rebukes the stationer's wife for her unwarranted jealousy—"Go and see Othello acted. That's the tragedy for you" (59: 708). In addition, some commentators have seen Tulkinghorn as a figure like Iago (see, e.g., G. Smith 125 and Dyson 162–63), a misogynist whom Coleridge believed was prompted by "motiveless malignity" (1: 149). Of course, as Senelick notices, Fagin, too, is like Iago in inciting a man to murder a woman who loves him (98).[8]

In each of the novels a climactic murder gives rise to an exciting chase: Sikes becomes a fugitive after his deed, and Lady Dedlock flees because she fears being under suspicion. Each crime is committed with a pistol, although in the earlier narrative it is used as a bludgeon, rather than as a firearm. In each case the motive is revenge, although the villain's female pawn in one instance is the victim, while in the other she is the murderer. Each crime arouses public outrage and the announcement of a monetary reward for the apprehension of the killer.

In *Oliver Twist*, Jacob's Island, a slum that is a source of misery and crime, serves as an important setting. In *Bleak House* another slum, Tom-all-Alone's, the location of the graveyard in which Hawdon is interred, gives rise to disease that spreads to wealthy, fashionable sections of London. As I have previously remarked, H. M.

Daleski regards the description of Jacob's Island in *Oliver Twist* as "a first version of Tom-all-Alone's," both areas having been ruined by involvement in Chancery litigation (64–65). David Paroissien observes that the location in *Oliver Twist* where Bumble and his wife go to meet Monks (38: 247–48) is based on a riverfront neighborhood in Chatham known as "Tom-All-Alone's," the name that Dickens was to employ for a slum in *Bleak House* (*Companion to OT* 226–27).

Other minor details from *Oliver Twist* also emerge in *Bleak House*. During Oliver's first attendance at a funeral with the undertaker Sowerberry, the narrator mentions that the grave-digger can readily follow the request, "fill up," since "the grave was so full, that the uppermost coffin was within a few feet of the surface" (5: 49). In *Bleak House* Nemo's corpse is buried by being lowered down only "a foot or two" (11: 137), and Jo later tells the disguised Lady Dedlock, "They put him wery nigh the top" (16: 202).

In Chapter 19 of *Oliver Twist*, we are told, "The mud lay thick upon the stones: and a black mist hung over the streets," as Fagin "glided stealthily along, creeping . . . like some loathsome reptile" (19: 132), a passage that seems to anticipate the remark in the opening of *Bleak House* that in the mud and fog of London "it would not be wonderful to meet a Megalosaurus" (1: 5).[9] All three images are significant: the mud endangers stability, since it makes for slippery footing, besides being malodorous and esthetically offensive, a mixture of dirt, refuse, and animal-droppings; the fog reduces visibility and pollutes the air, creating another kind of stench; and the reptilian Fagin or the imagined megalosaurus suggests primordial predatory instincts that threaten the city's status as a center of civilized life.

At the end of the earlier book, the narrator remarks that within the village church stands "a white marble tablet" bearing the name of Oliver's mother, Agnes (53: 360), and Cruikshank's etching shows Oliver and Rose standing reverentially before this spot. The novel's penultimate sentence speculates, "if the spirits of the Dead ever come back to earth, to visit spots hallowed by the love—the love beyond the grave—of those whom they knew in life, I believe that the shade of Agnes hovers round that solemn nook" (53: 360), a statement that seems to anticipate Esther's reaction when, after seeing Woodcourt for the first time since her illness, she momentarily takes the perspective of a ghost: "I felt for my old self as the dead may feel if they ever revisit these scenes" (45: 551). In the last chapter presented by the anonymous narrator who shares the telling of *Bleak House* with Esther, we find a brief description of Sir Leicester

Dedlock's daily ritual of riding with George Rouncewell, whom I have previously discussed as a surrogate for Esther, to stop before the door of the family mausoleum and pay respect to the dead Honoria (66: 764).

Rejecting the concept of inherited guilt is important in each narrative. Responding to Monks's use of the term "bastard," Brownlow asserts that this term, although "a reproach to those who have long since passed beyond the feeble censure of the world" (Oliver's parents), "reflects disgrace on no one living, except you who use it" (51: 343). In the later novel Esther eventually rejects with firmness the idea that she is "degraded" by "the sins of others" (3: 19) and decides that she herself is "as innocent of . . . [her] birth as a queen of hers" (36: 454).

In each book, moreover, Dickens is strongly concerned with dual or multiple perspectives. As we noticed in Chapter 1 of this study, the narrator in *Oliver Twist* at times uses an ironic tone and at other times is straightforward and literal.[10] In *Bleak House* the anonymous teller often employs bitter irony, while Esther is customarily plain-spoken and direct. Indeed, both narrators in this later novel include remarks introducing the interrelated themes of perspective and perception. The anonymous narrator displays an ability to look from afar with a wide focus—"Fog on the Essex marshes, fog on the Kentish heights" (1: 5)—and he suggests that he has the power to "pass from one place to the other, as the crow flies" (2: 10). Although the perspective of Esther usually appears to be limited, confined to herself and the people near her, she claims, despite her assertion that she is "not clever," to have had "always rather a noticing way" (3: 17). After repeating, "I have not by any means a quick understanding," she adds that feeling affection for someone can enhance her interest and perception: "When I love a person very tenderly indeed, it [her "understanding"] seems to brighten" (3: 17).

In *Oliver Twist*, too, perspective and perception are important themes. Occasionally, accounts of events are retold from a second viewpoint. The narrator describes the death of Oliver's mother (1: 18), and, considerably later, old Sally retells this story, adding details about Agnes's suffering and the gold locket she had saved for her child (24: 164–65). Another death, that of old Sally herself, is described from three perspectives—first, by the narrator (24: 164–65); next, by Mrs. Bumble (formerly Mrs. Corney), who is persuaded by Monks to tell about the pawn-broker's ticket (38: 251–53); then, by the two old women, who reveal that they overheard Mrs. Corney's interview with old Sally and who also indicate that old

Sally had told them of Agnes's desire to reach the grave of her child's father (51: 346). Perhaps the most striking instance of the use of multiple viewpoints, however, appears in the accounts of Oliver's being wounded in the attempt by Bill Sikes and Toby Crackit to gain entrance to the home of Mrs. Maylie. First, we are given Oliver's own impression of his being shot (22: 155). Afterwards, Toby tells of the boy's being left in a ditch (25: 170). Then, the narrator presents both his own account (27: 186) and a description from Sikes's point of view (28: 186–87). In offering four versions, Dickens emphasizes the incident and the different ways in which it is perceived.

In one later passage the narrator notes how Oliver's perspective and mood, which were adversely affected when the boy feared for Rose Maylie's life, respond to the good news of her recovery:

> The melancholy which had seemed to the sad eyes of the anxious boy to hang, for days past, over every object, beautiful as all were: was dispelled by magic. . . . Such is the influence which the condition of our own thoughts, exercises, even over the appearance of external objects. Men who look on nature, and their fellow-men, and cry that all is dark and gloomy, are in the right; but the sombre colours are reflections from their own jaundiced eyes and hearts. The real hues are delicate, and need a clearer vision. (34: 229)

The use of *jaundiced* in the penultimate sentence seems significant in anticipating the appearance in *Bleak House* of the name *Jarndyce*, which echoes this word: in the case of Tom Jarndyce, whose distress over the Chancery case led to suicide, the name is apt, but for John Jarndyce, the appellation is ironic, since he refuses to see bad in individuals by inventing the fiction of "the east wind."

Significantly, too, just as the ironic and straightforward styles of the narrator in *Oliver Twist* are in accord in terms of values endorsed and behavior condemned, so too, in *Bleak House*, the different perspectives of the anonymous narrator and of Esther are complementary, as many commentators have remarked (e.g., Harvey 95; Daleski 157–59; Frank 93; Davis, "Dickens and Significant Tradition" 59).

Looking at these two novels and considering all of the aforementioned similarities and recurrences in a group, we notice more fully the extent to which Dickens appears compelled to repeat motifs that deeply engaged him: illegitimacy, identity, degradation, guilt, redemption. By associating and linking various characters, he at times imparts a sense of a blurring or confusion of identities, and this technique emphasizes the theme of moral complexity. Each mother—Agnes and Honoria—is erring but also victimized, Agnes having been seduced by Edwin Leeford, Honoria having been deceived by her sister. Agnes is linked with her sister, Rose, and also with Nancy: the latter pretends to be Oliver's sister and then becomes maternal in attempting to protect the boy; Rose, at the end of the novel, after having been revealed to be the aunt of Oliver, is claimed by him as a "sister," his "own dear sister" (51: 348). If Rose is his sister, so is her sister, Oliver's mother, Agnes. In this way the three women are joined: one, Agnes, sinning, but misled—in Brownlow's words, "guileless" and "untried" (49: 327); another, Rose, idealized, unjustly slandered as illegitimate, and then adopted by the benevolent Mrs. Maylie; the third, Nancy, a prostitute and thief who loses her life in seeking to make amends for returning Oliver to Fagin. As I remarked in Chapter 2, Nancy may be seen as a surrogate for Agnes, whose name is etymologically related to hers, and, as I have also noted, Regina Barrecca points out that these two women are the only sexually active female characters of importance in the book (93). Another scholar, Keith Hollingsworth, suggests, however, that Nancy is also a surrogate for the virginal Rose, for he states that the latter is "allowed" by Dickens "to recover" from her nearly fatal illness because "Nancy dies in her place" (123). In effect, therefore, we may see Oliver as having three sisters—or mothers—ranging from seduced innocent to idealized virgin to prostitute, and since each assists him, even the sinful ones deserve forgiveness and reverence.

In *Bleak House* Lady Dedlock, duped into thinking that her child is dead, abandons the infant. Nevertheless, despite her guilt in having borne an illegitimate daughter, her grief and her desire for Esther's forgiveness make her a much more appealing character than her sister, Miss Barbary. Lady Dedlock, like Oliver's mother, is also linked with other women in the novel. At her death she is dressed in the clothes of Jenny, the brickmaker's wife whose child died as Esther was visiting. But even more important are her associations with her maid Hortense, whom she seeks to impersonate in visiting the grave of Hawdon, and with Esther herself. Indeed, Jo confuses the three, for Esther, before her disfiguring illness, bears a strong resemblance to her mother, and while Lady Dedlock has posed as Hortense, the latter, at Tulkinghorn's behest, has pretended to be Lady Dedlock acting as Hortense. Hortense, who has served as Lady Dedlock's maid, may be regarded figuratively as her employer's child, together with Esther. But Hortense may also be viewed as a surrogate for Lady Dedlock, for this passionate Frenchwoman later seeks to serve (or mother) Esther and then commits a murder desired by Honoria. Jenny, the bereaved parent of a child lost in infancy, is another surrogate for Lady Dedlock, as is Esther herself, for Esther creates her own persona and acts as mother to Dolly, a surrogate for herself. Again, as in *Oliver Twist*, we find that Dickens has linked some very different kinds of women: Lady Dedlock, sinning but loving and contrite, too; Jenny, a blameless sufferer; Hortense, immoral in committing murder and then seeking to implicate Lady Dedlock, but a woman who has received some provocation and does remove Tulkinghorn, a character who has mistreated the appealing George Rouncewell; and Esther, an exemplary figure. In any event, Esther's mother, her guilt notwithstanding, seems more sinned against than sinning, and after death she, like Agnes Fleming, is deemed worthy of forgiveness and respect. Perhaps in creating both Agnes, who abandons Oliver only because she dies, and Honoria, who deserts Esther only because of deceit, Dickens was trying to exorcise some of the resentment created in him by his own mother when she had wished to send him back to the blacking warehouse.

In each book, also, the protagonist's father, though not blameless, is shown to be decent and kind, his flaws notwithstanding. Each man is of genteel status, Edwin Leeford coming from a family that is well connected and Hawdon having social standing as an officer and therefore a gentleman. Each, too, reveals kindness and merit, for Leeford has won the devotion of his friend Brownlow, and Hawdon has earned the ardent loyalty of George Rouncewell. Furthermore, Brownlow in one narrative and Jarndyce in the other act as second fathers. Each is tenuously related or connected to the protagonist and offers guidance and protection. If Brownlow's fiancée, who was Edwin Leeford's sister, had lived, Brownlow would have been Oliver's uncle. In the other novel, John Jarndyce, in the days before Esther's birth, knew both her mother and her aunt, for his close friend Boythorn was to marry this aunt and would therefore have been Esther's uncle had the engagement not been terminated. While Brownlow encounters Oliver by providential coincidence (49: 328), Jarndyce is asked, in a pseudonymous letter from Esther's godmother, who knew of his generosity, to provide future assistance for the child (17: 213–14). In each case, the protagonist's actual father is a person to be forgiven, and in each case a surrogate provides paternal care. Dickens may be gesturing kindly

towards his own recently deceased father, also improvident finan-
cially but well-intentioned and good-hearted.[11]

In these two stories each protagonist may be seen as having, in
effect, two sets of parents: a pair of not-so-good biological parents
(Agnes Fleming and Edwin Leeford, Honoria and Hawdon) who
are guilty of sexual transgression, are unknown to their offspring
during the minority of these children, become therefore deprived
of the opportunity to display parental love, and suffer untimely,
distressing deaths (perhaps to satisfy Dickens's own views on retribution), but remain nevertheless basically worthy and therefore for-
givable; and another set of parental surrogates who are older,
celibate, and exemplary figures (Brownlow and Mrs. Bedwin, Jarndyce and Mrs. Rouncewell [if we regard her son George as a surrogate for Esther]), of whom the male provides guidance and material
assistance, while the female displays total, unquestioning faith and
confidence. Brownlow literally adopts Oliver, while Jarndyce becomes the legal guardian of Esther and plays his paternal role with
such care that at one point Esther wonders if he is actually her
father. Each protagonist may also be seen as having an evil stepmother: for Oliver, it is Edwin Leeford's first wife (mother of
Monks), who, although she never meets Oliver, seeks to harm him
by destroying his father's last will and slandering his mother's family; for Esther, this stepmother's role is filled by her aunt, whose
harsh religious views inspire extreme cruelty. Both of these witch-
figures die relatively young, in distressing ways. Indeed, because
Esther's aunt suffers a fatal stroke just after hearing the apocryphal
account in the Gospels of the woman taken in adultery, we may
speculate that she has suddenly understood the error of her ways
in casting stones. If she dies of a guilty conscience, this parallels the
later death of her sister, Honoria, Esther's mother. Oliver, but not
Esther, also has a wicked stepfather-figure, since on the way to the
attempted break-in at Mrs. Maylie's country house he is mistakenly
thought by two different carters to be the son of Bill Sikes (21:
147–48).

The double sets of parents seem to illustrate the psychological
concept of decomposition, for Dickens takes positive and negative
traits children may find blended in parents and separates these qualities. In doing this he implies that making assessments and judgments of morality is difficult and complex. Both Oliver and Rose
forgive Agnes any pain she has caused them, and both Oliver and
Brownlow remember Edwin Leeford only with affection. Esther and
Sir Leicester both completely forgive Honoria. If Hawdon wronged

Honoria, she certainly reveals no sense of grievance; if she deserted him, his retaining her letters implies persisting love. We never clearly learn why and how the love affair ended, and those who believe that Honoria deserted her captain to marry the older, wealthy Sir Leicester are merely speculating. Although neither the anonymous narrator nor Esther is explicit about her recognizing Hawdon as her father, the circumstances of Lady Dedlock's death make this realization virtually certain.

In *Bleak House* Tulkinghorn, whose threat to Lady Dedlock makes him for her and for her apprehensive daughter the main villain, is technically innocent of any crime and is a respected member of society, unlike Fagin. But just as Fagin is regarded as an outsider because he is a Jew and an outlaw, so Tulkinghorn is described by the anonymous narrator as "dwelling among mankind but not consorting with them" (42: 514). Both villains are eventually executed, Fagin by the law, Tulkinghorn by the murderous Hortense.

Each book strongly emphasizes the idea of links among human beings. Forster notices Dickens's insistence on parallels between the high and low strata of society: "Only to genius are so revealed the affinities and sympathies of high and low, in regard to the customs and usages of life" (*Life* 2: 2: 107). In *Oliver Twist* the narrator, after describing Noah Claypole's cruel, abusive condescension to Oliver, a "workhouse orphan" and therefore even inferior to him, a "charity-boy" born to "a washerwoman" and "a drunken soldier," comments, "It [Noah's behavior] shows us what a beautiful thing human nature sometimes is; and how impartially the same amiable qualities are developed in the finest lord and the dirtiest charity-boy" (5: 44). In *Bleak House* we find the famous passage in which the anonymous teller asks, "What connexion" exists between the Dedlock residences and "the whereabout of Jo the outlaw with the broom . . . ?" (16: 197). This motif is, of course, grimly echoed in a later passage showing how the contagion bred in Tom-all-Alone's finds its way to "the choice stream (in which chemists on analysis would find the genuine nobility) of a Norman house, and his Grace shall not be able to say Nay to the infamous alliance" (46: 553).

At the end of each novel, not only do the protagonist and his or her friends move from London to a rural setting, but there is a perhaps surprising oblivion regarding the social evils that have been depicted. In *Oliver Twist* no character will undertake to seek reform of the workhouse system that helped cause the death of little Dick, and no one speaks of trying to ameliorate the poverty responsible for a place like Jacob's Island and the criminal activities associated with it. In *Bleak House* neither Jarndyce nor Woodcourt plans to attempt to end the Chancery system that has harmed so many, nor does either seek any way to respond to the poverty that creates ills like Tom-all-Alone's and the deprivation that embitters people like the brickmakers who live near Bleak House.

Bleak House is a much fuller, more complex, more subtle, and more profound work than *Oliver Twist*. Complementing the affirmative story of Esther and the sad narrative of her mother, Lady Dedlock, is the account of the tragic destruction of Richard Carstone, the prey of Vholes. Moreover, while in *Oliver Twist* the principal villains—Fagin, Sikes, and Monks—operate separately from the workhouse, the main triad of wrongdoers in *Bleak House*—Tulkinghorn, Smallweed, and Vholes—are linked to Chancery.

As we have observed, *Bleak House* includes a noteworthy number of significant parallels to *Oliver Twist*. Of course, the later book's protagonist, Esther, is female and, through most of the novel, older. The government institution attacked, Chancery, was more of a danger to many of Dickens's readers than the workhouse system and seems more pervasive a threat to society in that it imperils the very purpose of law, the granting of justice. But while the later novel contains these and many other variations, it repeats the earlier book's concern with a modification of the family romance motif considered by Freud, a fantasy in which a child imagines being of higher birth than he or she has been led to believe. Both Oliver and Esther must confront their illegitimacy as each seeks the identity of his or her parents. Nevertheless, the two protagonists, starting out far lower than most persons, discover that, despite the stigma of illegitimacy, they were born to parents who were of gentle status. Moreover, as we have seen, the guilt of these mothers and fathers in producing illegitmate offspring is considerably mitigated by Dickens.

In the version of events in the later novel, Esther is subjected to abuse more subtle than that endured by young Oliver. Each, however, endures the trials of childhood and then eventually triumphs, but in the process each must become involved with questions of his or her own guilt and innocence. In using so great a quantity of echoes and reflections, Dickens reveals what seems a compulsion to repeat, to wrestle anew with his own persisting interests and anxieties. The constants in the two novels are significant: the survival of the abused child, the assistance of a generous, wealthy benefactor, the death of the erring mother, and forgiveness of her and reverence towards her. Although Dickens in these two novels disavows belief in hereditary guilt, he feels compelled to extenuate the offenses of the parents of Oliver and Esther. Such softening of faults serves to reassure those readers who might believe that character traits can be inherited. Indeed, according to Forster, Dickens himself revealed "a curious attraction" to the "question of hereditary transmission" of personal qualities (*Life* 8: 2: 636 [n.]). In *Oliver Twist* and *Bleak House* the goodness of the protagonists seems not only to save themselves but also to redeem after death their less worthy parents.

Notes

1. See K. Tillotson's edition of *Oliver Twist*, 1 (n. 1), and her comment in the introduction xxxiv. Axton, *Circle of Fire* 87, notices that the first of *The Mudfog Papers*, "Public Life of Mr. Tulrumble, Once Mayor of Mudfog," published in *Bentley's Miscellany* for January 1837, opens with a description of the town "in terms that anticipate in very primitive form the renowned introductory chapter of *Bleak House* nearly fifteen years later." House, who observes that Dickens in various works presents Rochester under several pseudonyms, including "Mudfog" (19), adds that "Bleak House was first going to be at Rochester instead of near St. Alban's" (19 [n.2]). In other words, both the original site of Oliver's birth and the original location of Bleak House were identical, suggesting a further link in Dickens's mind between the two novels. Paroissien carefully demonstrates that Chatham served as the model for Mudfog, but he points out that Dickens subsequently introduced details inconsistent with Chatham (*Companion to* OT 33–34, 79, and 87).

2. See, e.g., Daleski, who sees the account in *Oliver Twist* of Jacob's Island, a slum that has been "ruined by 'chancery suits,' " as "a first version of Tom-all-Alone's" in the later novel (64–65) and also compares the attack on Chancery in *Bleak House* with the "more limited denunciation of the workhouse" in *Oliver Twist* (167). Armstrong regards *Oliver Twist* as "a pre-photographic version of *Bleak House*" (131), remarks that each of these novels examines the protagonist's identity in relation to the identity of the mother and the circumstances of birth (131–32), and comments that each work "involves a sexual scandal, false identities, lost documents, disguises, and murder" (137). Westburg suggests that *Bleak House* includes many likenesses to the earlier work, but offers no specific comparisons (195).

3. Ghostly elements in *Bleak House* are examined by, among others, Newsom 8, 55, 57–58, 65–67, 155 (n. 4), and 156 (n. 10); Arac 126–28; Ragussis 253–80; Herbert 101–15; and Friedman, "A Considerate Ghost" 111–12.

4. For a fuller discussion of George as a surrogate for Esther, see Friedman, "A Considerate Ghost" 112–17.

5. This idea is suggested by Friedman, "A Considerate Ghost" 117, and by Sadrin 66–67.

6. Forster notes that Dickens's own friends Walter Savage Landor and Leigh Hunt were the respective models for these two characters (6: 7: 549).

7. One of Dickens's earliest literary efforts was a travesty of *Othello*, perhaps composed in 1833 (Haywood 67–88). Senelick oberves that Dickens's continuing interest in the play was stimulated by the performances of Macready (99–100).

8. Perhaps a further indication of Dickens's interest in *Othello* at the time of writing *Bleak House* is found in his use of "Barbary" for Lady Dedlock's maiden name, which is, of course, the surname of Esther's aunt, Miss Barbary; we may recall Desdemona's "Willow" song:

> My mother had a maid call'd Barbary;
> She was in love, and he she lov'd prov'd mad
> And did forsake her. . . .
> (4.3.26–28)

In *Bleak House* Miss Barbary, not her generous lover, Boythorn, proves "mad," for her reaction to Esther's birth (the concealment from Honoria of the child's survival and the cruel upbringing given Esther) is beyond reason.

9. As Ackroyd observes, this megalosaurus was anticipated by Dickens "just a few months before when in *Household Words* . . . he had imagined a 'scaly monster of the Saurian period' in a creek of the Thames" (644–45). Ackroyd earlier mentions the *Household Words* article (on a factory producing plate glass) in which this image appears (598).

10. Gilmour sees in *Oliver Twist* "two conflicting impulses . . .: a horror of the criminal underworld . . . and a sympathetic understanding . . . perspective" (113).

11. See Pratt 4–22 for a discussion of Dickens's ambivalence towards his own father.

Chapter 6

Sad Stephen and Troubled Louisa: Paired Protagonists in *Hard Times*[1]

The basic device of character doubling, often favored by Dickens, is used in *Hard Times* in ways that are both obvious and subtle and that become integral to the novel's narrative structure and thematic development.

In *Hard Times* the initial eight chapters, originally published as the first four of twenty weekly installments, start a narrative that seems as though it will be primarily concerned with Mr. Gradgrind, the apostle of facts. Moreover, a number of the twenty-five prospective titles considered for this novel definitely imply such an emphasis: for example, "Thomas Gradgrind's facts," "Hard-headed Gradgrind," "Mr Gradgrind's grindstone," and "Our hard-headed friend" (DWN 250–51). But Gradgrind, despite the importance of his eventual conversion, is not the focal center of *Hard Times*. In the fifth installment, two shifts of interest occur: the ninth chapter suggests that Sissy Jupe, the abandoned daughter of a circus clown, may become the main figure, and Chapter 10 introduces a new character who strongly commands our attention, Stephen Blackpool. Sissy, however, quickly fades from view and returns to prominence only late in the narrative. During the last fifteen of the original twenty installments, the role of protagonist appears to be divided between Stephen and Louisa, Gradgrind's restless oldest child, two persons whom Dickens connects in a truly extraordinary number of ways, their differences in age, sex, class status, and temperament notwithstanding.[2]

An odd couple, "Old Stephen," the forty-year-old mill-worker who has led "a hard life" (1: 10: 52), and young Louisa, the pretty daughter of the wealthy Mr. Gradgrind and later the wife of the even more affluent Mr. Bounderby, Stephen's employer, serve as paired protagonists, alike in some respects, complementary in others, victims of an ethos that cherishes facts, statistics, and reason, while showing a concomitant disregard for imagination and feeling. As the fates of both Stephen and Louisa demonstrate, men and women in diverse social strata may suffer greatly in a nation marked by an insensitivity to basic emotional needs.

Stephen's difficulties with his debased, alcoholic wife, his co-workers, and Bounderby, as well as his falling under suspicion of bank theft and his accidental death, make up a story that Dickens interweaves with an account of the perils faced by Louisa because of her upbringing and the actions of her brother Tom, Bounderby, and Harthouse. Although the narrator gives much more attention to Louisa than to Stephen, the latter's death-scene seems to be the novel's main climax. Furthermore, throughout most of *Hard Times* both of these characters are very closely linked, not only by the obvious fact that each is caught in a disastrous marriage, but also by many other parallels in situations and in relationships, as well as by similar details in settings and imagery. A reader may not consciously note every connection, but the cumulative effect of these numerous ties helps to unify the story. While Dickens wishes to make *Hard Times* an attack on some features of utilitarianism, he seems not wholly comfortable writing a "thesis-novel."[3] Consequently, he seeks to give his narrative greater coherence and impetus by inducing us to care about the interwoven destinies of Stephen and Louisa.

—1—

Just as David Copperfield is susceptible to the antithetical influences of a "good angel" and a "bad" one—Agnes and Steerforth (ch. 25)—so each of the two protagonists in *Hard Times* is menaced by a diabolical character and assisted by a saintly one. Stephen, contemplating his marital plight, thinks that he is "bound hand and foot, to a dead woman, and tormented by a demon in her shape" (1: 12: 65), and the narrator later calls this person Stephen's "evil spirit" (2: 6: 117). Similarly, when James Harthouse, the man who will try to seduce Louisa, first appears to Bitzer and Mrs. Sparsit, "it was to be seen with half an eye that he was a thorough gentleman, made to the model of the time; weary of everything, and putting no more faith in anything than Lucifer" (1: 2: 91–92). After meeting Tom, Harthouse behaves "as if he knew himself to be a kind of agreeable demon who had only to hover over him, and he must give up his whole soul if required" (2: 3: 102). The narrator refers to this character as Tom's tempter (2: 3: 103) and his "powerful Familiar" (2: 7: 132), but the diabolic qualities are given even more emphasis in the account of the ways in which Harthouse approaches Louisa:

> When the Devil goeth about like a roaring lion, he goeth about in a shape by which few but savages and hunters are attracted. But, when he is trimmed, smoothed, and varnished, according to the mode; . . . then, whether he take to the serving out of red tape, or to the kindling of red fire, he is the very Devil.   (2: 8: 135)

When subsequently reproached by Sissy, Harthouse concedes, "I . . . have glided on from one step to another with a smoothness . . . perfectly diabolical" (3: 2: 172).

Stephen is tortured by his "evil spirit," a woman who suddenly just "went bad," as he expresses it (1: 11: 58). In the original installment version of the novel in *Household Words*, Bounderby opens a very brief description of her decline with the statement that she "found other companions," but later editions omit this detail, the only semblance of an explanation for the great change.[4] As Stephen's dream indicates, his anguish over this abusive woman tempts him to violate the divine commandment against murder.[5] Soon after, when his wife is about to make the fatal error of drinking a poisonous liniment, the weaver finds himself powerless to speak or move (1: 13: 69).

Stephen is saved from the guilt of his inaction by Rachael, to whom he twice declares, "Thou'rt an Angel," and then adds, "it may be, thou hast saved my soul alive" (1: 13: 70). Earlier, the narrator has mentioned that, to Stephen, Rachael "looked as if she had a glory shining round her head" (1: 13: 67). Later, speaking to Louisa in his room, the weaver once more calls Rachael "th' Angel" of his life (2: 6: 120).

Rachael, at a time before she prevents Stephen's wife from drinking the poison, had ministered to the ailing woman and then remarked, "When she gets better, Stephen, 'tis to be hoped she'll leave

thee to thyself again, and do thee no more hurt" (1: 13: 68), a hope
that is later evidently fulfilled. In a sense, therefore, the good angel
tends to the bad one and then dismisses her.

While Stephen's "evil spirit" tempts by tormenting, Louisa's devil
torments by tempting. Harthouse, learning from Tom of her strange
upbringing and marital discontent, uses her affection for her brother
in trying to lead her to break the commandment against adultery.
Although Louisa has the strength to resist and flee to her father's
home, the prospect of love brings her to a mental crisis. Telling
Gradgrind for the first time that she grew up with "a hunger and
thirst . . . which have never been for a moment appeased," she refers
to the conflict his system created by requiring her to struggle to
suppress her instincts: "In this strife I have almost repulsed and
crushed my better angel into a demon" (2: 12: 162). This remark
refers to her own inner qualities rather than to persons—to her
angelic desire for emotion and imagination and to the demonic traits
of doubt and aloofness—but the comment seems to recall the very
recent escape from Harthouse, a diabolical seducer, and to anticipate the renewal of Louisa's relationship with the saintly character
who will assist in her recovery, Sissy.

Although Sissy is not explicitly called an angel, she clearly deserves this appellation. An early review of *Hard Times*, after noting
that Rachael, "a fellow 'hand' of pattern goodness," is Stephen's
"guiding star," adds, "A star of the same kind is supplied to poor
Louisa, in her trouble, by Sissy Jupe."[6] Gradgrind himself senses
Sissy's mysterious power: "Somehow or other, he had become possessed by an idea that there was something in this girl which could
hardly be set forth in a tabular form" (1: 14: 72). When Sissy subsequently comes to offer comfort to the remorseful, distraught Louisa,
the latter "fell upon her knees, and clinging to this stroller's child
looked up at her almost with veneration," before making a prayer-
like request: "Forgive me, pity me, help me! Have compassion on
my great need, and let me lay this head of mine upon a loving
heart!" (3: 1: 168). Significantly, just as Rachael, Stephen's good
angel, handles his problem with his "evil spirit," so Sissy, Louisa's
good angel, performs the task of persuading the devil, Harthouse,
to retreat. Sissy's angelic status is again emphasized when Louisa,
seeking to comfort Gradgrind after Tom's crime has become known
to him, promises that his three younger children "will be different,"
then adds, "*I* will be different yet, with Heaven's help," and gives
"her hand to Sissy, as if she meant with her help too" (3: 7: 203).
Upon later learning that Sissy has found a means of saving Tom

from arrest, Gradgrind "raised his eyes to where she stood, like a good fairy in his house" (3: 7: 204).

Of course, the two good angels—Rachael and Sissy—eventually join forces to find Stephen and to seek assistance for him. After the mortally injured Blackpool is brought up from the mine-shaft, Sissy induces Sleary's troupe to shield Tom, whose attempt to cast blame for the bank theft on Stephen caused the weaver to embark on the trip leading to the fatal accident. Being victimized by Tom further ties Stephen to Louisa, since she has also been betrayed by this "whelp," who induced her to marry Bounderby, extracted money from her, and then made Harthouse aware of her marital unhappiness.

Stephen and Louisa are additionally linked in that each is caused anguish by an outsider who comes to Coketown, the ugly Slackbridge and the handsome Harthouse. In the chapter in which Harthouse first appears, he is referred to only as a "stranger" (2: 1: 91–94). Although we are meant to laugh at Bounderby's later attempt to attribute the workers' unrest to Slackbridge, whom the employer calls one of "the mischievous strangers who are always about" (2: 5: 111), the organizer ironically is actually a mischievous stranger, and he encourages the ostracism of Stephen, a punishment that leads directly to the weaver's second interview with Bounderby, his dismissal from the mill, the visit to his room by Louisa, the plot concocted by Tom, whom Louisa took as an escort, and Blackpool's subsequent death. When Stephen is suspected of complicity in the bank theft, belief in his guilt is expressed by both Harthouse (2: 10: 152–53) and Slackbridge (3: 4: 182–83). Both outsiders also leave Coketown suddenly, Harthouse being persuaded to depart by Sissy (3: 2: 172–75) and Slackbridge seeming simply to disappear from the scene after convincing the union members to condemn the missing Stephen as a "proscribed fugitive" (3: 4: 183).

—2—

Just as Stephen's close escape from committing murder occurs soon after he has a nightmare about being on the executioner's scaffold, so Louisa's avoidance of adultery is preceded by descriptions of Mrs. Sparsit's frequent daydreams expressing a desire for the younger woman's sexual disgrace. The narrator observes that Mrs. Sparsit, although "not a poetical woman," develops "an allegorical fancy": "She erected in her mind a mighty Staircase, with a dark pit of shame and ruin at the bottom; and down those stairs, from day to day and hour to hour, she saw Louisa coming" (2: 10: 150–51). This figurative "dark pit," towards which Louisa gradually descends, is analogous to the "black ragged chasm" (3: 6: 196), the abandoned mine-shaft, into which Stephen suddenly drops.[7] Even though Louisa avoids a "fall," which would have made her an outcast like Blackpool, she does collapse, "an insensible heap" (2: 12: 163), at Gradgrind's feet, and Stephen is later brought up from the pit "a poor, crushed, human creature," a "form, almost without form" (3: 6: 199).

Other parallels also connect Stephen and Louisa. The watchful Mrs. Sparsit first sees Blackpool lurking near the bank (2: 8: 139), an observation that leads to his unjustly falling under suspicion of theft, and Mrs. Sparsit subsequently, after extensive spying on Louisa, wrongly accuses her of adultery. During the rainstorm, Louisa has fled to her father and avoided misconduct, and we may recall the earlier rainstorm during which Stephen, with Rachael's assistance, escapes from the temptation to commit murder.

When the distressed Louisa asks Gradgrind to shelter her, the meeting provides an ironic contrast with the prior scene between father and daughter in the same room, at the time that they discussed Bounderby's marriage proposal. These two highly significant interviews between Louisa and her father seem balanced by the two climactic confrontations between Stephen and his employer: during the first meeting Blackpool is told there is no help for his marital problems (1: 11: 60), and during the second he is dismissed from his job (2: 5: 115). Although Stephen requests the first meeting, he is summoned to the second, a pattern that is reversed in Louisa's two interviews with her father. For each protagonist—Stephen and Louisa—the second meeting leads to a separation from Bounderby. During Stephen's first interview, Bounderby's callous indication that the law cannot help a poor man seeking divorce leads the weaver to remark several times "'tis a muddle" (1: 11: 61), an assessment that he restates during the second meeting with Bounderby (2: 5: 113–14) and reiterates when dying (3: 6: 200–01). Louisa's first long discussion with her father leads the young woman to a comparable expression of moral confusion—her repeated query, "What does it matter?" (1: 15: 78), a question to which she returns when she afterwards wonders how to respond to Harthouse's overtures (2: 7: 125).[8] Of course, Blackpool's view of life as a "muddle" gives way to his dying affirmation of faith in a guiding star, while

Louisa eventually finds strength and comfort in the love offered by Sissy.

These two sets of interviews—one set between Stephen and Bounderby, the other between Louisa and her father—are also connected by a few other features. Stephen's initial meeting with Bounderby takes place during a rainstorm (1: 11: 56), as does Louisa's second interview with her father (2: 12: 160). Stephen's temptation to murder occurs on a night soon after the first discussion with his employer, while Louisa's near-seduction directly precedes her second climactic scene with Gradgrind.

During this second meeting, Gradgrind experiences a conversion, a change that leads him to acknowledge the inadequacy of his prior philosophy. Shaken and sorrowful, he seeks to offer reparation to Louisa, beseeching her, "What can I do, child? Ask me what you will" (2: 12: 162), and then arranging for her to stay in his home and be cared for by Sissy (3: 3: 178). Similarly, Gradgrind is later the one to whom the dying Stephen turns for reparation: "Sir, yo will clear me an' mak my name good wi' aw men. This I leave to yo" (3: 6: 201).

The vulnerability of each protagonist—Stephen and Louisa—is increased because of affection for another person. Since Stephen adores Rachael, he promises her not to join the union, a promise that results in his being ostracized, while Louisa's love for her brother Tom induces her to marry Bounderby. To underscore the resemblance, the narrator ends one of the two chapters in the seventh weekly installment with a night scene in which Stephen, in the road outside the building where he dwells, watches Rachael walk away (1: 13: 71), while the other chapter in the installment concludes as Louisa stands at night outside the door of her father's home and listens to Tom's "departing steps" (1: 14: 74).

—3—

Nearly all of the dramatic intensity in the tenth through the nineteenth of the twenty original weekly installments is created by two immoral schemes: Harthouse's attempt to seduce Louisa and Tom's plot to have Stephen blamed for the theft from the bank. Although both plans ultimately fail, Tom's leads, as we have noticed, to Stephen's death, while Harthouse's ironically produces a beneficent result, since the crisis it creates for Louisa brings about her reconciliation with Sissy and her separation from Bounderby. But although

Louisa then proceeds to cultivate the emotional life that she was previously trained to suppress, Dickens stresses the fact that her future happiness remains limited.

Both Stephen and Louisa can be seen as victims of the "Facts" philosophy's effects on the nation and on individuals. Blackpool suffers because a political system made insensitive by excessive enthusiasm for rationality, statistics, and the doctrine of laissez faire fails to assist him in three important areas: Parliament tolerates unfair divorce laws that aid the rich but offer no redress to the poor; it does not provide adequate supervision of working conditions, a neglect exemplified by the lack of legislation requiring proper fencing in of dangerous machines (like the one that maimed Rachael's younger sister); and it does not compel owners of coal mines to close up abandoned pits. In addition, Stephen is betrayed by the callous cruelty of Bounderby and the calculating treachery of Tom, two coldly selfish men who also do great harm to Louisa.

Nevertheless, while the sufferings of Stephen and Louisa support the validity of Dickens's views about the danger of Gradgrind's philosophy, these two victims also make us notice some of the limitations of this thesis. Although Louisa has been damaged by her father's destructive system of education, she nevertheless shows notable kindness in her early relations with Sissy. When the latter, speaking of her father's recent deterioration, starts to sob, Louisa "kissed her, took her hand, and sat down beside her" (1: 9: 50). Later, when Sissy asks Gradgrind if he has received information about her missing father, Louisa's eyes follow her "with compassion" (1: 9: 51). Louisa's subsequent withdrawal from Sissy seems prompted mainly by shame at having accepted Bounderby's proposal. Moreover, despite the change in behavior towards Sissy, Louisa continues to display generous impulses. Stephen Blackpool, harassed during his second interview with Bounderby, begins "instinctively addressing himself to Louisa, after glancing at her face" (2: 5: 112), for he correctly senses her sympathy.

Stephen himself is also kind and considerate. Despite his "instinctive propensity to dislike" Mrs. Pegler (2: 6: 116), an impulse probably attributable to his unwitting recognition of some physical resemblance to Bounderby, her son, Stephen treats this strange old woman with great gentleness and tact, apologizing when his question "Onny children?" seems to cause distress (2: 6: 118). Very soon after—in the same chapter—Louisa, after asking Stephen whether Rachael is his wife, blushes and states reassuringly, "It was not my meaning to ask a question that would give pain to any one here"

(2: 6: 119), another minor detail tying the two protagonists together. Even though Stephen has not, as far as we know, been oppressed by an education like Louisa's, we may wonder if his upbringing included any specific nourishment of his fancy, the kind of instruction that Dickens believes will lead to compassion and unselfish concern for others. Bluntly denying that Stephen is "a particularly intelligent man" (1: 10: 52), the narrator nonetheless notices that the weaver's room includes a "few books and writings ... on an old bureau in a corner" (1: 10: 54), but we never learn what these texts are. Certainly, the daily environment of Coketown is not responsible for Stephen's unselfishness and sensitivity.

As Blackpool is dying, he mentions his prayer "that aw th' world may on'y coom toogether more, an' get a better unnerstan'in' o' one another" (3: 6: 201), a reference to the need to close the rift between classes in mid-Victorian England. In responding, Louisa affirms, "your prayer is mine" (2: 6: 201), as the novel's two main victims join in hoping for national redemption.

The account of Stephen's final comments and of his death may be regarded as the major climax of *Hard Times*, for most of the one remaining weekly installment (the novel's last three chapters) seems somewhat perfunctory, despite the excitement of Bitzer's last-minute apprehension of Tom, the amusement provided by Sleary's story of the ensuing escape, and the pathos in the ringmaster's speculation that the reappearance and demise of the dog Merrylegs are an almost certain sign of the death of Sissy's father. In Dickens's brief concluding chapter, the dismissal of Mrs. Sparsit is followed by a short survey of the subsequent lives of this woman, Bitzer, Bounderby, and Gradgrind. We then are invited to contemplate Louisa, "watching the fire as in days of yore, though with a gentler and a humbler face" (3: 9: 218). Asking what she sees of the future, the narrator notes the broadsides and the tombstone epitaph exonerating Stephen, the continued saintly serenity of Rachael, and the remorseful death of Tom. But the three final paragraphs in *Hard Times* are strangely unsettling. First, we are teased by a possible prospect for Louisa: "Herself again a wife—a mother—lovingly watchful of her children, ever careful that they should have a childhood of the mind no less than a childhood of the body... ?" (3: 9: 219). We are soon surprised, however, by the stern, severe words, "Such a thing was never to be."

The fate then described—the view of Louisa winning the love of "happy Sissy's happy children" and of "all children" through her dutiful efforts to foster "imaginative graces and delights"—reminds us not of the future awarded to Esther Summerson, the protagonist of Dickens's immediately preceding novel, *Bleak House*, a heroine who gains happiness despite her dismal childhood, but of the lot assigned to Em'ly, the tarnished fallen woman in the yet earlier *David Copperfield*, a character whose life in Australia is celibate and saintly, a model of penance.

Both Stephen and Louisa remain victims, characters whose destinies are lamentable, since the emphasis is on loss, not fulfillment, even though the narrator provides religious consolation for Stephen and some degree of secular solace for Louisa in the redemptive satisfactions of her vicarious maternal role. The sad life and premature death of one figure, as well as the unfortunate youth and limited later happiness of the other, illustrate the shortcomings of a society that hinders instead of assisting the search of men and women for emotional nourishment. By skillfully keeping our attention fixed on these two examples of suffering humanity, Dickens seeks to win for them a sympathy that will induce us to stand against the forces that diminish sensitivity and compassion. As Stephen and Louisa confront nearly simultaneous crises, their fates are intricately interwoven, for *Hard Times* finally stresses not the differences that divide the social classes but the kinship that unites them.

Notes

1. This chapter was originally published in slightly different form in *Dickens Quarterly* 7: 2 (June 1990): 254–62, and is reproduced with the permission of The Dickens Society.
2. Oddie, who studies the stories of Stephen and Louisa from a perspective different from mine, also concludes, "Together, these two narratives determine . . . the vision and total structure of *Hard Times*" (60).
3. Among the critics noticing inconsistencies between the novel's ideology and the implications of the narrative is Winters, who observes that Bounderby, although "brought up in an atmosphere of love and compassion," becomes "a monster" (222), while Jupe, despite his circus background, behaves in an "essentially selfish" manner (234). Winters proceeds to notice that various characters in the book "fail to support" the thesis of "the superiority of Fancy over Fact, of Heart over Head" (236). Coles directs attention to the ways in which *Hard Times* endorses

positions contrary to those affirmed in essays published in *Household Words*.

4. See Ford and Monod's "Textual Notes" (245: second note for 58.10).

5. Many critics agree with Winters, who believes that the nightmare reveals Stephen's wish to destroy his wife (230).

6. Portions of this article, which appeared in *The Rambler*, October 1854, n.s. ii, pp. 361–62, are reprinted in *Dickens: The Critical Heritage* (303–04). Collins attributes the review to Richard Simpson.

7. Handley states that "we cannot help but contrast" Mrs. Sparsit's image of Louisa's going down the staircase with "the factual descent of Stephen Blackpool into the mine-shaft; Louisa does not fall" (43).

8. Handley considers Louisa's query an "equivalent" to Stephen's view of life as "a muddle" (92).

Chapter 7

Estella's Parentage and Pip's Persistence: The Outcome of *Great Expectations*[1]

By definition, coincidence involves some type of noteworthy duplication—a matching or correspondence of identities or actions or
places or times (or of some combination of these). Forster declares,
"On the coincidences, resemblances, and surprises of life, Dickens
liked especially to dwell," for he insisted that the "world . . . was
so much smaller than we thought it" and that "we were all so
connected by fate without knowing it" (*Life* 1: 5: 76). Central to *Great
Expectations* is a series of coincidences that shape the lives of many
of the novel's characters and complicate a reader's responses to
Pip's unfolding narrative.

   Late in the book, Pip sinks into despair on learning that his true
patron is the convict he once helped on the marshes: "it was not
until I began to think, that I began fully to know how wrecked I
was, and how the ship in which I had sailed was gone to pieces"
(39: 243). Even though he goes on to describe as his "sharpest and
deepest pain" the awareness that "for the convict" he "had deserted
Joe" (39: 243), his greatest cause of distress actually seems to be the
feeling that he has lost any chance of gaining Estella. During a later
visit to Satis House, Pip tells her of his continuing affection, but
adds, "I have no hope that I shall ever call you mine" (44: 270). He

remains in extreme depression until his own observations and reports from others lead to a startling realization: "the man we have in hiding [Magwitch] . . . is Estella's Father" (50: 303). This extraordinary coincidence strangely induces Pip to find new hope and greatly affects his subsequent behavior. By focusing closely on the ways in which Pip's attitude and actions are influenced by his discovery, we can, I believe, gain a clearer understanding of the outcome of the entire narrative. For the hero's new awareness plays an especially significant part in forming his responses to the failure of his plan to marry Biddy and to the mysterious appearance of Estella on the site of Satis House in the ending that Dickens decided to publish.

—1—

As Neil Forsyth observes, the revelation of Estella's parentage has been slowly prepared for (164). In Chapter 22, originally published as the fourteenth of the novel's thirty-six weekly installments, we are for the first time clearly told that Estella is only Miss Havisham's adopted child. In various succeeding installments, Pip gradually perceives the resemblance between Estella and Molly, Jaggers's housekeeper, and eventually asserts, "I felt absolutely certain that this woman was Estella's mother" (48: 292). Nevertheless, he afterwards seeks further information about Molly from Wemmick and then asks Miss Havisham about Estella's background. Later, when Magwitch's disclosures about his own past are reported by Herbert, the revelations conveniently dovetail with material previously gained from other sources and enable Pip to identify the convict as Estella's father. Surprising though this realization is, its credibility has been enhanced by the very deliberate manner in which diverse hints have been developed, for these are found in no fewer than eight of the seventeen installments published from March 2 through June 22, 1861.

Of course, Pip's discovery creates retrospective irony when we recall his earlier feelings about the "abyss" between Estella and Magwitch (43: 264), and the coincidence also makes the young woman still another link between her father and Miss Havisham, who have been previously connected not only through their interest in Pip, their alienation from society, and their employment of Jaggers, but also through their concidental victimization by the same villain, Compeyson. Even more interesting, however, is the way in which learning of Estella's true parents affects Pip. Seeking to corroborate his guesses, he himself does not understand why he is intent on "tracing out and proving Estella's parentage" (51: 303). A clue, however, seems present in the timing of his perception about Molly. Just before this realization, we are told that Pip, eager to avoid proof that Estella has married Drummle, has refrained from reading newspapers. But a chance meeting with Jaggers leads to a dinner, during which the lawyer refers to Drummle's having "won the pool" and speaks of Estella as "Mrs. Bentley Drummle" (48: 291). Just after hearing this distressing news, Pip looks at Molly and decides that she is Estella's mother.

Although the protagonist later speculates that his urge to confirm that Estella is the daughter of Magwitch may stem from a desire to "transfer" to the latter "some rays of the romantic interest" long associated with Estella (51: 304), his excitement may be attributable to two other causes: first, a satisfaction in finding Estella to be the child of a convict, since the discovery would make her less lofty and possibly more within reach, even though her very recent marriage has seemingly made her truly inaccessible; and, second, Pip's wish to find a coincidence so extraordinary as to justify a faith in the possibility of miracles. If Magwitch's daughter, lost, according to his words, for "a round score o' year" (50: 303), can be found, may not Pip's Estella, just lost to Drummle, still be recovered? Such may be Pip's implicit reasoning, perhaps similar to that of Sir Leicester in *Bleak House*. In Chapter 58 of that novel the stricken baronet finds in the marvelous reappearance of the long-lost George Rouncewell a cause for hope that the missing Lady Dedlock will also be safely returned. Pip, despite his earlier renunciation of all thought of winning Estella, and despite his later statement that he has "lost her and must live a bereaved life" (51: 306), seems after discovering her parentage to act as though his optimism had been rekindled, even though she has married Drummle.

In previous remarks Pip has repeatedly described his love for Estella as an obsession. Even after her marriage, Pip tells Jaggers that "whatever concerned her was still nearer and dearer . . . than anything else in the world" (51: 306). Although he evidently accepts the lawyer's advice that Estella's background be kept secret, Pip's devotion to Magwitch, already strong by this time, appears intensified by the knowledge of the latter's relationship to Estella. We may wonder whether Pip seeks to prove his own worthiness to himself by aiding her father to escape. For there may be significance in the fact that Pip does not even mention the "vague something lingering in . . . [his] thoughts" (55: 335), later disclosed to be the intention of proposing to Biddy (57: 349–50), until after Magwitch has been mortally injured and captured. Indeed, before this, Pip's first fear when his life is threatened by Orlick is, "Estella's father would believe I had deserted him" (53: 316)—Pip here refers to his benefactor as "Estella's father," instead of using either the convict's name or the pseudonym "Provis."

Later, Pip feels compelled not only to tell the dying Magwitch that his daughter, thought dead for many years, is alive, but also to add, "She is a lady and very beautiful. And I love her!" (56:342). But Pip seems misleading in not mentioning Estella's apparent failure to return his affection and in omitting any reference to her marriage, by what she calls her "own act" (44: 271), to Drummle, who is considered "a mean brute, . . . a stupid brute" by Pip (44: 272) and is seen as a potential wife-beater by Jaggers (48: 291). Then, too, in his avowal to Magwitch of love for Estella, the protagonist intimates that she and he will eventually be married, an idea that he evidently believes will please her dying father.[2] At this point, Pip appears to forget that in the preceding chapter he told us of harboring a "vague something" in his thoughts. Only later do we learn that this refers to a plan to marry Biddy, but if we then remember the scene with the dying Magwitch, we must concede that Pip's loyalty, even while he is supposedly thinking of marriage to Biddy, is not to her but to Estella; and his avowal of love for a married woman certainly raises questions of propriety. Perhaps even after the failure of the attempt to help Magwitch escape, Pip still clings to the hope that his devotion to this man will, as in a fairy tale, miraculously win the hand of the latter's daughter. Pip, who once "resolved" never to "breathe" a "word of Estella to Provis" (43: 265), now seems to seek the old convict's blessing for a marriage that appears no longer possible. Estella's parentage adds irony to her marriage to Drummle, "the next heir but one to a baronetcy" (23: 150), but she is, of course, unaware of her background, and her reasons for marrying Drummle remain undisclosed. Mrs. Oliphant, in an attack on *Great Expectations*, asserts that Estella "breaks nobody's heart but Pip's," does not carry out Miss Havisham's vindictive plans, and "only fulfils a vulgar fate by marrying a man without any heart to be broken, and being miserable herself instead" (DCH 440). But this choice of Drummle can be regarded differently. William F. Axton sees Estella's marriage as "a masochistic union" intended to be a "perverse revenge on the woman who has warped her" ("*Great Expectations* Yet Again" 290), while Lucille P. Shores argues that Estella selects Drummle because "she feels he is the only sort of husband to whom she can do no harm" (97).

One other possibility, however, is that Estella wishes to achieve her foster-mother's revenge on a victim who is like the betrayer Compeyson in being a false gentleman. Jaggers believes that the marriage may turn out to be difficult for Drummle (48: 291), and we certainly would not grant the latter the status of "a true gentleman at heart" which Herbert's father denied to Compeyson (22: 142). Karl P. Wentersdorf has discussed the connection between Orlick and Drummle (212, 217–19): the former, given to "slouching after" (17: 104), and Drummle, described as "lagging behind" (26: 167), are linked later in the narrative, for Orlick is evidently the man that Pip sees lighting Drummle's cigar (43: 268). Because Orlick subsequently reveals that he has become Compeyson's employee (53: 318–19), he serves to connect the two false gentlemen. Moreover, Jaggers's repeated references to Drummle as "the Spider" (26: 164, 168; 48: 291) create an association between this character and the spiders on Miss Havisham's wedding-table (11: 69; 38: 229), emblems of ruin caused by the cruelty of Compeyson, whom we may also consider a spider if we recall the "nets" in which he entrapped Magwitch (42: 262). Drummle seems, therefore, a substitute for Compeyson and a suitable object on whom to obtain revenge for Miss Havisham. Although Estella does not escape unscathed from her marriage, she does survive her husband.

In addition, a few details raise the possibility that Dickens wishes us to link Estella with Drummle's death. After encountering Pip at the Blue Boar, Drummle is seen "seizing his horse's mane, and mounting in his blundering brutal manner" (43: 267). Later, we learn of his death, "from an accident consequent on his ill-treatment of a horse" (59: 356). Since Pip has just previously reported that Estella had been "separated from her husband, who had used her with great cruelty" (59: 356), we may tend to associate her with the horse, despite our not knowing the animal's gender, for both Estella and the horse are harshly treated by Drummle, and the prior image of mounting may carry sexual connotations. Just as Tolstoy, over a decade later, was to use Vronsky's mare, a creature ridden to death, to symbolize Anna Karenina (Part 2, ch. 25), so Dickens is perhaps suggesting that Estella, daughter of physically violent parents, may in some vague way be responsible for Drummle's destruction, thereby avenging Miss Havisham on a surrogate for her betrayer. Dickens does not wish to make Estella clearly a killer like her mother, but he may want to hint that Drummle's death is an answer to Jaggers's toast concerning the marriage, "may the question of supremacy be settled to the lady's satisfaction!" (48: 291).[3]

Although speculations like these do not seem to be considered by Pip, he never escapes the effects of his startling discovery that Estella is Magwitch's child. His response to this coincidence evidently shapes his subsequent reactions to two crucial coincidences of timing: first, his arrival in the village for the purpose of proposing to Biddy occurs just after her marriage to Joe; and, second, in the revised ending, his return after eleven years to the site of Satis House is on the same evening that Estella has chosen to visit this location.

—2—

The idea of Biddy as a possible mate for Pip is thought of and rejected by him early in the story (17: 102–05), before he learns of his "expectations." Apparently he first begins to reconsider this option at about the time that Herbert, after the shock of Magwitch's capture and before the trial, mentions the possibility of obtaining a clerkship for him (55: 334–35). But, as we have noticed, Pip's first reference to his intention of proposing to Biddy is so veiled—"a vague something"—that it is incomprehensible; and between this reference and the subsequent explanation we find him affirming his love for Estella to the dying Magwitch. Since at the time of this avowal the covert reference to marrying Biddy has not yet been clarified, we are prevented from initially regarding the comment about loving Estella as disloyalty to Biddy. Certainly, however, we may later view the hero's statement as indicating a lack of any deep attachment to the latter. Pip, despite his genuine remorse about his treatment of both Biddy and Joe (52: 312; 53: 316–17), has never had any feelings for her other than those of respect and brotherly affection, her early residence in the same household having perhaps created an incest-prohibition similar to that which David Copperfield must overcome before recognizing his desire for Agnes.

Following Magwitch's death, Pip, having fallen ill and been nursed back to health by Joe, plans to tell the latter of the previously mentioned "vague something." Joe leaves unexpectedly, however, and only then are we told that the "something" involves proposing to Biddy. After three days, Pip travels to the village, but finds that Joe and Biddy have just been married.

Fainting at the surprise, the protagonist then reacts in an unusual way: his "first thought" is not one of disappointment but, instead, "one of great thankfulness" that he "had never breathed this last baffled hope to Joe"(58: 354). Pip may be truly grateful that he has caused his brother-in-law no discomfort, but he is perhaps also pleased that he has *not* given Joe a chance to relinquish Biddy in a display of noble-hearted generosity. The coincidence that Biddy's marriage comes just before Pip can propose saves him not only from potential rejection but also from the prospect of actually becoming Biddy's husband. He perhaps feels relieved to have escaped Biddy, for he may not really wish to face even the possibility that she would ask him to work at the forge.[4] Indeed, his previously declared intention of leaving all decisions to Biddy, should she accept him (57: 350), seems a plan to resign from adult responsibility. Most important, Pip has not overcome his obsession with Estella. At the time when she, after disclosing her plans to be married, told him that he would soon get over his disappointment, the response was really a promise, "Never, Estella!" (44: 272). His final words to Magwitch, while evidently meant to cheer the dying man, are perhaps also intended to comfort Pip himself. Many years before, when Pip once tactlessly exclaimed to Biddy, "If I could only get myself to fall in love with you," she perceptively replied, "But you never will, you see" (17: 103)

After learning that Biddy and Joe are married, Pip undertakes to cleanse himself by begging their forgiveness and then announces his intention to return almost immediately to London, where he will accept Herbert's offer of a clerkship and go, a voluntary exile, to Cairo. Although Pip's eagerness to depart hastily from Biddy and Joe may reflect either a wish to avoid obtruding on their early days of marriage or a desire to conceal his own disappointment, his behavior may also be prompted by an impulse to flee the scene of a close escape from a future that he did not really want, a future that would have been a final acknowledgment of the loss of the woman he still loves. With Biddy safely married, Pip is free to wait indefinitely for Estella.

Earlier, Pip has been dramatically saved from the murderous Orlick in a rescue made possible by two coincidences: Herbert's opportune finding of the letter summoning his friend to the marshes, and the availability of Trabb's boy to serve as a guide after Herbert and Startop reach the village. In Victorian fiction, such fortunate circumstances are often attributed to divine intervention.[5] Pip evidently sees his survival as a providential response to his remorse concerning his treatment of Biddy and Joe and to his sincere prayers for divine pardon (53: 317, 319). Right after the rescue, he offers a "thanksgiving" (53: 320).

The subsequent coincidence that prevents Pip from even proposing to Biddy may also seem to him—and to us—a miraculous phenomenon that allows him to continue defying reason and hoping for further miracles. For, after "losing" Biddy, he considers no alternative other than bachelorhood. His eleven-year stay "in the East" (59: 355) seems a penance, a punishment like the one that society unfairly gave Magwitch, but Pip's removal from ordinary life is also like Miss Havisham's in being self-imposed. In fact, he may appear as emotionally arrested as the heiress, whom Maire Jaanus Kurrik believes he resembles (175–76), and we may wonder whether he has welcomed exile in the exotic East because it has reduced his chances of meeting women whom British society would consider suitable marriage partners. Significantly, after the return of Pip to England, his assurance to Biddy that he does not long for Estella (59: 356) seems disingenuous—possibly a self-deception if read with the novel's original ending (never published by Dickens), for even that conclusion is marked, as John C. Kucich observes, by "the prominence Pip gives Estella at the end of his narrative" (102). When considered with the revised conclusion, the statement to Biddy is clearly a falsehood, for Pip concedes in the next sentence that, while speaking to her, he was "secretly" intending "to revisit the site" of Satis House, for "Estella's sake" (59: 356). In addition, both the original and revised endings contradict the last paragraph in Chapter 57, which affirms that the result of Pip's intention of going to the village to propose to Biddy is "all" that he has "left to tell" (57: 350).

—3—

Both conclusions describe a coincidental meeting with Estella when Pip returns to England. In the original version he has this encounter on Piccadilly after two years have passed, while in the revised ending the meeting is much more remarkable, taking place on the very evening of Pip's homecoming visit to Biddy, Joe, and their children, and occurring at the deserted, desolate site where Satis House once stood. Not only is the location of the reunion in this revised ending far more significant than Piccadilly; in this version both Pip and Estella have coincidentally chosen to visit this particular place for nostalgic reasons, and they have picked the same time. In the original conclusion the only point of the meeting is that Estella, who has remarried after Drummle's death, conveys "in her face and in her voice, and in her touch, . . . the assurance, that suffering had been stronger than Miss Havisham's teaching, and had given her a heart to understand what . . . [Pip's] heart used to be" ("The Original Ending": 359). Pip, in employing the words "used to be," suggests that by the time of this meeting his heart has changed, has perhaps become less romantic or less sensitive. But his insistence on bachelorhood in the preceding talk with Biddy may make us doubtful that any such change has occurred, and we may also wonder why in this final meeting, in the original version, Pip does not correct Estella when she mistakenly assumes that young Pip is his child.

In the revised ending Pip stresses the extraordinary nature of the encounter: he first perceives "a solitary figure," "the figure of a woman" that, on seeing him, falters "as if much surprised"; on hearing his name "uttered," he recognizes Estella and later remarks, "After so many years, it is strange that we should thus meet again, Estella, here where our first meeting was!" (59: 357). Nevertheless, he seems less astonished than she, as though he possibly regards the meeting as a wonderful but not wholly unexpected event. Both he and Estella, in this revised ending, have lost their fortunes, but each has been improved by adversity.

In this conclusion, the one that Dickens decided to publish, the intention is, despite much speculation to the contrary by some commentators, to unite Pip and Estella in marriage. Indeed, any attempt to deny this must begin by countering the fact that Forster includes in his biography a reference to "an objection taken not unfairly [by some critics] to the too great speed with which the heroine, after being married, reclaimed, and widowed, is in a page or two again made love to, and remarried by the hero" (*Life* 9: 3: 737). Forster adds that Dickens changed the conclusion because of Bulwer-Lytton's "objecting to a close that should leave Pip a solitary man" (*Life* 9: 3: 737). Morever, when *Great Expectations* appeared in 1862 in the Illustrated Library Edition of Dickens's works, it contained wood engravings prepared by Marcus Stone under Dickens's supervision. The final illustration, captioned "With Estella After All," shows Pip and Estella reunited at the site of Satis House and seems to suggest that the two will remain together, for Estella's right hand firmly grasps Pip's left arm, while her left hand rests on top of that arm, as he, head uncovered and hat held in his right arm, looks protectively at her face (fig. 2). With Marcus Stone, as with his predecessor, Hablot Browne, Dickens exercised control over the content and the style of each illustration, and a letter to the publisher

Frederic Chapman refers approvingly to the selection of "With Estella After All" as the frontispiece for the new edition of the novel
(PL 10: 121–22 [1 Sept. 1862]—cf. 445 [to William Day, 25 Oct. 1864]),
a choice that seems surprising in its hint about the narrative's conclusion. Those who dispute the idea that Pip and Estella are to
marry seem to neglect both Forster's opinion and the implications
of Stone's engraving.

Moreover, various details in the second ending seem to confirm
Forster's belief that it implies the protagonist's marriage. On sitting
down with Estella, Pip thinks of his last words to Magwitch, a
farewell expressing love for the convict's daughter. Moreover, Estella discloses that she has "often thought" of Pip and then makes
an admission even more gratifying to him: "There was a long hard
time when I kept far from me, the remembrance of what I had
thrown away when I was quite ignorant of its worth. But, since my
duty has not been incompatible with the admission of that remembrance, I have given it a place in my heart" (59: 358). Pip has finally
gained an answer to the question he had asked many years before:
"When should I awaken the heart within her, that was mute and
sleeping now?" (29: 187). He has never believed her cold words, "I
have no heart" (29: 183), and in this reunion she openly refers to
her heart and the place in it devoted to the remembrance of Pip's
love. Furthermore, her statement suggests that prior to Drummle's
death—which released her from wifely "duty"—she had to exert
an effort to keep the remembrance of Pip's love "far" from her. As
for the hero, he immediately responds, "You have always held your
place in my heart" (59: 358)—no ambiguous reference here by Pip
to her understanding "what my heart used to be." Although Estella,
in the revised conclusion, does comment that she now comprehends
what Pip's "heart used to be" (59: 358), her remark seems not a
recognition of change in the protagonist, but merely a defensive
gesture, for she may fear—in her new vulnerability—that Pip, despite his reassuring words, no longer loves her.

There is significance, too, in the fact that Estella's proposal that
she and Pip "will continue friends apart" (59: 358) elicits no response from the hero except for his taking of her hand. The final
clause published in the installment version in *All the Year Round*, "I
saw the shadow of no parting from her," seems less satisfactory
than the emended wording Dickens provided for the 1868 edition—"I saw no shadow of another parting from her"—for the prior
statement ("I saw the shadow of no parting from her") may bring
to mind the humorous possibility that the prospect of not being able

Fig. 2. With Estella After All

to part from Estella ("no parting") might now be seen as a "shadow," a problem, facing Pip.[6]

But, if the book's revised conclusion includes an anticipation of marriage, we may question why Pip, as narrator, is not more lucid and direct. Since he continues to use the past tense, we may surmise that he has had time to discover whether his expectation of "no shadow" was correct. As Milton Millhauser asks, "Why . . . does he not tell us what he knows?" (274). Nevertheless, the echo at the end of *Great Expectations* of the closing lines of *Paradise Lost*, noticed by Edgar Johnson (2: 993–94), suggests a parallel to Milton's poem, in which a reconciled Adam and Eve go forth together, united, to face the world, and implies that we should regard the outcome of Dickens's novel as basically positive. Just as Milton's epic narrator states that Adam and Eve depart from Eden "hand in hand with wand'ring steps and slow" (12: 648), so Pip writes of Estella and himself, "I took her hand in mine, and we went out of the ruined place." Moreover, the degree of improbability or surprise in the revised conclusion's coincidental meeting is so much greater than that in the corresponding encounter in the original version that Pip and we are likely to see some supernatural cause at work once more—providence or destiny.

Pip is a decent, honorable, kind man, one whose sufferings seem disproportionate to his earlier moral errors. For him to be again disappointed would be a cruel conclusion, one that would condemn him to a life of only limited involvement with others. Marriage with Estella, who, like Pip, is in her mid-thirties, would perhaps give the protagonist a chance to have a child of his own, a desire that Biddy surmises he has when she replies, in response to his request that she "give" or "lend" her son to him, "No, no," and adds, "You must marry" (59: 356). Clearly, for Pip, only Estella can be his mate.

—4—

Pip's early romantic delusions serve in many ways to create his problems, but his views are in part imposed upon him by circumstances and by his understandable misinterpretation of these. Christopher Ricks, after referring to Jaggers's dual roles and to Magwitch's being Estella's father, asserts, "these improbabilities are gross enough," but maintains that they act to win sympathy for the protagonist: "The odds against him are shown to be pretty terrifying" (203). As a result of his own temperament, the expectations mysteriously announced to him, and his misunderstanding concerning Miss Havisham, Pip has become, in Herbert's words, "a good fellow, with impetuosity and hesitation, boldness and diffidence, action and dreaming, curiously mixed in him" (30: 190). Although Pip at the end of the novel appears to retain an unrealistic romantic outlook, it is largely purged of selfishness. As Robert A. Greenberg persuasively argues, the revised conclusion is more appropriate than the original one to "the total coherence of the book" (154).[7] And this ending is meant to be a happy one, even though Pip carefully avoids a totally clear account. Indeed, the remaining tinge of ambiguity may perhaps be Dickens's conscious or unconscious acknowledgment of a conflict. There is, on the one hand, the fear that Pip's moral education has come too late to save him from a saddened, diminished life, while, on the other hand, there is the intuition, first suggested by Bulwer-Lytton, but nevertheless endorsed by Dickens himself, that, in the case of Pip, one more last-minute rescue is not too much to hope for. In addition, another element makes the revised ending particularly suitable. From the early chapters on, the novel seems to place great emphasis on the theme of revenge. Magwitch, Compeyson, Miss Havisham, her half-brother, Molly, Orlick, Pip himself—all of these figures display vindictiveness.[8] Despite this extensive concern with revenge, however, the value that the narrator, Pip, eventually comes to embrace is forgiveness. He learns that his sister, before her death, asked his pardon (35: 215–16), and his forgiveness is also sought by another erring mother-figure, Miss Havisham (49: 297, 301). Earlier, despite his own pain, Pip has readily forgiven Estella, even without being asked (44: 272). In turn, he himself, when threatened by the murderous Orlick, requests divine pardon (53: 317) and, after his rescue, subsequently begs forgiveness of Biddy and Joe (58: 355). That Pip knows he will receive this is suggested by his earlier praise of Joe as "this gentle Christian man" (57: 344), an expression indicating the narrator's recognition that Joe is "a true gentleman at heart."

The forgiving of Miss Havisham—by Pip and by us—seems earned by her sincere repentance and by the expiation of her death from shock after she has been burned in a kind of purgatorial fire. But her regret and suffering may also make us wish her to be given a relatively full moral exoneration, and this seems to require a softening—a retroactive reduction—of the wrong she has done to both Estella and Pip. In effect, *only* the romantic reunion intimated in the revised ending can achieve this, since Estella has long been, in Pip's words, "part of my existence, part of myself" (44: 272), and is "impossible . . . to . . . separate . . . from the innermost life of my life" (29: 182). We may be reminded here, too, of *Paradise Lost*, in which Eve reports Adam's words to her: "Part of my soul I seek thee, and thee claim / My other half" (4: 487–88). The discovery of Estella's parentage lifts Pip from despair, reawakens his hope, and creates in him, and perhaps in us, the readers of his story, expectations that Dickens was later persuaded to satisfy. After recognizing Estella's relationship to Magwitch, Pip once again appears confident about the possibility of the miraculous in life. He therefore is free to persist in his desires and to interpret subsequent events such as his escape from Orlick, the removal of Biddy as a potential mate, and the meeting with Estella at the site of Satis House as confirmation of providential design. As his story concludes, his expectations, though modified, remain great.

Notes

1. This chapter was originally published in slightly different form in *Studies in the Novel* 19: 4 (Winter 1987): 410–21, copyright 1987 by the University of North Texas, and is reproduced with the permission of the publisher.
2. Dabney maintains that Pip is giving Magwitch "a final illusion to die on" (147), while H. Stone asserts, "One part of Pip's rebirth consists in recognizing and accepting Estella's true identity and then confessing to her debased father—now under sentence of death—that he loves her" (*Dickens and the Invisible World* 311).
3. Forster, in his biography, observes of Dickens, "The question of hereditary transmission had a curious attraction for him, and considerations connected with it were frequently present to his mind" (*Life* 8: 2: 636 [n.]).
4. Millhauser maintains that Pip "would probably have made a rather condescending husband for the Biddy he had determined on marrying, country school-teacher or no" (271), while Young states that "experience and education have made him unsuited to a life at the forge (or anything similar with Biddy)" (212). Pearlman sees snobbery in "Dickens' unwillingness to allow his hero to sacrifice himself" by marrying Biddy (200), but a very different view is offered by Rawlins, who affirms that Dickens intends the loss of Biddy to be "a bitter pill" for Pip and does not realize that the reader will "gasp with relief" (679).
5. See, e.g., Nelson, "Dickens' Plots" 11–14, and Goldknopf 164, 174. Sucksmith asserts that Dickens's "most important use of coincidence" is "to

create an ironic effect" and to suggest "fate or design" (237). See, too, the stimulating chapter on coincidence in Reed 126–41.

6. Calder, in his edition of the novel, suggests that Dickens, by emending the version in *All the Year Round*, may have wished to make "the last phrase less definite, and even ambiguous" (496), since the shadow may have been there even though Pip did not see it.

7. Miller also finds the second ending "much truer to the real direction of the story" (*Charles Dickens* 278), as does Gregory 407–08. Sucksmith, in defending this revised version, maintains, "If we accept the account of Estella's regeneration in the rejected ending, then we should also accept the reconciliation between Pip and Estella in the new ending, since this is only a logical development of that regeneration" (112). Meckier also supports this second ending ("Charles Dickens' *Great Expectations*," esp. 53–54). For arguments endorsing Dickens's earlier, unpublished conclusion, see Rosenberg, "Last Words," and the expansion of this essay in his edition of *Great Expectations*, 491–527, an edition that also includes Rosenberg's selected bibliography of discussions considering this dispute (743–44).

8. Among the commentators who discuss Pip's covert desires for violent revenge, expressed through such surrogates as Orlick and Drummle, are Moynihan 71–77 and Wentersdorf 206–07, 214–16, 219–21.

Chapter 8

Mr. Boffin and Mr. Riah: Strange Symmetry in
Our Mutual Friend

In discussing *Our Mutual Friend*, John Forster remarks that Mr. Riah, "the benevolent old Jew," whom Dickens "makes the unconscious agent of a rascal, was meant to wipe out a reproach against his Jew in *Oliver Twist* as bringing dislike upon the religion of the race he belonged to" (*Life* 9: 5: 740). As various commentators have noticed, Riah obviously offers a strong contrast to Fagin (Fisch 65; Naman 79; Heller 40). Although both elderly men are unusual in attire and appearance, Fagin, we are told, has a "villanous-looking and repulsive face" (8: 65), while Riah, according to the narrator of *Our Mutual Friend*, is "venerable" (2: 5: 273). More important, Fagin, while seeming to be hospitable and nurturing, a beneficent provider of food and shelter, is actually greedy, treacherous, and cruel. Riah, on the other hand, in acting for Fledgeby, whom he serves not as an "unconscious agent"—Forster's assertion notwithstanding—but as a fully aware representative, appears to be hardhearted and grasping, yet nevertheless proves kindly and protective. Fagin, the tor*mentor* of Nancy and Oliver, gives way in the later novel to a Jew who becomes the true *mentor* of Lizzie and Jenny Wren (as Fanny Cleaver calls herself). In *Our Mutual Friend*, however, Riah acts not merely as an admirable Jew who contrasts with Fagin, but serves as a significant parallel to Boffin, whose pretense of being a miser enables Bella Wilfer to shed her materialistic exterior and discover her real self.

Just as the Golden Dustman acts as a catalyst in the John (Rokesmith) Harmon-Bella Wilfer plot-line, so Riah helps bring a happy resolution to the Lizzie Hexam-Eugene Wrayburn story. Connections between Boffin and Riah have been noticed by scholars like Edwin M. Eigner (*The Metaphysical Novel* 189), Thomas Leitch (155), and Goldie Morgentaler (155), but the two characters reveal considerably more similarities than have previously been discussed. Indeed, Mr. Boffin and Mr. Riah, both seen by "society" as outsiders, a former servant (as well as a dustman) and a Jew, emerge as complementary figures who enable Dickens to emphasize important links between the novel's two main plot strands and to explore the theme of fatherhood, a subject holding deep personal resonance for him as son and as parent. Although literary critics have often disparaged both Boffin and Riah, I find them more complex and more successful artistic creations than do their detractors. In the presentation of Boffin, many features, including his background as a servant, his interest in literacy, and his attitude towards wealth, make the extended pretense of miserhood credible, while Riah can be defended by considering particular perspectives offered by social history and psychology. There are sound reasons why Mrs. Eliza Davis, the Jewish lady whose complaint about Fagin helped beget Riah, despite her minor criticisms of this figure's depiction, expressed gratitude to Dickens after reading No. 7, the installment in which Riah is introduced. For Mrs. Davis, the creation of this character was "a great compliment paid to myself and to my people" (*Anglo-Jewish Letters* 307; PL 10: 269 [n. 5], 454 [nn. 1, 2, 3]; Johnson 2: 1012). In 1867 she sent Dickens as a gift a copy of a Hebrew and English Bible, with the inscription, "Presented to Charles Dickens, in grateful and admiring recognition of his having exercised the noblest quality men can possess—that of having atoned for an injury as soon as conscious of having inflicted it" (Johnson 2: 1012). We may assume that by then Mrs. Davis had finished reading *Our Mutual Friend*, the serialization of which had been completed in November 1865, and that she did not object to the way in which Riah is developed in the remainder of the novel.[1]

—1—

Boffin enters the narrative well before Riah. In the second chapter, Mortimer Lightwood refers to the elder John Harmon's "old servant" as the inheritor of a dust-mountain (1: 2: 26), and we encounter Boffin himself in the opening of the second monthly installment (1: 5: 54). Riah, however, is neither mentioned nor presented until five months later, in the seventh monthly number (2: 5: 273), after approximately one-third of the novel had been published. In addition, since Boffin has a much more prominent role in the narrative, he appears in twenty of the novel's sixty-six chapters and is mentioned in nine more, while Riah is depicted in only eight chapters and referred to in just five others. Nevertheless, numerous details link "the Golden Dustman" (1: 17: 208) and "the gentle Jew" (2: 5: 276) and highlight the noticeable symmetry in their actions.

First, each is exotic, decidedly strange in appearance. The narrator calls Boffin a "very odd-looking old fellow" (1: 5: 54), a person "of an overlapping rhinoceros build," with a "broad-brimmed hat" (1: 5: 54).[2] Later, we encounter Riah, "an old Jewish man," who wears "an ancient coat," is "bald and shining at the top of his head, . . . with long grey hair flowing down at its sides and mingling with his beard," and has a "rusty large-brimmed low-crowned hat" (2: 5: 273), a character who, in Jenny Wren's words, looks "unlike the rest of people" (3: 2: 429). Although Dickens often gives characters recognizable verbal mannerisms and speech patterns that set them apart from other figures, the dialogue created for Boffin and Riah seems particularly distinctive. When we first meet Boffin, his speech is exuberant ("Morning, sir! Morning! Morning!" [1: 5: 54]), ingenuously and tactlessly direct ("How did you get your wooden leg?" [1: 5: 55]), and marked by malapropisms or blunders ("we live on a compittance, under the will of a diseased governor" [1: 5: 58], "His name is Decline-And-Fall-Off-The-Rooshan-Empire" [1: 5: 59]). Later, when Riah is introduced, the language attributed to him in his conversation with Fledgeby is noticeably noncolloquial—formal, deferential, at times stilted: "Generous Christian master, it being holiday, I looked for no one" (2: 5: 273), "The son inheriting, was so merciful as to forgive me both [principal and interest], and place me here" (2: 5: 274).

When Boffin and later Riah first appear, each man is connected to the theme of literacy, an important motif in this novel.[3] Boffin approaches Silas Wegg, who has attracted his attention while singing a ballad to a butcher's boy who has just purchased a copy, and proposes that Wegg serve as a paid reader to help Boffin compensate for his inability to read (1: 5: 56–58).[4] Subsequently, Riah is found in the company of Lizzie Hexam and Jenny Wren, whom he has allowed to use the roof of Pubsey and Co. as a refuge in which to study reading, since Eugene Wrayburn has been paying to provide tutoring that will allow them to become literate.

Boffin formerly worked for the elder Harmon, a harsh master, whom Mrs. Boffin once denounced as "a flinty-hearted old rascal" (1: 8: 95); Riah serves Fascination Fledgeby, a secret usurer, who is the son of a now dead moneylender. Since the front for Fledgeby's usury business is Pubsey and Co., a house that stocks "mock beads," "cheap clocks," "cheap vases of flowers" (2: 5: 273), and evidently some fabrics, Riah, in the course of his employment, sells to Jenny Wren items from the company's "damage and waste" (2: 5: 278), while Boffin, as a person formerly involved in the dust-contracting business, also once dealt with waste. In the novel, each older man is the recipient of pleas for financial assistance: Boffin is sent begging letters (1: 17: 209–11), while Fledgeby deceitfully forwards to Riah the appeals of the Lammles and Twemlow for delays in paying debts (3: 12: 549–52; 3: 13: 558–59). We also may find a link in the perceptions held of each character by the public: Boffin is regarded in an anomalous way as being a "Dustman" who is "Golden," since he has suddenly been enriched (1: 17: 208), and Riah, despite his "shabby" appearance (2: 5: 273), is thought to be wealthy, although he is actually poor (2: 5: 274–75). Of course, for many in Dickens's original audience, the idea of a "gentle Jew" (2: 5: 276) would have seemed as paradoxical as that of a "Golden Dustman." In mid-Victorian England, Jews and dustmen were usually regarded as being on the periphery of society. Significantly, in Volume 2 of Henry Mayhew's enlarged 1861–62 four-volume edition of *London Labour and the London Poor*, a chapter entitled "Of the Street Jews" (115–35) is directly followed by one called "Of the Street-Finders or Collectors" (136–81), a category including "dustmen" (159–79).

As Boffin observes, his wife has renamed the home inherited from old John Harmon "Boffin's Bower" (1: 5: 60), a designation perhaps suggested by the "lattice-work Arbour" atop the High Mound that is nearby (1: 5: 64); Riah, who lives in the building owned by his employer, has "made a little garden" on the roof (2: 5: 275). Both the bower and the rooftop garden may be considered unusual refuges. The narrator explicitly praises the Boffins as "honest and true," "trustworthy in all things from the greatest to the least" (1:

9: 106), and directly commends Riah with such adjectives as "grateful"(2: 5: 280) and "good" (3: 2: 429).

During the course of the novel, both Boffin and Riah assume roles as surrogate fathers—the first to Bella, the second to both Lizzie and Jenny. Moreover, Boffin also gives parental counsel to young John Harmon, while Riah at one point offers fatherly advice to the male protagonist in the other major narrative strand, scornful Eugene Wrayburn. Each elderly man, although presently childless, has had paternal experience: Boffin and his wife gave parental care and affection to their irascible employer's two motherless childen (1: 8: 95; 1: 15: 185); and Riah, as he tells Jenny, has lost a wife, a daughter, and a son (3: 2: 430).

Soon after the apparent death of young John Harmon, the Boffins, motivated by sympathy for Bella Wilfer, whose expectations of wealth have been ended, invite the young woman to leave her parents' modest home and live with them. Eventually, Mrs. Boffin promises her that when she marries "with their consent they will portion" her "most handsomely" (3: 4: 454). As the Boffins's surrogate daughter, Bella becomes convinced, she believes, of the preeminent importance of riches. Speaking to her actual father, she confides, "I have made up my mind that I must have money, Pa. I . . . have resolved that I must marry it" (2: 8: 317). Shortly before this statement, the narrator asserts that Bella has been "doubly spoilt . . . : spoilt first by poverty, and then by wealth" (2: 8: 305), an assessment indicating that the Boffins, despite their commendable intentions, have in a short time adversely influenced this young woman. Subsequently, her materialistic goals prompt her to reject the courtship of the man she knows as John Rokesmith, Mr. Boffin's secretary (2: 13: 369–71).

Not until ten months later, in the novel's concluding double-number, did the original readers of Dickens's serialization learn that the night after this rebuff the Boffins became aware that the distressed Rokesmith was actually young Harmon. The husband and wife together proposed the elaborate stratagem of Noddy Boffin's pretended miserhood, a ruse designed both to teach and to test Bella (4:13: 752–53). As Edwin M. Eigner observes, Boffin has great confidence in the young woman and wishes to demonstrate her merit to her and to young Harmon, while simultaneously proving to the latter his own worth ("Pious Fraud" 19). Before the long-delayed revelation of this scheme, termed a "pious fraud" in Dickens's working notes (OMF 874; DWN 363), the novel's readers receive no clear clue and are likely to be fooled by Boffin's behavior. Certainly,

Bella is deceived, for soon after her rejection of Rokesmith she tells her father of Boffin's change "for the worse" (3: 4: 455).

At almost exactly the same time that Boffin begins this benevolent deception to assist Bella, whom Mrs. Boffin later calls his " 'special favourite' " (4: 13: 752), Riah comes to the aid of the novel's other heroine, Lizzie Hexam, by arranging for her to flee London. On the evening after hearing Bella's refusal, Rokesmith, apparently just prior to being recognized as John Harmon by Mrs. Boffin, meets with Bradley Headstone to employ him as a tutor for Sloppy (2: 14: 379), whom the Boffins have asked to share their home (2: 10: 332). In hiring Headstone, Rokesmith is prompted by a desire to learn whether Lizzie has been harmed by the false accusation of murder directed against her father (2: 14: 381). Of course, Rokesmith is unaware of Headstone's infatuation with Lizzie and merely assumes that the schoolmaster will know about her because of his association with Charley Hexam, her brother. Headstone, "very soon after his interview with the Secretary [Rokesmith]" (2: 15: 384), goes to propose to Lizzie, and her rejection of him (which appears in the monthly installment just after that containing a parallel, Bella's refusal of Rokesmith as a suitor) leads to the schoolmaster's threat concerning Eugene and to Charley's angry repudiation of his sister. In utter distress, Lizzie is approached by Riah, for, even before knowing her identity, the old man has been moved by his "gentleness and compassion" to offer comfort to a seeming stranger (2: 15: 396). When Lizzie recognizes him—a friend who has allowed Jenny and her to study in tranquility on the house-top of Pubsey and Co., from which Jenny purchases damaged "strings of beads and tinsel scraps" for her dolls (2: 5: 276–78)—Riah addresses her as "My daughter" and, on learning how her brother has acted, instantly denounces Charley as "a thankless dog" (2: 15: 396).

Although Lizzie accepts the old man's invitation to rest at his home before being escorted to her own residence, they soon meet Eugene. After Wrayburn unsuccessfully tries to dismiss Riah with a series of condescending, anti-Semitic remarks, both men take Lizzie directly to her lodging. When Eugene and Riah part, the old man comments, "I give you good night, and I wish that you were not so thoughtless" (2: 15: 400), advice that anticipates Lizzie's later plea to Wrayburn, "You have not thought. But I entreat you to think now, think now!" (4: 6: 676). Unlike John Harmon, who readily accepts Boffin's proposal about testing Bella, Wrayburn derides Riah's admonition. After Eugene leaves, Riah sits watchfully for an hour on some steps near Lizzie's residence, a protective figure who will soon after devise a plan to assist the young woman. Indeed, in the very next chapter we learn of her disappearance from London (2: 16: 404–06), and in the succeeding chapter Fledgeby induces Riah, who acknowledges "a father's" feeling for Lizzie, to admit that he has advised her to run away, since she was "beset by the snares of a . . . powerful lover [Eugene]" and "by the wiles of her own heart" (3: 1: 426). He reveals only that she is "at a distance—among certain of our people" (3: 1: 426). Acting as a surrogate father, Riah has "counselled flight" to lessen the "moral danger" faced by Lizzie (3: 1: 426) and has found her a safe place of refuge. Just as Boffin will keep his reasons for acting like a miser undisclosed from all but Mrs. Boffin and young John Harmon, so Riah is furtive in concealing Lizzie's new location. As we have already noticed, Dickensian coincidence makes the devising of these two secret plans to assist the heroines almost simultaneous.

Boffin, during his role-playing, pretends to be rude to Rokesmith, while Riah, in compliance with the ruse orchestrated by Fledgeby, is eventually compelled to act as a harsh creditor towards Eugene, even though this intention is indicated to Mortimer Lightwood rather than directly to Wrayburn (3: 10: 525–26). In addition, each paternal figure—Boffin and Riah—clearly influences the heroine with whom he is involved. Each older man arranges a change of residence: Bella departs from her parents' home and thereby escapes the domination of her mother, while Lizzie leaves London to live in a quiet country town away from both Headstone and Eugene. By posing as a miser, Boffin induces Bella to choose love over money, so that she may become romantically attracted to young Harmon and be rewarded for her proper choice by ultimately getting both affection and wealth. By arranging for a safe retreat for Lizzie, Riah protects her from the sexual threat posed by Eugene and affords her a chance to gain some tranquility and increased self-confidence.

—2—

The chapter following that in which we learn of the assistance given to Lizzie by Riah continues the development of the latter character, as he provides paternal care to another surrogate daughter, the twelve- or thirteen-year-old Jenny Wren (2: 1: 224), who sees him as "so like the fairy godmother in the bright little books" (3: 2: 429). By regarding Riah as her "fairy godmother," who calls her "Cinderella" (3: 2: 428), Jenny can acknowledge her true identity as a victimized child (rather than the parent of a troublesome son), can recognize Riah's unselfish benevolence and helpfulness, can depict him as an exotic figure who seems to possess extraordinary powers, and can express a hope that her story will be like a fairy tale in leading her, like Cinderella, from hardship to happiness.

At the end of the installment in which this chapter appears (No. 11), we find Bella's comment to her father about a deterioration she sees in Boffin (3: 4: 455), a change much later revealed to be a hoax. Bella is misjudging her benefactor because of his own playacting, but Jenny similarly soon comes to a false assessment of Riah because of the deception imposed on him by Fledgeby. A few chapters before, at the beginning of the same installment in which Bella describes the change in Boffin, we have witnessed Riah playing the part of a severe usurer (3: 1: 420–21). Boffin is first actually shown behaving harshly in the initial chapter of the next monthly number (3: 5: 456–60). Although we are always aware that the seeming cruelty of Riah is an act, we have no reason to suspect that Boffin is merely feigning. The latter's role-playing is voluntary, a pedagogic device, but Riah's pretense is not, for the old man feels he must follow the dictates of Fascination Fledgeby, to whom Riah feels deeply grateful because Fledgeby had forgiven a debt owed to his late father, the former proprietor of the family's money-lending business (2: 5: 274). Nevertheless, this gratitude, expressed privately to Fledgeby, is not the only motivation for Riah's subservience, for the old man later reveals that he has been legally bound to "certain months of servitude" and had intended upon their expiration to disclose the ruse to Jenny (4: 9: 708). We may assume that had Riah not agreed to this legally sanctioned servitude, he would have suffered imprisonment, the prospect subsequently used by Fledgeby to torment Twemlow (3: 13: 558). By casting Riah as a grasping usurer, Fledgeby cleverly masks his own cruelty and greed. Even though the old man tells clients that he acts merely on behalf of the business's owner, this claim is, ironically, always disregarded (2: 5: 274–75). As Robert Newsom observes, the fact that "Riah pretends most when he tells us the literal truth" is "possible precisely because he inhabits a world in which deception is the norm" (" 'To Scatter Dust' " 47). Jenny, misled by Fledgeby's contention that his being called "master" is merely a jest (3: 13: 554), overhears the stern refusal of Twemlow's wish for leniency and then denounces her once-beloved "godmother" as "the wicked Wolf" (3: 13: 562), an outburst anticipating Bella's repudiation of Boffin as "a Monster," "a Demon," in the succeeding installment (3: 15: 584).

Just as Jenny reacts to mistreatment of Twemlow, so Bella responds to abuse of Rokesmith. In the case of Boffin, Bella is a surrogate daughter who is assisted and is also misjudging. For Riah, these functions are divided between two surrogate children: Lizzie is the "daughter" to whom he gives major assistance, while Jenny misjudges him. Interestingly, as Adrian Poole notices (OMF xviii), the working notes to the first installment reveal that Dickens considered as names for Gaffer Hexam's daughter first "Jenny" and then "Lizzie" (OMF 847; DWN 335).

Each of the two pretenders—Riah and Boffin—is linked with the image of a dog. A chapter-title describes Fledgeby's casting of Riah in a derogatory role—"Give a Dog a Bad Name, and Hang Him" (3: 13: 553), and Fledgeby subsequently, in his farewell note, calls Riah "an unthankful dog of a Jew" (4: 9: 709). In the other strand, Boffin, after assuming his pretense, is reported by the narrator to have "eyed" Wegg "as a dog might eye another dog who wanted his bone" (3: 6: 483), and Noddy also later does a canine imitation when pretending to ridicule Rokesmith's admission of a desire to win Bella's affection—"Mew says the cat, Quack-quack says the duck, Bow-wow says the dog!" (3: 15: 583). In each case, too, the behavior that creates the misleading impression has to do with seemingly avaricious attitudes towards money: Boffin pretends to be a miser, while Riah acts the part of a merciless usurer. Each pretense, moreover, is prolonged. Even after Bella has chosen to marry Rokesmith, Boffin delays ending his ruse, for he wishes to help John test Bella's acceptance of a modest life-style. Riah, after belatedly realizing that his role-playing serves to confirm anti-Semitic stereotypes, decides he cannot quit until his legally binding term of service has expired. In addition, during each deception, both Boffin and Riah may have been lawbreakers. In the novel's penultimate chapter, we learn that Mortimer Lightwood makes Fledgeby realize that he is "in danger of being blown into the air by certain explosive transactions in which he had been engaged" (4: 16: 782), a reference either to legal jeopardy or else simply to the peril of public exposure. If legal problems are involved, Riah, as Fledgeby's agent, would be implicated. Earlier, we have discovered that Boffin, before learning Rokesmith's true identity, had found in a Dutch bottle old Harmon's "latest will," a document leaving the entire estate to himself, and had concealed the will (4: 14: 767). There seems to be technical impropriety in that no one should have kept this will hidden, least of all old Harmon's "sole executor" (1: 2: 26).

The parallel denunciation scenes, which are nearly simultaneous (appearing in juxtaposed numbers), are balanced by a pair of reconciliations. Recalling various clues that point to Fledgeby's deceit (4: 8: 700–01), Jenny returns to Riah, who leaves the usurer's employment and then accepts the dolls' dressmaker's invitation to move into Lizzie's old room (4: 9: 710). After Jenny witnesses the death of her natural father, whose dipsomania had made him his own daughter's "poor unfortunate child" (4: 9: 713), she refers, when speaking with Sloppy, to Riah as "my second father" or "my first, for that matter," an acknowledgment of her actual father's weakness (4: 16: 787). Boffin, too, regains the good opinion of his surrogate daughter, Bella, but his wife must first disclose his ruse (4: 13: 751–53). In starting to tell the story of the impersonation, Mrs. Boffin begins, "Once, twice, three times, and the horses is off" (4: 13: 751), an expression that seems comparable to the comment by Jenny after she, with the help of statements by Riah, has gained awareness of the pretense imposed upon him: "And now the murder's all out" (4: 9: 708). Both Boffin and Riah may be categorized by the title of a comedy by Bulwer-Lytton that Dickens and his troupe of amateur actors produced years before, in 1851 and 1852: *Not So Bad As We Seem* (Johnson 2: 734–37). In the two reconciliation scenes, presented in successive installments of *Our Mutual Friend*, each young woman warmly kisses the older man. Earlier, the parallelism in these paternal roles has been emphasized by the narrator's describing Boffin walking alone with Bella (3: 5: 461–63), for previously Riah was depicted accompanying Lizzie (2: 15: 396–98), before Eugene joined them, and Riah was also shown escorting Jenny through the London streets (3: 2: 429–33). At the end of the novel, each of these two elderly men lives in the home of a surrogate daughter: Boffin and his wife with Bella and her husband, Riah with Jenny.

In addition to being protectors of surrogate daughters, Boffin and Riah are also linked in that each is a potential or actual victim of an extreme hypocrite who is a monster of avarice—Boffin's employee and Riah's employer. The newly rich Golden Dustman becomes the target of the "friendly move," the extortion scheme of Silas Wegg, who defames Boffin when talking to Mr. Venus (2: 7: 296, 301); and the needy Riah is slandered by Fledgeby (3: 1: 420–21, 423; 3: 12: 550; 3: 13: 556, 559), another type of extortionist, a usurer, and is induced to behave so reprehensibly that he finds himself "hateful" (4: 9: 707)—indeed, Fledgeby may be seen as "extorting" cruel behavior from him. Each of the two conniving villains, however, is physically chastised by a "child" of his victim. Fledgeby, after being thrashed by Lammle, whose wife has discerned that Riah is only an agent, is further punished when pepper is placed on his wounds by Jenny,[5] who is soon to see herself clearly as the "daughter" of the abused Jew, while Wegg, in being exposed and denounced for plotting against Boffin, is treated roughly by the latter's surrogate son, John Harmon, and then thrown into "a scavenger's cart" (4: 14: 770) by the young man whom the Boffins have adopted, Sloppy. Just as we witness the parallel vindications of Boffin and Riah, so we observe the unmaskings of the scoundrels who have schemed against them.

Because Riah is surprisingly slow to recognize that his forced behavior brings "dishonour" on his "ancient faith and race" and reflects unfavorably on "the Jews of all conditions and all countries" (4: 9: 707), we may find unconvincing his excuse of having been legally bound to servitude. Nevertheless, we should also recall that Boffin willingly remained for many years in the service of an ogre, an "awful Tartar" who had disowned his wife and children and had even once acted insultingly towards Mrs. Boffin (1: 8: 94–95). Both Boffin and Riah are alike in being generous, long-suffering, honest, and loyal servants of despicable employers.

Dickens further connects these two figures through their relationships with various other characters. Besides being assisted by Riah, Lizzie Hexam attracts the interest of Boffin, who asks Rokesmith to determine whether she has been harmed by Riderhood's false accusation of her father, a statement that was later retracted (3: 9: 511). Lizzie, having been sent Riderhood's retraction by Harmon, whom she later refers to as her "unknown friend" (3: 9: 515), has forwarded the document to Boffin (2: 16: 405) and has also given a copy to Riah and Jenny to take to show to Miss Abbey Potterson (3: 2: 434–35). Mortimer Lightwood has dealings first with Boffin, who has retained him for legal assistance, and later with Riah, before whom he represents his friend Eugene, who has fallen into debt to Fledgeby (3: 10: 525–26). Soon after, we find a chapter in which Sophronia Lammle is first observed plotting with her husband to victimize the Boffins (3: 12: 546–49) and then seen appealing to Fledgeby to use his "well-earned influence" to obtain indulgence from Riah (3: 12: 549). When Eugene meets Boffin, the young man offers mildly mocking conversation (1: 8: 98–99), and Wrayburn afterwards, on meeting Riah, delivers some insulting banter. Still another link appears in the novel's penultimate chapter, when Jenny, one of Riah's two surrogate daughters, and Sloppy, whom the Boffins have adopted, first meet (4: 16: 786–89).

—3—

Although each of the two heroines—Lizzie and Bella—has great love for her biological father, each greatly benefits by receiving affectionate guidance from a surrogate father who helps her face a crisis. Nevertheless, each young woman must act for herself to determine her future, for neither Riah nor Boffin can provide solutions by himself. Riah perceives that avoiding the company of Eugene is important if Lizzie is to regain her composure, but the rural refuge he helps her to obtain provides only a temporary respite. Before she can gain lasting serenity and happiness, Lizzie must overcome two problems: the illiteracy forced upon her by Gaffer and the sense of guilt induced by her participation in her father's scavenging on the river. This remorse has led her, after she finds work as a seamstress, to befriend Jenny, the granddaughter of a drowning victim whose body was recovered by Hexam (2: 1: 227). In her first meeting with Bella, however, Lizzie again alludes to her guilt (3: 9: 518). The feeling is not eradicated until she finds late in the novel that the skills developed in the river outings with her father may enable her to save Eugene's life (4: 6: 683–84). Her other disadvantage, illiteracy, was overcome, presumably even before she left London, through the lessons arranged and paid for by Eugene (2: 2: 234–37): Lizzie demonstrates her accomplishment when she reads the message carried by the dying Betty Higden (3: 8: 506) and later writes a "short letter" informing Mrs. Boffin of Betty's death (3: 9: 511). In addition, Lizzie shows impressive social confidence when meeting Bella, "the boofer lady," with whom she was momentarily confused by the stricken Mrs. Higden (3: 8: 505).[6]

Lizzie, by first acquiring literacy and then becoming free from guilt about her help to her father on the river, can overcome her feelings of unworthiness in relation to Eugene. Bella, however, needs to surmount the materialism that prompts her to reject Rokesmith. Since the narrator asserts that Bella, before being spoiled by the Boffins' wealth, was "spoilt first by poverty" (2: 8: 305), her natural father, Reginald Wilfer, evidently would bear some responsibility for this, even though blaming him for lack of wealth seems contradictory to the values endorsed by the novel. Wilfer, although likeable, warm-hearted, and highly moral, is depicted as a timid, shy man who cowers before his domineering wife. Indeed, the narrator sees him as a grown cherub (1: 4: 41), a character who is "like a boy" (2: 8: 313). In the eyes of Bella, he is not so much a parent as "a sort of a younger brother" (2: 8: 317), but his paternal short-comings are, of course, much less harmful than those of Jenny's father, who is viewed by his daughter as a refractory child. Nevertheless, Wilfer is linked to Mr. Dolls in that each uses the excuse offered by that flawed father Mr. Micawber (DC 49: 490) about being dominated by "circumstances over which" he has "no control" (2: 2: 241 [for Mr. Dolls]; 2: 8: 312 [for Wilfer]). When Bella informs Wilfer of her desire for a mercenary marriage, he objects only in an extremely mild, ineffectual way (2: 8: 317–18). Later, however, Bella, when upset by Boffin's abuse of Rokesmith, thinks of Wilfer as a source of comfort ("good little Pa," "Nobody else can understand me" [3: 15: 584]), and he will subsequently offer speedy, strong approval of Bella's renunciation of materialism (3: 16: 593–94).

Nevertheless, he is not the one who guides Bella to this new position. Acting as a surrogate parent, Boffin thinks of a forceful way to lead her to interpret properly a living drama. In feigning miserliness, Boffin consciously takes the risk that Bella will approve of his feigned greed and imitate his example, and such a response is, indeed, evoked from Silas Wegg, although this scoundrel does not really need further incentive to avarice. Indeed, Wegg's extortion plot, the "friendly move," originated well before Boffin devised his plan, and, even earlier, young John Harmon had quickly become suspicious of Wegg (4: 14: 767). Late in the novel, Boffin states that his pretense was designed not only to show Bella the danger of mercenary values, but also to provide "for the punishment of . . . Wegg, by leading him on in a very unhandsome and underhanded game that he was playing" (4: 13: 755). Unlike Riah, who hurts people by performing Fledgeby's bidding, Boffin does not really harm anyone with acting, since Wegg's charge that his own mind has been "lowered by unwholesome reading on the subject of Misers" (4: 14: 769) is clearly absurd. Mr. Venus listens regularly to the tales of misers (3: 14: 562), but still decides to abandon his part in the extortion scheme and to warn Boffin.

Of course, responses to the stories of characters like the misers are bound to be subjective. Sir Walter Scott, in *The Lives of the Novelists*, includes in his essay "Tobias Smollett" the following comment on *The Adventures of Ferdinand Count Fathom*:

> To a reader of a good disposition and well-regulated mind, the picture of moral depravity presented in the character of Count Fathom is a disgusting pollution of the imagination. To those, on the other hand, who hesitate on the brink of meditated iniquity, it is not safe

to detail the arts by which the ingenuity of villany has triumphed in
former instances; and it is well known that the publication of the real
account of uncommon crimes, although attended by the public and
infamous punishment of the perpetrators, has often had the effect of
stimulating others to similar actions.   (83)

The fact that the misers in the tales Boffin has read to him can
be regarded as exemplary in either a positive or negative sense is
emphasized by the reaction of Rokesmith upon being asked if he
knows of these strange characters: "They lived and died very miser-
ably. Did they not, sir?" (3: 5: 468). In *Oliver Twist* Fagin attempts
to use narratives of notorious criminals as inducements to emulation
of wrongdoing, but Oliver, who represents, as Dickens asserts in a
preface, "the principle of Good surviving through every adverse
circumstance, and triumphing at last" (3), is repelled, not attracted,
by the book, probably the *Newgate Calendar*, that is given to him (20:
140–41). Interestingly, however, even virtuous Oliver has previously
found amusement in Fagin's stories of his own youthful criminal
career (18: 131).

Although Bella is asked to help purchase books about misers,
she is evidently never urged to read these volumes, but is instead
subjected to watching Boffin act as a living example, a "glaring
instance," a "fingerpost . . . pointing out the road" that she "was
taking and the end it led to" (4: 13: 754–55). Boffin apparently thinks
that a living negative example might be more effective pedagogi-
cally than just the act of reading, and he also presumably realizes
that he and young John Harmon have been made more conscious
of the dangers of avarice as a result of their having witnessed the
abhorrent behavior of old Harmon. Since Boffin exaggerates the role
of miser to the point of caricature, the test for Bella may seem easy,
but its difficulty is actually great, since the young woman is dependent on Boffin's favor, is treated with kindness by him, and is out-
wardly encouraged by him to accept mercenary values. Bella passes
the test, for besides being sensitive to Mrs. Boffin's discomfort at
her husband's harsh, insulting treatment of Rokesmith, the young
woman subsequently, during the journey with the secretary to attend Betty Higden's funeral, expresses her desire to converse with
him "on equal terms" and asks forgiveness for leading him to believe that he need act "constrained" with her (3: 9: 510). Mrs. Boffin
has asked Bella to provide a "small report" about Lizzie (3: 9: 510),
while Rokesmith has been asked by Boffin to learn if the retracted
false accusation "still leaves any stain" upon Lizzie (3: 9: 511). The

Boffins have sought to bring the two young people together by giving them similar missions. Bella readily accepts John's suggestion that she speak privately with Lizzie and clearly indicates to Rokesmith disapproval of Boffin's new behavior (3: 9: 512–13). During a long meeting with Lizzie, Bella, despite her previous assertions to her father about her inclination to be mercenary (2: 8: 317; 3: 4: 455), disregards the young woman's lower-class status and treats her with kindness, compassion, and candor. The interview concludes with Lizzie's assertion that she has seen from her reading in the fire that Bella has "a heart well worth winning" (3: 9: 520).

For H. M. Daleski, Lizzie "serves as a mirror, revealing to Bella what she really is," and Lizzie also offers to Bella "an image of what she may become," thereby teaching a lesson to which Boffin's is "complementary" (323). Edwin M. Eigner makes a similar comment, remarking that Bella is aided not only by Boffin's ruse, but by "the influence of Lizzie Hexam, the Madonna or redeeming heroine of the parallel plot" (*The Metaphysical Novel* 206). Dickens himself, in the working notes for No. 13, which includes chapters 8–10 of book 3, writes, "Lizzie to work an influence on Bella's character, at its wavering point" (OMF 870; DWN 359 [CD places double underscoring beneath this line]). Just as Lizzie needs to develop a stronger sense of her own worth, so Bella, in addition to having to shed her materialistic tendencies, must come to believe that she is not "a nasty little thing" or a "limited little brute," a person restricted by base mercenary desires (3: 9: 520). Climactically, when Bella finds that her earlier folly in telling Sophronia Lammle of Rokesmith's proposal leads to the dismissal of the secretary, she immediately condemns Boffin's actions, leaves his household, and soon after agrees to marry Rokesmith and accept the modest lifestyle he offers. Her willingness to relinquish the Boffins as benefactors may be regarded as a heroic act that in some ways parallels Lizzie's later rescue of the wounded Eugene. As Humphry House observes, Boffin's "pretended miserhood" suggests that Dickens believed there was a "need . . . for some very elaborate artifice to get the mercenary ideas out of Bella's head in the kind of society she was living in" (169). When John Harmon, after Mr. Inspector comes to take him for questioning, decides on even further delay before revealing his true identity as Harmon, Bella passes this final trial and validates the prediction about her loyalty made long before by Lizzie Hexam (3: 9: 520).

As Jennifer Hayward observes, both young women at their meeting recognize that they are "pawns in the Harmon murder case,

... that both have no female friends, and that both have love interests which they are too modest . . . to discuss directly" (77–78). Earlier, in successive installments of the novel, each young woman has fancifully speculated about love. Bella, while dining with her father at Greenwich, looks at the ships and imagines being married to various men, each of whom is very wealthy (2: 8: 315–16). Lizzie, in response to questions by Jenny, "looks at the hollow by the flare" of the fire and projects her own suppressed feelings onto a rich lady who might love Eugene (2: 11: 343–44).[7] Moreover, Jenny, who, as we have seen, is at times almost an alter ego for Lizzie, occasionally wonders about her own future suitor or husband (2: 2: 233, 242–43).

Both Bella and Lizzie, as well as Jenny, have unusual relationships with their biological fathers. Lizzie has been a substitute for her dead mother in showing Charley both sisterly and maternal care (1: 3: 37; 1: 6: 79) and in acting as housekeeper and companion to her father. Bella, according to Arthur A. Adrian, acts towards Wilfer as a "mother cum lover" (134), and she refers to him as a "younger brother" (2: 8: 317). Jenny, however, sees her father, "Mr. Dolls," as a troublesome child (2: 2: 239–41). Significantly, two of the most intensely emotional passages in the entire novel occur when the narrator, after the discovery of Gaffer's body, directs at the corpse a lengthy apostrophe beginning, "Father, was that you calling me?" (1: 14: 175), an echo of Lizzie's earlier anxious call (1: 13: 166), and when Jenny, late in the narrative, mourns the death of her father, her "poor boy," her "poor unfortunate child," her "poor lost boy" (4: 9: 712–14).

Later, when Lizzie is to marry Eugene, she asks Bella to attend the wedding (4: 11: 724), a ceremony which, like Bella's, is private. In the novel's penultimate chapter, the narrator indicates that "the greatest event of all," in the "new life" led by Bella and John after the latter's disclosure of his true identity, "was a visit from Mr and Mrs Eugene Wrayburn" (4: 16: 789), a remark implying a continuing relationship between the two heroines. The two plots have, of course, been joined as well by Lizzie's having helped her father take from the Thames a body wrongly thought to be that of young John Harmon (a misidentification that makes possible the latter's lengthy pose as Rokesmith) and also by Lizzie's later pulling from the river the injured Eugene.

The extraordinarily cruel upbringing received by young Harmon has so damaged his self-esteem that he evidently needs even further proof of his wife's total and unquestioning fidelity than her willingness to forego the Boffins's material assistance and to live economically: he declines to explain to her his business with Mr. Inspector until all problems have been satisfactorily resolved. The hero of the other major plot-strand, Eugene, although evidently not at all victimized as a child in the manner that young Harmon was, nevertheless also reveals a need for an increased sense of his own worth in that his view of himself as languorous and lacking direction is certainly negative and reveals self-doubt, despite his facetious tone (2: 6: 292–93). Both of the male leading characters in the novel's two main strands—the Bella-John and Lizzie-Eugene love-matches—undergo similar immersions in the Thames, nearly fatal "baptisms," or "deaths" and rebirths, that lead to greater moral strength and also enable the victims to marry for love. Before being attacked, John Harmon had intended to conceal his identity only for "a few hours or days" (2: 14: 372). The misidentification of George Radfoot's body leads to the prolonged deception. Later, the discovery that the latest will of the elder Harmon leaves the entire estate to the Boffins frees John Harmon of any need to marry Bella in order to gain his father's wealth, since the restrictive will is no longer binding and the Boffins insist on being his benefactors without setting any conditions. John's choice of Bella, therefore, can be based solely on his being attracted to her. Similarly, after being seriously injured by Headstone, Eugene decides to propose marriage to Lizzie, since he believes that he is near death anyway. The overall situation gives him the courage to defy society: Headstone, through his crime, has ironically made possible the union of his enemy Eugene and Lizzie. Before being assaulted, Eugene regards marriage to Lizzie as "out of the question" (4: 6: 682). For both Harmon and Wrayburn, a violent assault eventually leads to freedom to be guided by love alone (Ermath 204).[8]

These two characters, moreover, are linked in still other ways. Just after Boffin has been presented by Mortimer to Eugene (1: 8: 98–99), Noddy is stopped in the street by Rokesmith, who proceeds to introduce himself (1: 8: 99–102). Each young man distrusts Riderhood, whom Eugene dislikes instinctively (1: 12: 157) and whom John recognizes as having been involved with Radfoot in underhanded dealings (2: 13: 361–63). Each of the two young men seeks to protect Lizzie Hexam from harm that could be caused by Riderhood's false accusation of her father, and this interest is emphasized: both Eugene and Lizzie mention Wrayburn's efforts to exonerate Gaffer (2: 2: 234, 236; 2: 11: 343; 2: 15: 391–92), and Rokesmith / Harmon forces Riderhood to sign a retraction (2: 12: 357–58; 2: 14: 378–79, 381), a document that is later, at Lizzie's request, taken by Riah and Jenny to Miss Abbey Potterson, proprietress of the

Six Jolly Fellowship Porters (3: 2: 434–45). Dickens also, as Michael Greenstein notices, employs humorous wordplay to connect Harmon and Wrayburn (129). When Rokesmith visits the Boffins to discuss his desire to act as a secretary, Noddy asks for an explanation, observing that he and his wife had "always believed a Secretary to be a piece of furniture, mostly of mahogany" (1: 15: 180), and soon after we hear Eugene use the word in that way when he describes his "Secrétaire" with its "abstruse set of solid mahogany pigeon-holes, one for every letter of the alphabet" (2: 6: 282).

Each of the two young men—Harmon and Wrayburn—is in search of himself, of his authentic identity, Eugene in installment No. 7 (2: 6: 292–93), John in No. 9 (2: 13: 359–67), and each man is a puzzle to Mortimer Lightwood. For he questions the behavior of his friend Eugene, who sees himself as a "troublesome conundrum" (2: 6: 293), and Mortimer is also baffled by the identity of John Harmon, since the solicitor, after trying unsuccessfully to locate the missing Julius Handford, is surprised to find that Handford and Rokesmith are the same (4: 12: 737).

Moreover, as Jack Lindsay and Gwen Watkins observe, the amatory relationships in both major strands of this novel include problems reminiscent of those facing Dickens himself at this time (Lindsay 346, 382, 384; Watkins 136–39). John Rokesmith / Harmon must prove to himself that the beautiful young woman whose love he seeks is not really mercenary and can love him for himself, not for his wealth, while Eugene must acquire the courage to disregard the opinion of "society" and marry a woman beneath him in the social scale, a woman who has saved his life. Dickens clearly would have wanted to believe that Ellen Ternan valued him for more than materialistic reasons, he may have seen her as having in a sense "saved" his life in prompting him to end a marriage that he had come to perceive as stifling,[9] and he would have been aware that in having a sexual (or even a close platonic) relationship with her he was challenging social opinion in an even more extreme way than he had defied it in arranging the separation from Catherine.

—4—

Both Boffin and Riah, after being misjudged, respectively, by Bella and Jenny, are eventually seen as truly virtuous men: in each case, an apparently selfish and cruel "father" is recognized as being actually benevolent and self-effacing. Indeed, when Riah desires to help the badly thrashed Fledgeby, Jenny remarks in an annoyed way, "One would think you believed in the Good Samaritan" (4: 9: 708), a comment indicating that Riah's behavior reflects the idealism of the Gospels more clearly than do the deeds of many alleged Christians, including Riderhood, who, after extorting money from the ailing Betty Higden, is sarcastically described by the narrator as a type of "the Samaritan in his latest accredited form" (3: 8: 502). Certainly, there is a sharp contrast between Riah and Fledgeby, who separates himself from Christianity not only by his bedroom garb—"Turkish slippers, . . . Turkish trousers . . ., and a gown and cap to correspond" (3: 1: 419), all of which are later replaced by "Christian attire" (3: 1: 428)—but also by his disdainful references to fellow Christians (3: 1: 424, 427–28). Those readers who regard Riah as unrealistic in his goodness may have similar difficulty in accepting Boffin, for the Golden Dustman, who pretended to be intent on humiliating Rokesmith / Harmon, is later revealed to be an extravagantly kind benefactor, a person who, after discovering that the will concealed in the Dutch bottle was the elder Harmon's final testament and left everything to him, insists on relinquishing all but one mound to young John Harmon (4: 14: 768). Dickens's response to skeptics may be found in his preface to the original volume-edition of *Nicholas Nickleby* (1839):

> It is remarkable that what we call the world, which is so very credulous in what professes to be true, is most incredulous in what professes to be imaginary; and that while every day in real life it will allow in one man no blemishes, and in another no virtues, it will seldom admit a very strongly-marked character, either good or bad, in a fictitious narrative, to be within the limits of probability.   (4)

Boffin, the wealthy benefactor, and Riah, the needy one, are like the Uncommercial Traveller in representing the firm of Human Interest Brothers (*Uncommercial Traveller* 1).

For various commentators, however, credibility remains an issue with each of these characters. G. K. Chesterton, for example, asserts that Dickens initially meant the Golden Dustman's deterioration to be real (215). Of course, the working notes, not readily available to Chesterton, totally disprove such a supposition (Shea 38). As Jennifer Hayward suggests, "Boffin's transformation is paired with the John Harmon / John Rokesmith doubling" (73). Boffin and his wife, when planning the elaborate pretense, may well have been prompted by learning of Harmon's masquerade as Rokesmith, an impersonation that John later describes in the final double-install-ment (Nos. 19–20) by employing the same expression that Dickens

used in the working notes for an earlier installment (No. 15) to
designate Boffin's ruse—a "pious fraud" (4: 13: 751; OMF 874;
DWN 363).

Arnold Kettle calls the device of Boffin's feigned miserhood "one
of Dickens's happiest inspirations," since through it "Dickens gets
it both ways" and can reveal "the alternative possibilities before
Boffin" (215). Moreover, Noddy's pretense itself becomes more
plausible when we examine several other factors. First, we may
assume that in order to have continued working for many years for
an obnoxious figure like old John Harmon, Boffin had to develop
great control of his own behavior, control not unlike that of an
actor. In addition, his employer provided an extraordinary model
of avaricious conduct. By imitating this kind of man, Boffin could
find, as Masao Miyoshi proposes, a cathartic outlet for any dark
urges he himself might have: "it [the pose of miserliness] served
Boffin himself as well, as a way of obviating an unpleasant new self
that could very well have emerged from his sudden condition of
wealth" (8). Then, too, because the pretense was partly conducted
to tease and punish Wegg, a truly greedy person, the ruse could
have been for Boffin a kind of retroactive revenge against old Harmon, since Wegg, who has been designated to oversee the former
Harmony Jail, now Boffin's Bower, may be regarded as a surrogate
for Boffin's avaricious dead employer. Among the qualities suggesting that Boffin might have potential skill as an actor is the fact
that he does reveal imaginative ability, for he, unlike Wegg, finds
that he is "severely punished" by hearing of "the confounding enor-
mities of the Romans" and categorizes these characters as "scarers"
(1: 5: 66). Indeed, Boffin's sensitivity is indicated by his very desire
for vicarious literacy—to be provided by his "literary man," who
will enable him to find "a new life" (1: 5: 60).

Boffin is also intended to be regarded as having more intelligence
than may first be apparent, even though the narrator at one point
refers to him and his wife as "ignorant and unpolished" (1: 9: 105).
The Golden Dustman himself indicates that he is "a pretty fair
scholar in dust" who "can price the Mounds to a fraction" and
knows "how they can be best disposed of" (1: 15: 186). Even in
literacy, he seems to be more proficient than he at first claims he is
when speaking to Wegg (1: 5: 57–58): we later find Noddy attempting, although with little success, to review various business
papers and make notes about them (1: 15: 179); when Mr. Venus
shows him the will found by Wegg, Boffin, we are informed,
"slowly spelt it out aloud" (4: 3: 644); and Boffin has evidently been

able to understand without help the meaning of the will in the Dutch bottle and to decide to keep this document concealed (4: 14: 767).[10] An important reason for Noddy's enthusiasm in his role-playing is his sincere belief that excessive devotion to gaining wealth can be extremely harmful. Describing to Lightwood the cruelty of old Harmon, Boffin remarks, "It's a'most a pity . . . that he ever went and made so much money. It would have been better for him if he hadn't so given himself up to it" (1: 8: 94). As an actor, Boffin shows imagination and skill, especially when he feigns being intimidated by Wegg (4: 3: 639–46), and his intelligence allows him to see through and respond effectively to the Lammles' scheme to have Alfred replace Rokesmith (4: 2: 628–37), a plan inspired in part by the Lammles' having been led by the pretense of Boffin to believe that he was "turning very suspicious and distrustful" (3: 12: 546).

Further anticipation of Boffin's prolonged ruse may also be provided by his first name, Nicodemus, which, as both Jane Vogel and Robert Bledsoe notice, seems to refer to a character in the Gospel According to John. Dickens, however, apparently uses the name not to suggest that Boffin needs to awaken and ask "the right questions" (Vogel 41) or to indicate that Noddy must be "born again spiritually" (Bledsoe 101), but to hint that Boffin is a secret follower of Jesus (John 3: 1–21; 7: 50–52; 19: 30): in other words, while pretending to be a harsh miser, Boffin is actually benevolent and generous.

Not only Boffin, but Riah, too, has been attacked as an unsuccessful literary creation. Edward N. Calisch calls him "an unconvincing, spineless saint" (128), while Esther L. Panitz regards Riah as "a paragon of virtue" who is "completely unbelievable" (111). But saints, while they may submit passively to abuse, are not "spineless," since their faith gives them a courage that accepts the risk of martyrdom. In the novel, moreover, Riah, despite his estimable qualities of forgiveness and kindness, is weak. He is a sinner rather than a "paragon of virtue," for he knowingly assists Fledgeby, an evil man. In addition, in the context of mid-Victorian life, Riah's extreme submissiveness may appear very credible. Critics have neglected the previously mentioned detail about the old man's being legally bound to Fledgeby, as well as the fact that Riah, if his debt had not been forgiven, would have faced imprisonment.

Passivity also is induced by the prevalent anti-Semitism of the time. Morgentaler considers the old man's docility a link "to the history of his people as a vanquished race" (152). On first meeting Riah, Eugene treats him in a demeaning, insulting way, by repeatedly and pointedly calling him "Mr. Aaron" (2: 15: 398–400). This device, as H. M. Daleski remarks, is typical of Wrayburn, who later uses "the invention of a name as a ready means of scorn in his reception of Jenny's father" (304), a figure that Eugene disparagingly refers to as "Mr Dolls" (3: 10: 527). We may, of course, add to Daleski's comment the point that Eugene has previously used a similar tactic by insultingly giving Headstone the appellation "Schoolmaster" (2: 6: 287). But in addressing Riah, who is encountered assisting the distraught Lizzie, Wrayburn also gratuitously indulges in other anti-Semitic references besides the assignment of the name "Aaron": after remarking that he himself has been "lingering about like a bailiff," Wrayburn looks at Riah and adds, "or an old clothesman" (2: 15: 398), a major occupation for Jews in Victorian London (Mayhew 2: 116), and then observes that by leaving Lizzie Riah can become "quite free for any engagement he may have at the Synagogue" (2: 15: 399). In allowing himself to be subjected to such remarks, Riah is meek. But what recourse is available? Given the prejudices of the era, what action could be taken by an elderly Jew against a young gentleman who happens to be a barrister? In such a social situation, a target of abuse who is not submissive readily runs the risk of even more extreme victimization. Just as Boffin, in his role as a servant to old Harmon, had to exercise restraint and control, so did Riah as a member of a society permeated by anti-Semitism. If we are aware of the pervasiveness of this bigotry, which has been described by Mayhew (2: 117), as well as in Harry Stone's "Dickens and the Jews" (esp. 225–28) and in the study of Georgian Jews by Todd M. Endelman (86–117), a work examining English Jewry during Dickens's formative years, we may find Riah's behavior much more comprehensible. As Esther Summerson's defenders have cogently observed, degradation is very likely to damage the victim's self-image (see, e.g., Zwerdling, esp. 429–30). In depicting Riah, Dickens shows the same kind of psychological insight that is evident in the earlier presentation of Esther. As a Jew, Riah must constantly seek to protect his self-esteem against a society that denigrates him.

Besides passivity, the other attribute of Riah's that has been questioned is his great benevolence. But, as we have previously suggested, Riah's kindness is not very different from that displayed by other Dickensian characters. Indeed, Harold Fisch finds that "Mr. Riah has little to distinguish him from the hundred other kindly old gentlemen in humble occupations invented by the same author" (65). Although "hundred" may seem an overstatement, and although most Dickensian benefactors are not "in humble occupations," the general point seems valid. Nevertheless, we must remember that for most readers in Dickens's contemporary audience Riah's being identified as a Jew would have sharply differentiated him from other kindly old men. Indeed, there was a stereotypical image of the elderly Jew as a sexual predator like Isaac Rapine in Smollett's *Roderick Random* (Fisch 45). In a study of anti-Semitic stereotypes, Frank Felsenstein refers to attempts to link Jews with lasciviousness and sexual immorality (118, 122). Dickens is careful to separate Riah from this kind of negative role by having such a possibility raised and rejected even by the odious Fledgeby, who asserts, "You can't be a gallivanting dodger. . . . You're one of the Patriarchs; you're a shaky old card; and you can't be in love with this Lizzie?" (3: 1: 425). Such badinage elicits from Riah the statement that he is "too old and broken to be suspected of any feeling for her but a father's" (3: 1: 426).

One of the most interesting attacks on Riah comes from G. K. Chesterton, who cannot resist using Eugene's name for Riah and stating, "Old Aaron is not an exaggeration of Jewish virtues; he is simply not Jewish because he is not human" (xi). But Chesterton quickly contradicts himself. After asserting that *Our Mutual Friend* is "literally full of Jews," among whom he includes such worthies as Veneering, Lammle, and Fledgeby (xi), Chesterton goes on to maintain that Riah "looks like one particularly stupid Englishman pretending to be a Jew among all that crowd of clever Jews who are pretending to be Englishmen" (xii). So locked is Chesterton into his anti-Semitism that he overlooks the inconsistency—Riah goes from being "not human" to being like a "particularly stupid Englishman," a designation that Chesterton might consider superior to that of a Jew. Of course, we are given no explanation as to why Fledgeby, if he is secretly a Jew, indulges in anti-Semitic banter and also refers, in a soliloquy, to his "fellow-Christians" (3: 1: 427–28), nor are we told why Lammle refers slightingly to Jews (3: 12: 545, 549). Moreover, Veneering's successful campaign for Parliament should have attracted more attention, since not until 1858, only six years before Dickens began writing *Our Mutual Friend*, had that assembly agreed to seat a Jew as a member (Roth, *Essays* 281). When we realize that Chesterton's comments seem to be based on nothing but the belief that deceitful financial schemers must be Jews, we understand more clearly the social position of Riah decades before.[11]

We should note, however, that despite the seeming acceptance of a victim's role, Riah does show dignity and even some defiance. He calmly but firmly rejects Wrayburn's request that he leave Lizzie: "I will hear only one voice to-night, desiring me to leave this damsel before I have conveyed her to her home" (2: 15: 399). Moreover, in calling Eugene "Christian gentleman" (2: 15: 399), an appellation like the expression "Generous Christian master" that was previously applied to Fledgeby (2: 5: 273), Riah appears intent on differentiating himself from both of these men. Although Riah dutifully follows Fledgeby's instructions regarding the money-lending business, the old man steadfastly refuses to reveal to his employer the place to which Lizzie has been sent for refuge: "that it was hopeless to question him [Riah] on that one reserved point, Fledgeby . . . saw full well" (3: 1: 426). Earlier, when Fledgeby asserts that "Your people [Jews] . . . lie enough," Riah, "with quiet emphasis," replies that there is "too much untruth among all denominations of men" (2: 5: 274). When Fledgeby then sarcastically asks, "who but you and I ever heard of a poor Jew?" Riah immediately retorts, "The Jews," and adds, "They hear of poor Jews often, and are very good to them" (2: 5: 274).[12] Of course, Riah's most forceful rejection of anti-Semitism comes when he expresses to Jenny his realization that by following harsh orders he was "doing dishonour to . . . [his] ancient faith and race," a statement followed by the remark, "Men . . . take the worst of us [Jews] as samples of the best" (4: 9: 707).

Dickens himself wishes in *Our Mutual Friend* to reject anti-Semitism, and therefore the abuse that Eugene directs at Riah is relatively mild and seems intended to be seen as another of the personal deficiencies that Wrayburn must modify. Moreover, Eugene's anti-Semitism is slightly tempered by his later quip on hearing, from Mortimer, that he has "fallen into the hands of the Jews": "having previously fallen into the hands of some of the Christians, I can bear it with philosophy" (3: 10: 525). Interestingly, except for Eugene's early remarks and for the casual identification of Jews and usurers by Mortimer Lightwood (3: 10: 525), as well as Alfred Lammle's references to his apparent creditor, Riah, as "a Jew" and "the Jew" (3: 12: 545, 549), the only expressions of anti-Semitism in the novel come from the odious Fledgeby and from the Reverend Frank Milvey's wife, who is depicted as a comic figure. Deborah Heller quotes the conversation with Mrs. Milvey in which Lizzie, after acknowledging that her employers, the husband and wife who own the paper-mill, are Jews, adds that she herself "was first brought to their notice by a Jew" [Riah] (3: 9: 508). Citing Lizzie's next sentence, "But I think there cannot be kinder people in the world," Heller observes, "The 'but' may not please us, but it certainly is candid: the frank admission of prior expectations happily confuted" (52). We cannot, however, unhesitatingly attribute such an attitude to

Lizzie, since she appears to be using the "but" merely to counter the overt suspicion and obvious prejudice shown by Mrs. Milvey. More important is Lizzie's strong testimony to the benevolence of her Jewish employers, figures whose altruism has led them to assist Lizzie in making arrangements for Betty Higden's funeral.

Murray Baumgarten states that because of the "isolation" of Riah in the novel, there is an "impossibility of any kind of Jewish story being told about him . . . , for the Jew is defined via his or her Jewish reference group, with its customs, festivals, traditions, and cultural values" (52). But we should observe that Mr. and Mrs. Boffin, too, are isolated, evidently with no friends or even close acquaintances, and they apparently belong to no religious congregation. Riah, at least, does have friends at a distance that he can call upon when he leaves Fledgeby's service and must depart from the building of Pubsey and Co., where he has been living. Before accepting Jenny's invitation to share her home, Riah has thought of going to the Jewish couple that owns the paper-mill at which Lizzie has been given employment (4: 9: 709), a business located in a town slightly further from London than Riderhood's Plashwater Weir Mill Lock, which is over twenty-five miles away (3: 11: 540).

In considering Riah, Baumgarten also states that the old man wears "skirts" that give him "the mark of his Judaism as feminization" (52), and Goldie Morgentaler maintains that the idea of Riah's inferiority is "further underlined by his feminization" (152). But the narrator, in introducing Riah, remarks that he wears "an ancient coat, long of skirt" (2: 5: 273), then refers to his "coat-skirt" (2: 5: 275) and later to his "long-skirted coat" (2: 15: 396). This coat-skirt is what is designated by the expression "his long black skirt, a very gaberdine" (2: 5: 276) and by the subsequent reference to "the Jewish skirts" (4: 9: 712). All of the three illustrations by Marcus Stone that include Riah, "The Garden on the Roof" (bk. 2, ch. 5), "A Friend in Need" (bk. 2, ch. 15), and "Miss Wren Fixes her Idea" (bk. 4, ch. 9), clearly show this long-skirted coat, with trousers visible below its bottom (see fig. 3 for this third illustration). Henry Mayhew, writing several years before Dickens composed *Our Mutual Friend*, states that "Fifty years ago" the Jew "not infrequently wore the gabardine, which is never seen now in the streets, but some of the long loose frock coats worn by the Jew clothes' buyers resemble it" (2: 119), and the illustration in Mayhew's work of "The Jew Old-Clothes Man" (facing 2: 118) presents a person whose garments and beard (fig. 4) resemble those in Stone's depictions of Riah. Moreover, the idea of feminization, while suggested by Jenny's use of the name "godmother" for Riah (3: 2: 428), is countered by Riah's beard, mentioned in the text and evident in Stone's illustrations, by Mortimer Lightwood's description of Riah as "quite a Patriarch" (3: 10: 525), by the mention of the wife, daughter, and son that Riah has lost (3: 2: 430), and by Jenny's seeing him as her "second father" (4: 16: 787).

Conceding that "Riah's character seems particularly restricted because he must represent the Jews," Anne Aresty Naman asserts, "most of Dickens's good men are in fact dull, one-dimensional characters," and cites such examples as Brownlow, Jarndyce, and Boffin (94). In trying to explain why George Eliot's Daniel Deronda is not a "round," or well-developed, character, Barbara Hardy suggests that, in depicting him, "George Eliot created an individual in a way we may understand by looking at our feelings for a whole class of people" (Introduction 19–20). Hardy goes on to propose that the "automatic sympathy" we extend to "classes of people . . . who are unprotected, vulnerable, or persecuted" can, "in life, as in literature, deflect our attention from individual members of the class and produce that insensitive response to individuals which is one of the things we mean by sentimentality" (Introduction 20). For Hardy, Deronda's "deadness" is explained by the belief that "George Eliot's feelings for her character . . . are all determined by her view of him as a Jew" (Introduction 20–21). Perhaps even more than Deronda, Riah is designed as a representative. Indeed, Morgentaler argues that "Dickens cannot conceive of Jews as individuals" (156). Significantly, both Riah himself and Fledgeby usually think of Jews as a class. Barbara Hardy claims that Eliot's "contemporary Jewish reader was in the same position as the author, in naturally responding to the class rather than to the individual" (Introduction 21). If we accept this view, Mrs. Davis's approbation of Riah is more understandable.

As someone who has suffered insults because of religious prejudice, Riah seems sensitive to the needs of the two young women he "adopts," both of whom are at a disadvantage—Lizzie because of her illiteracy and her feelings of guilt, Jenny because of her physical disability and her alcoholic natural father. As Naman comments, "Riah's position as an outcast enables him to serve as a haven of refuge for his two friends, Lizzie Hexam and Jenny Wren, who may also be considered outcasts" (81). Mrs. Eliza Davis, in her letter to Dickens on November 16, 1864, maintains that Riah's "kindness to the two girls [Lizzie and Jenny], the indifference whether they be of his own faith or another is very truthful," and adds, "I believe we [Jews] do perform the enjoinder to 'show kindness unto the

Fig. 3. Miss Wren Fixes her Idea

Fig. 4. The Jew Old-Clothes-Man.
Clo', Clo', Clo'.

stranger because ye know the heart of the stranger for ye were strangers in the land of Egypt' [Exodus 22:21–22, 23:9; Leviticus 19:33–34]—and, to a certain extent, we are yet strangers here" (*Anglo-Jewish Letters* 308). Explaining the impulse to assist even the injured Fledgeby, Riah tells Jenny, " it is the custom of our people to help" (4: 9: 709), in an installment published in May 1865. In an early description of Mr. and Mrs. Boffin, the narrator also ties their goodness to faith by emphasizing their "religious sense of duty and desire to do right" (1: 9: 105).

In December 1863, a few months after Dickens began planning *Our Mutual Friend*, he learned that his fourth child, Walter, who had been sent more than six years before to serve with the army in India, had suddenly died five-and-one-half weeks before his twenty-third birthday (Johnson 2: 1012–13). The ages of Dickens's eight surviving children ranged from nearly twenty-seven to slightly under twelve. As Dickens reached fifty-two in February 1864, his concerns about his offspring, especially his sons, certainly focused his attention on the difficulties of being a parent. Several years later, when Edward, the youngest child, departed in 1868 at the age of sixteen and one-half to seek employment in Australia, Dickens addressed to his son a letter with a revealing comment: "I hope you will always be able to say in after life, that you had a kind father" (Forster, *Life* 11: 3: 819).

In 1865 Dickens had repeated, with slight verbal changes, his estimate of his own father, John Dickens, that was written soon after the latter's death, in early 1851: "The longer I live, the better man I think him" (PL 6: 343 [n. 3]). For despite the older Dickens's financial irresponsibility, a shortcoming that led to his son's being removed from school and sent to work at the blacking factory and to his own disgraceful imprisonment in the Marshalsea, John Dickens was evidently redeemed by his warmth and affection. Later in life, when Charles had achieved success as a writer, he was often disturbed by his father's continued improvidence and requests for monetary assistance. Nevertheless, like Boffin and Riah, the surrogate fathers in *Our Mutual Friend*, John Dickens was eventually viewed by his famous son as a positive figure, appearances to the contrary notwithstanding.

There seems great significance in the fact that the main storylines of *Our Mutual Friend* emerge from the actions of one bad father and one misguided one: old John Harmon, an utterly despotic parent who disowned his wife and then both of his children and left a punitive, restrictive will, and Gaffer Hexam, who kept his daughter from becoming literate and induced her to participate in activities that she regarded as immoral and degrading. As Adrian Poole suggests, the novel presents such other poor examples of fathers as Mr. Dolls, Riderhood, and Podsnap (xvii). We may note, too, that Eugene Wrayburn's father tries to be dictatorial but apparently accepts his son's resistance, and, as we have previously observed, Wilfer, despite Bella's praise of him as "the best of fathers" (3: 4: 454), is not wholly exemplary in that he provides love but not a full sense of protection. Not one of the actual fathers is without limitations, but the novel includes two remarkably admirable surrogate fathers whose actions help resolve major problems. Although these two men, Mr. Boffin and Mr. Riah, never meet and are mentioned in the same chapter in only two cases late in the novel (bk. 3, ch. 12; bk. 4, ch. 16), one or both figures are referred to or actually appear in all but the fourth, sixth, and fifteenth of the twenty installments, and one or both of these characters play an important part in half of the twenty numbers (Nos. 3, 5, 8, 10, 11, 12, 14, 15, 16, and 19). Freud, in a letter written in 1883 to his fiancée, includes in a list of Dickens's limiting "mannerisms" "the fact that all the good people immediately become friends as soon as they meet and work together throughout the whole book" (quoted by Jones 1: 174). Boffin and Riah are among the exceptions to this habit. Indeed, the fact that they never meet may be seen as emphasizing their complementarity. As Poole comments, both men are "benign fathers," "despite their ugly disguises" (OMF xvii).

Both Boffin and Riah are motivated entirely by kindness and a desire to be benevolent. As substitute fathers, they are devoted and unselfish, but each feels a need to pretend and, therefore, invites misunderstanding by a young person whom he wishes to assist. Although parallel in their roles as protective parental surrogates and in their status as childless outsiders, they also reveal major differences. Because of newly inherited wealth, Boffin has gained some acceptance from society: calling cards are left by the Veneerings, the Podsnaps, Lady Tippins, Twemlow, and others in that circle—indeed, "All the world and his wife and daughter leave cards" (1: 17: 208). Nevertheless, the Boffins are in an anomalous social position in that their inheritance of vast wealth, while it gains them a solicitation signed by a titled aristocrat like the Duke of Linseed (1: 17: 209), does not protect them from being treated with condescension by "the great visiting authorities who agreed that the Boffins were 'charmingly vulgar' " (2: 8: 304). Indeed, Mrs. Boffin at times makes "a slip on the social ice on which all the children of Podsnappery . . . are required to skate" (2: 8: 304). Boffin, when first mentioned by Lightwood, is referred to as Harmon's "old servant" (1: 2: 26). Although Noddy later states that he was the "foreman" in Harmon's dust business (1: 8: 94), his work certainly involved physical labor, for he uses a revealing metaphor when stating that he is too old "to begin shovelling and sifting at alphabeds and grammar-books" (1: 5: 58), and Mr. Venus comments later on Boffin's adeptness at using a shovel (3: 6: 480).

We get the sense, too, that Boffin was also a domestic servant, since Mrs. Boffin appears to have been old Harmon's housekeeper, and both husband and wife cared for their employer's children and grew "older and older in the old man's service, living and working pretty hard in it" (1: 8: 96). Despite their wealth, the Boffins' having been "in service" prevents them from gaining full social acceptance. As an *Examiner* review attributed to John Forster by Philip Collins ("Dickens' Self-Estimate" 190 [nn. 31, 37]) observes, the Boffins are "social nobodies" (682). Significantly, the narrator depicts three major social occasions held after the Boffins have received their inheritance: the Lammles' celebration of their first anniversary (2: 16: 400–11), the dinner party at the Veneering home following the Lammles' bankruptcy (3: 17: 604–14), and the Veneerings' dinner some time after the marriage of Lizzie and Eugene (4: 17: 792–96). In the accounts of these three events there is no indication that the Boffins are present or were even invited.

Nevertheless, Riah, as a Jew and a person lacking wealth, is far lower in social status than the Golden Dustman. Speaking to Twemlow, Fledgeby comments, "You cultivate society and society cultivates you, but Mr. Riah's not society" (3: 13: 557). Although Fledgeby's next statement—"In society, Mr. Riah is kept dark" (3: 13: 557)—suggests that he refers to Riah here as a moneylender rather than as a Jew, the two terms are equated, as is shown by the previously mentioned remarks of Mortimer Lightwood and also of Alfred Lammle.

In the novel's penultimate chapter, we learn that Riah, who, after having to move from Pubsey and Co., has gone to live with Jenny as her "second father," is employed by John Harmon to continue acting the role of a moneylender, albeit one who has suddenly become "mild" (4: 16: 782), a development that John Glavin describes as reflecting "no real change" (61). Glavin later asks, "Why can't

Riah just come clean with Twemlow? What use can that fiction serve—except the uses of anti-Semitism? For that matter, why can't Harmon-Boffin just pay the debt [of Twemlow]?" (76). We may also ask whether Twemlow has forgotten that Sophronia Lammle has previously sought to enlighten him about Fledgeby's use of Riah as "his mask" (3: 17: 608). On the other hand, young John Harmon's decision to have Riah continue to maintain a pretense, but this time in a benevolent role, may be intended to preserve Twemlow's pride and independence, since the debtor might be embarrassed if his payment were made by John Harmon. Nevertheless, Riah does seem in the post-climactic sections of the novel to remain much more of an outsider than Boffin, who, with his wife, is "staying indefinitely" with the Harmons (4: 16: 789). Although at the end of the novel Riah, like Boffin, is living with a surrogate daughter, that person is Jenny, not Lizzie. Indeed, we are not encouraged to think that Riah is ever likely to be invited to the home of Lizzie and her husband, the previously insulting Eugene. For, earlier, Lizzie evidently does not even think of asking Riah to attend her wedding to Eugene, as Deborah Heller reminds us (58). Yet Lizzie previously referred to Riah as "a good old man" who was her "true friend" (3: 9: 518), and he has been for her an extremely beneficent figure. Lizzie, in speaking to Charley, states that she was led into the company of Jenny, the granddaughter of a drowning victim whose corpse was recovered by Gaffer, "by something more than chance" (2: 1: 227)—in other words, by providence. Through Jenny, who purchased waste materials at Pubsey & Co., Lizzie met Riah.

Each of the two elderly men, Boffin and Riah, is, as Edwin M. Eigner remarks, a "Prospero or Oberon figure," a "quasi-mystical" character (*The Metaphysical Novel* 189). Indeed, after assisting the distraught Lizzie, Riah seems to the narrator to be "like the ghost of a departed Time" (2: 15: 400), and later, at the beginning of the chapter in which the ruse of Boffin is disclosed, Noddy is described as being "like some jovial good spirit" (4: 13: 749). Earlier, Miss Abbey Potterson, after meeting Riah and Jenny, wonders if she has "dreamed those two rare figures" (3: 2: 435). Arnold Kettle's observation that the role-playing of Boffin is an extremely effective way of presenting "the alternative possibilities" before him (215) may also be applied to the forced pretense by Riah, who is and at the same time is not a merciless usurer, the Jew as demon and the Jew as positive moral exemplar.

In posing as a miser, Boffin shows an inventiveness and a histrionic flair not unworthy of Dickens himself, and, like the novelist,

Boffin was previously the recipient of many begging letters (1: 17: 209–11; Cotsell 124–25). Riah also reveals qualities that link him to the Inimitable: just as the elderly Jew had lost a wife, a daughter, and a son (3: 2: 430), so Dickens had lost his daughter Dora in 1851, his son Walter in 1863, and—by his own choice—his wife, Catherine, in 1858. Just as Dickens in 1858 suggested in the so-called "violated letter" that his relationship with an unnamed young woman— usually thought to be Ellen Ternan—was untainted by sexual desire, since she was "innocent and pure, and as good as . . . [his] own dear daughters" (PL 8: 741), so Riah denies any amatory interest in Lizzie when he is interrogated by Fledgeby (3: 1: 425). As Morris Golden suggests, Dickens saw himself as like Riah in being wrongly misjudged as a result of slander (*Dickens Imagining Himself* 218). Perhaps we can also add another, lesser resemblance: Dickens, an amateur magician, has Jenny playfully attribute magical qualities to the old man she calls her "fairy godmother," for she asserts that Riah looks "so unlike the rest of people," as if he had "changed . . . into that shape" and could even change her derelict father (3: 2: 429). Like a magician, Riah has made Lizzie vanish (3: 1: 425–26). Dickens's great concern with the names of his characters lends added interest to the fact that nearly twenty-five years before, in August or September of 1849, he had composed a playbill for one of his conjuring entertainments in Bonchurch, on the Isle of Wight, and had referred to himself as "The Unparalleled Necromancer RHIA RHAMA RHOOS" (PL 5: 706), the first of the three appellations being an anticipation of Riah's name.

Of course, Dickens appears to project himself not only into John Harmon, who must learn if the woman he loves is mercenary, into Eugene Wrayburn, who defies society in following the dictates of his heart, and into the benevolent surrogate fathers Boffin and Riah, but also into the villains. As Lindsay and Watkins suggest, Headstone's obsession with Lizzie, as well as Eugene's fascination with her, seems to reflect Dickens's infatuation with Ellen Ternan (Lindsay 384; Watkins 137–39). The lengthy night walks undertaken by both Wrayburn and Headstone at the former's instigation may remind us of Dickens's own appetite for prodigious nocturnal pedestrian feats in London (Johnson 1:466; Ackroyd 624). Moreover, like Dickens, the scoundrel Wegg invents characters (" 'Miss Elizabeth,' 'Master George,' 'Aunt Jane,' 'Uncle Parker' " [1: 5: 53], figures repeatedly mentioned [2: 7: 294, 303; 3: 7: 484; 4: 3: 646; 4: 14: 769]) and gives readings for profit; and Fledgeby, like the novelist, is a creator of a script for Riah to follow (3: 12: 552; 3: 13: 559–61). Just

as Dickens had years before devised a Jew who—in the opinion of
Mrs. Davis and many others—evoked anti-Semitic responses, so
Fledgeby shapes Riah into a character likely to bring all Jews into
disrepute. And, like another Charles—the young Hexam—Dickens
at one time distanced himself from a beloved older sister when
he disapproved of Fanny's behavior in not telling him that Maria
Beadnell's friend Marianne Leigh had claimed to be his confidante
(PL 1:22–23 [to Maria Beadnell, 14 May 1833]), but, of course, unlike
Hexam, Dickens was soon reconciled with his sister.

As the novel progresses, Mr. Riah and Mr. Boffin emerge as moral
centers. Both older men are childless, Riah having lost his children
and the Boffins having lost their surrogate children, the son and
daughter of old John Harmon. But Boffin and Riah emerge as the
most supportive parental figures in the novel, even though each of
the three young women that they assist—Bella, Lizzie, and
Jenny—must also help herself. Each surrogate father, moreover, is
far, far better than he at times seems, and this point appears to have
great significance. Dickens may, in a sense, be seeking to make
amends to John Dickens, before his death the model for some of the
weaknesses and also some of the lovable traits of Micawber, and
after his death the inspiration for some qualities of the selfish but
wronged William Dorrit. Fred Kaplan comments that Wilfer, whom
he regards as an "idealized version of John Dickens," is "ineffectual
but loving," while "the benevolent Mr. Boffin completes the resolution of Dickens' lifelong effort to reconstruct out of the materials of
John Dickens a satisfactory father figure"(476). As we have observed, Dickens revised his disapproving view of his father and
came to a more appreciative opinion. Like Boffin and Riah, John
Dickens was eventually recognized by his eldest, famous son as a
good father, far better than he once seemed. And perhaps, too, the
eventual recognition of the merits of Boffin and Riah reflects the
hope of Dickens that his own children would in time come to regard
him as having been a benevolent and supportive parent. According
to his daughter Mamie, he expressed tearful guilt in July 1860 at
the time of his daughter Kate's marriage—"But for me, Katey would
not have left home" (Storey 106)—and, as I have remarked, a farewell letter to his youngest son, Edward, on the latter's departure
for Australia in September 1868 expresses earnestly the wish to be
remembered "in after life" as having been "a kind father" (Forster,
Life 11: 3: 819).

In *Our Mutual Friend* Dickens confronts a basic fear—that the
father will (or did) prove unsatisfactory in providing one or both

of a child's two basic needs—love and protection. But while dealing with this anxiety, Dickens presents stories that offer comfort and reassurance: if the father does (or did) fail in some ways, the virtuous child may nevertheless hope to receive proper parental care from a surrogate. Moreover, even if this second father seems to reveal serious failings, a dark side, the child may in time discover that the perceived faults were illusory.

In this long novel, while Boffin and Riah never meet, some of the characters closely involved with each older man do become acquainted, and these two unlikely benefactors—perhaps because they do not encounter each other—may at times seem like parts of one character. The many resemblances between the wealthy Boffin and the needy Riah further suggest that the two main plot-lines both offer the same basic tale, despite variants. This sameness is further implied by the close proximity of many incidents and climaxes in the two narratives, for in many cases we find a near-simultaneity in events. In each story, a young woman whose self-esteem needs strengthening is helped to achieve this and becomes joined with a young man who also needs to bolster his self-image. Although one hero, John, is far more virtuous than the other, Eugene, Bella, the woman in Harmon's life, is less exemplary than Lizzie, the heroine in the other love-match. Both young women, however, are enabled to find self-assurance, a mate, and apparent happiness because of the assistance of surrogate fathers and their own ethical decisions and actions. As Robert Morse maintains, in *Our Mutual Friend* "the principle of doubleness" is a feature that "shapes, colors, and binds this novel together no less radically than the theme of money" (206). The ultimate effect of all the doubling is to impart emphasis to the affirmative, optimistic tale that Dickens is creating for himself and his audience. The elaborate symmetry also implies that there is a controlling design or plan not only in the novel but also in human life itself.

Notes

1. In the letter of June 22, 1863, Mrs. Davis, after complaining that the creation of Fagin has "encouraged a vile prejudice against the Hebrew," writes, "[while] Charles Dickens lives the author can justify himself or atone for a great wrong on a whole though *scattered nation*." Her intent was not, however, to urge Dickens to create an admirable Jew to balance Fagin, but to persuade the novelist to allow his name

to be included in "the list of Donors to the Lady [Judith] Montefiore Memorial" (*Anglo-Jewish Letters* 304–05). Although Dickens in his reply denied that Fagin should be a cause for Jews to take offense, he did forward a donation (PL 10: 269–70), and in the seventh number of *Our Mutual Friend*, an installment appearing in November 1864, he introduced the character of Riah. As the inscription in the gift suggests, for Mrs. Davis the creation of Riah was perhaps an even more effective way of "atoning" for Fagin than was Dickens's response to her appeal for the Lady Montefiore Memorial.

2. In a letter of May 5, 1864, sent to Marcus Stone with instructions for the etching "The Boffin Progress," intended to accompany bk. 1, ch. 9 ("Mr. and Mrs. Boffin in Consultation"), Dickens writes, "I want Boffins oddity . . . to be an oddity of a very honest kind, that people will like" (PL 10: 391).

3. For discussions that develop this point, see Friedman, "The Motif of Reading in *Our Mutual Friend*," and Altick, "Education, Print, and Paper in *Our Mutual Friend*."

4. McMaster (374 and 381 [n. 8]) and Nelson ("Dickens's *Our Mutual Friend*" 207–22) both suggest that Gaffer Hexam may be in part derived from Henry Mayhew's *London Labour and the London Poor*, but neither mentions the possibility that some of Mayhew's details about dustmen may be relevant to the creation of Boffin. Mayhew, in his study, notices that illiteracy is prevalent among dustmen ("Among 20 men whom I met in one yard, there were only five who could read, and only two out of that five could write, even imperfectly" [2: 176]), and he also remarks, "The dustmen are very partial to a song, and always prefer one of the doggerel street ballads" (2: 176).

5. The sadism Jenny reveals in her chastisement of Fledgeby is anticipated when she tells Charley Hexam how she would choose to punish the children who tease her because of her deformity (2: 1: 224) and also is suggested in a later conversation with Lizzie, when Jenny describes what she would do if her future husband "should turn out a drunkard," like her father (2: 2: 242–43).

6. Later, Lizzie, in pleading with Eugene to leave the country town where she is residing, likens her resolve to continue fleeing from him to the determination of Betty Higden to keep moving to avoid the workhouse (4: 6: 677). Poole, referring to Lizzie and Betty, finds significance in the names' being "different forms of Elizabeth" (OMF xviii).

7. Lizzie's indirect method of disclosing affection for Wrayburn may remind us of Amy Dorrit's covert revelation of her love for Clennam by telling the story of the Princess and "the poor little tiny woman"(1: 24: 286–89).

8. While the comic wrongdoers, Wegg and Fledgeby, work, respectively, against Boffin and Riah, we may note that Riderhood and Headstone, the more ominous villains, are involved in physical mistreatment of the

two heroes, John Harmon and Eugene Wrayburn. Headstone attacks Eugene, and Riderhood was evidently a participant in the drugging of Harmon (2: 13: 362). Riderhood, however, does not seem to be guilty of the murder of George Radfoot, despite the suspicions of Lizzie (1: 6: 74–75) and of Miss Abbey Potterson (3: 2: 435). When Harmon indicates that Radfoot is dead, Riderhood appears to express genuine surprise (2: 12: 353–55), a reaction suggesting that he at least did not know that both Radfoot and Harmon had been thrown into the river. While this detail may not completely remove doubt as to whether Rogue threw Harmon into the water, the former is never clearly charged with this crime. Muir writes that Riderhood "possibly murders" (99), and this is as far as we can go, even though Davis asserts that Riderhood is "the real murderer" (*The Flint and the Flame* 268). Another possible suspect mentioned in Harmon's soliloquy recalling the crime, "a black man . . . wearing a linen jacket, like a steward" (2: 13: 362), is never referred to again in the novel. Collins's claim that Jacob Kibble and Job Potterson are "Radfoot's murderers," since "they start and stagger when confronted with the 'dead' man" (*Dickens and Crime* 284), seems to be refuted by Dickens's working plans for No. 1, which contain the following notation on the left side:

> Work in two witnesses by name: For end of story:
> ship's steward—Potterson
> Job Potterson
> Passenger   Mr Jacob Kibble
> (OMF 846; DWN 335)

The text and the working notes include no indication that Kibble and Potterson are anything but witnesses, and their surprise appears to be a natural reaction rather than a sign of guilt. For a fuller discussion of this matter, see Friedman, "A Loose Thread in *Our Mutual Friend*," which argues that Radfoot's murder is never definitely solved. There is a possibility, however, that one other death can be blamed on Riderhood: the ostracism imposed on Hexam because of Riderhood's having borne false witness against him may have led to Gaffer's being distracted and careless enough to meet his fatal mishap. (Of course, young John Harmon is also indirectly responsible for the false accusation, as is Boffin, who offered an immense reward.)

9. Kaplan states that marital distress made Dickens believe "that he faced a life-and-death struggle for survival" (376).

10. Hill states that Boffin "must have been able to read to choose the books he later brought home for Wegg to read aloud; and it remains a puzzle how he could have known so much about the misers and books like Rollins's history and the Wars of the Jews" (88 [n. 9]). We may assume, however, that booksellers have given Boffin information about his purchases. In speaking to Wegg about stories of misers, Boffin refers to

"the bookseller that sold me the Wonderful Museum" and mentions that the bookseller read to him from this book (3: 6: 478). Moreover, Bella accompanied Boffin on his expeditions to acquire books about misers (3: 5: 461–63). Nevertheless, Boffin's ability to read seems greater than he at first indicates to Wegg.

11. Rosenberg maintains that "the Veneerings, Lammles, and their sort, who have adopted all the sordid upstart traits associated with 'Jewish capitalism' . . . are probably themselves thinly veiled portraits of Jews" (*From Shylock to Svengali* 269), but such a claim ignores the fact that most Victorian capitalists, many of whom displayed "sordid upstart traits," were not Jews. Had Dickens wished to make the Veneerings and the Lammles Jewish, he could readily have done so in a direct manner, pointing to Riah as a contrast to some of his coreligionists.

12. Mayhew observes, "The Jewish charities are highly honourable to the body, for they allow none of their people to live or die in a parish workhouse," and later adds, "If a Jew be worn out in his old age, and unable to maintain himself, he is either supported by the contributions of his friends, or out of some local or general fund, or provided for in some asylum, and all this seems to be done with a less than ordinary fuss and display, so that the recipient of the charity feels himself more a pensioner than a pauper" (2: 127–28). As I have observed in n. 4, the influence of Mayhew on Dickens may have extended beyond the depiction of Gaffer Hexam to include Boffin, and Dickens may also have responded to some of Mayhew's comments about Jews, such as the passage just quoted and also the point that "There are few fonder fathers than they are" (2: 120). Mayhew's praise of the Jews' benevolence and sensitivity in assisting fellow Jews in need was later to be echoed in Mark Twain's 1899 essay "Concerning the Jews" (356).

Chapter 9

Resolutions and Implications

As we have seen, in fiction composed at different stages of a lengthy career, Dickens displays remarkable virtuosity in introducing duplicating devices such as repetition, paradox, and multiple perspectives in varied and subtle ways. By retelling the same story or by employing recurrent characters and motifs within a work or in more than one narrative, he can reinforce or qualify or subvert a resolution—or sometimes a re-solution or irresolution—to a problem concerning human needs and desires. Of special significance are the implications that the narratives convey about the consequences of virtuous actions or of immoral ones.

In the eight books considered, the moral values expounded by the narrators and by the admirable characters are not always supported by the events described. Although the outcomes of stories often suggest prescriptions for behavior, Dickens's fiction is complicated by exceptions to patterns and by ambiguities. Poetic justice often seems incommensurate or flawed. Affirmation and optimism are juxtaposed with grim, sad events, for in Dickens's imaginative world we find reflections of unfortunate realities, and we realize that the solutions to moral problems are often neither simple nor assured. These ambiguities, which are at times inconspicuous or even covert, may be regarded as ramifications of the theme of diverse perspectives, for they suggest that the viewpoints of the narrator and the virtuous characters should perhaps not always be accepted without qualification. Even though Dickens's basic morality remains clear and constant, some problems are not resolved, but merely evaded.

In *Oliver Twist* and *Nicholas Nickleby*, the adventures of each protagonist intimate that providence will protect the innocent and expose the guilty, who will be punished. In both *Oliver Twist* and *Nicholas Nickleby* we find a virtuous protagonist gaining the protection of generous parental surrogates, benefactors who also contribute in some manner to the uncovering of past misdeeds and the defeat of current plotting. But while the survival of goodness and the revelation of hidden guilt may be in large part attributable to providential care, operating at times through chance events or human goodness or the conversion of reprobates, there remain in each novel victims who cannot be rescued or saved, sacrifices to ruthless greed and unfeeling cruelty—in *Oliver Twist*, little Dick, Nancy, her friend Bet, who goes mad; in *Nicholas Nickleby*, Smike, other children irreparably harmed at Dotheboys Hall, Lord Frederick Verisopht, who dies in an attempt to redeem past moral errors.

Although some sufferers are innocent, while others are flawed, the happiness of the survivors is accompanied by a degree of sorrow: *Oliver Twist* concludes with a reference to Agnes Fleming, Oliver's mother, and at the end of *Nicholas Nickleby* we are reminded of the loss of Smike, first cousin to and surrogate for Nicholas. Moreover, in *Oliver Twist*, despite the discomfiture of Bumble, the destruction of Fagin and Sikes, and the defeat of Monks, the workhouse survives, poverty persists, the slums and crime remain. Similarly, although the story of Nicholas Nickleby exemplifies the victory of virtue through Nicholas's triumphs over villains like his Uncle Ralph, Sir Mulberry Hawk, Arthur Gride, and Squeers, the victory depends largely on the extreme benevolence of the Cheeryble brothers and comes much too late to save Smike, nor does it serve to eradicate avarice, deception, and cruelty. In each novel, too, some malefactors proceed with impunity: in *Oliver Twist*, Noah Claypole, the workhouse board (except for the particularly odious "gentleman in the white waistcoat," who dies prematurely), Mrs. Mann, and Mrs. Sowerberry; in the later novel, Sir Mulberry's henchmen Pyke and Pluck, Snawley, who falsely claims to be Smike's father, and the Wititterlys, who employ and mistreat Kate. Moreover, *Nicholas Nickleby*, although it reaffirms the same moral principles endorsed in *Oliver Twist* and includes more comic material than the earlier book, seems in some respects darker, for while the flaws of Oliver's parents are largely extenuated, the misdeeds of Smike's parents bring to their son undeserved pain and early death.

In *A Christmas Carol*, Dickens's tale affirms that even a sinner and reprobate like Scrooge can reform late in life, a parallel to the parable in Matthew 20: 1–16 of the laborers hired "about the eleventh hour" to work in the vineyard. Since the narrative's conclusion, however, is marked by Scrooge's exuberance over escaping his worst fears, he and we, too, are led to overlook the waste of most of his prior life. And moral puzzles remain: while we are guided by the narrator to understand the reasons for Scrooge's late reformation from spiritually dead sinner to newborn believer and benefactor, we never get a satisfactory explanation of the reasons for the earlier change in the protagonist. Once Mr. Fezziwig's enthusiastic young apprentice, Scrooge had previously survived a lonely, sad childhood with the aid of an imagination that enabled him to find comfort by conjuring up Ali Baba and other fictional characters. But Scrooge then becomes a hardened materialist who is willing to allow Belle—beauty—to depart from his life. We are induced also to overlook nearly all the suffering that Scrooge causes others over many years, since this damage is kept almost entirely implicit. No heed is given the fact that the benevolence shown the Cratchits at the end is probably made possible by money gained through Scrooge's earlier misdeeds. The story also, while noticing the harm brought to Scrooge himself by his past behavior, the loss of the chance to have a family of his own, as well as his failure to avail himself of the opportunities to enjoy the hospitality of his nephew and niece-in-law, places emphasis, like the Gospels, not on paradise lost, but on paradise regained, the finding of salvation.

In *David Copperfield* many equivocal chapter-titles introduce ambiguity and in some cases ambivalence: we are made more aware of subjectivity in responses and of the need for frequent reassessment of our judgments. The book asks us to question the behavior of ourselves and others, for persons we encounter may change for better or worse, and our early perceptions may be either valid or misguided. Nevertheless, some characters like Agnes and Clara Peggotty remain constant exemplars. Other complications also emerge, however, for, despite the emphasis placed by David on the providential care that has enabled him to survive and flourish, innocent characters like Dora and Ham meet harsh fates, and penitents like Emily and Martha Endell find only incomplete redemption: Emily is destined by Dickens to a life of selfless celibacy, while Martha, though permitted to marry, lives with her mate, as Mr. Peggotty reports, in a place "fower hundred mile away from any voices but their own and the singing birds" (63: 731). Martha seems to be considered less guilty than Emily, for the latter transgressed despite having the shelter and loving guidance of her uncle, while the former had neither parents nor surrogates for them (47: 577). But, significantly, Martha and her mate are in effect exiled within the place of exile from England; and the distance from other persons, originally set by Dickens at three hundred miles, was increased to four hundred miles when he revised his manuscript and proof (Burgis ed. DC 63: 744 [n. 2]). Furthermore, while the major wrongdoers are punished, since we are meant to agree with the second Mrs. Chillip's judgment that the Murdstones "undergo a continual punishment; for they are turned inward, to feed upon their own hearts" (59: 701–02), no retribution is meted out to lesser villains like the friendly waiter, Creakle, Tungay, the young man with a donkey cart who steals David's box, or the abusive tramp encountered on the road to Dover. Exceptions, however, do not shake the protagonist's faith, since faith is belief not based solely on demonstrable evidence. In the concluding installment of the novel, David points to his own life as a sign of providential benevolence.

In *Bleak House* Dickens re-views issues of identity, guilt, heredity, and imperiled goodness that he explored in *Oliver Twist*, but in the later book these problems appear even more grim and more complicated, despite Esther's triumphant survival with the assistance of a generous parental surrogate. At the end of *Bleak House*, Chancery, an evil force, remains strong, the conflagration so fervently desired by the anonymous narrator not seeming at all imminent, while admirable characters like the loving and compassionate Esther, the benevolent John Jarndyce, and the devoted Allan Woodcourt all retreat, seeking neither retribution for the death of Richard Carstone nor prevention of future predation. Moreover, although Woodcourt has been the forceful hero of a shipwreck in distant seas, he is remarkably ineffectual in England: he is unable to save Hawdon, or Gridley, or Jo, or Richard. Indeed, to establish his own medical practice, to obtain a comfortable home, and to win Esther, he must depend on Jarndyce's aid. Although Tulkinghorn has died at the hands of Hortense, the villainous Vholes and Grandfather Smallweed remain free to practice their wickedness. Moreover, while Captain Hawdon, Lady Dedlock, and Richard Carstone are indeed erring, their fates, as well as those of a less guilty character like Gridley and an innocent like Jo, seem unduly harsh. At the same time, offenders like the Reverend Mr. Chadband, Mrs. Rachael, and Mr.Turveydrop remain completely unscathed.

In *Hard Times* deep flaws in society hurt both the wealthy and the poor, and the power of virtuous figures is severely limited. Rachael cannot help Stephen survive, and her persuading him to vow not to join the union, evidently because she fears violence, proves ironically destructive. Sissy Jupe's empathy enables her to comprehend, statistics notwithstanding, that any loss of life in a shipwreck is deeply meaningful (1: 9: 48), and her wisdom of the heart enables her to overcome the pain of her own father's desertion and the initial obtuseness of Mr. Gradgrind. But, when Sissy seeks to repay Gradgrind for his kindness to her, she is able to assist Tom temporarily but cannot save him from later ruin, and she removes James Harthouse as a threat but cannot lead Louisa to a fate less circumscribed and bleak than that anticipated in the novel's closing paragraphs. For Stephen and Louisa, co-protagonists, retribution seems severe indeed, for the former perishes even though he has sinned only in failing to act immediately and expeditiously to keep his wife from drinking poison, a rescue that is achieved by Rachael, while Louisa never fully recovers from her marriage to Bounderby, a mistake for which there clearly were extenuating circumstances in her misguided upbringing and her misplaced devotion to her brother Tom.

Although in the published ending of *Great Expectations* Pip seems finally to achieve his hopes of union with a miraculously transformed Estella, ambiguities arise about other matters. Pip, after coming to recognize Joe Gargery as a "gentle Christian man" (57: 344), a true gentleman, remains in both the first and second endings on friendly terms with Biddy and Joe, but in neither conclusion do we get the impression that he will see them frequently. One of the trio of major villains, Orlick, is imprisoned for robbing Pumblechook, but suffers no penalty for his murderous assaults on Mrs. Joe and Pip. Moreover, much earlier, Pip has quietly accepted the fact that his guardian Jaggers at times suborns witnesses (20: 133–34), and Pip himself later readily disregards the law by harboring a fugitive, with the knowing help of Herbert Pocket, and also by obtaining a forged passport for Magwitch (52: 310). In a suburban retreat at Walworth, Wemmick supposedly seeks to exclude all traces of his law office employment in Little Britain (25: 162), work that carries the stain of guilt, but Pip does not indicate awareness that Wemmick violates his own rule by keeping in the castle that is his home "curiosities" (25: 162)—mementoes of criminals with whom he has had dealings in Little Britain.

In *Great Expectations* we find various tales of misdeeds and punishments—Magwitch's lawbreaking and transportation, Compeyson's betrayals and eventual death, Drummle's spousal abuse and violent demise, Mrs. Joe's harsh handling of Pip and her victimization by Orlick, Pumblechook's pompous folly and later mistreatment by Orlick. The novel offers a bildungsroman that emphasizes deprivation and frustration, for its protagonist-narrator tells of a denying "mother," a "father" who is affectionate but cannot provide protection, and a persistently rejecting love-object in Estella. Nevertheless, with the revised ending Pip's narration is, I believe, an attempt to convince his readers and himself that the age of miracles and of joyful redemption is not past. In this sense, like *A Christmas Carol*, Pip's story, which also begins on Christmas Eve, stresses wonder and paradox.

Our Mutual Friend, remarkably complex and full, also stresses the need to believe in miracles, especially saving acts performed by angelic human beings. In this novel the narrator traces the trials and triumphs of four co-protagonists, for young John Harmon, the title-character, shares the stage with Bella Wilfer and also with another pair of seemingly mismatched lovers, Lizzie Hexam and Eugene Wrayburn. Help comes from two unlikely sources—a newly wealthy former servant who is an erstwhile dustman and a needy Jew who works for a scoundrel. Harmon is deserving, for he displayed unselfishness in his youthful attempt to defend his sister when their father disowned her (1: 2: 25), and Lizzie is also a noble figure in sacrificing her interests to those of her father and brother, but each is attracted to someone not entirely worthy who must be tested and reformed—the self-centered, initially materialistic Bella and the often insensitive, sexually predatory Eugene.

Despite the evidently happy resolutions, questions arise when we consider the Lizzie-Eugene and Bella-John love-matches in *Our Mutual Friend*. To what extent is the continuance of Bella's reformation from a mercenary stance dependent on the fact that her married life with John, even before the acceptance of enormous wealth from Boffin, is marked by a reasonable degree of material comfort? As for Lizzie, will her new husband open their home to visits from her benefactor and friend, Mr. Riah? Indeed, will Eugene drop his fondness for anti-Semitic insults? Functioning as benevolent parental surrogates, Boffin and Riah compensate for the shortcomings of biological parents but their powers remain limited, and at the end

of the novel both are enabled to do good because of financial resources left by the cruelly avaricious old Harmon. Nevertheless, the
doubling of the parental surrogate—Mr. Boffin and Mr. Riah—
serves to make more universal the implications: if the natural father
is not wholly satisfactory, a surrogate may miraculously appear to
offer assistance and guidance.

Ambiguities and unresolved questions in these narratives notwithstanding, Dickens's moral values are always clear. Although a
repeated situation or duplicated story may sometimes cause us to
have queries about the moral scheme implied by a book's outcome,
and although paradoxes and diverse perspectives may lead us to
very complex responses, Dickens, like Shakespeare, eschews moral
relativism. In a letter to the Rev. David Macrae, he maintains that,
in practicing his "art," one of his "most constant and most earnest
endeavours has been to exhibit in all . . . [his] good people some
faint reflections of the teachings" in the Gospels and that his virtuous characters are therefore "humble, charitable, faithful and forgiving" (PL 9: 556 [1861]). Dickens affirms honesty, love, kindness,
generosity, and courage; he condemns cruelty, deceit, greed, hypoc-
risy, and snobbery. At times the duplicating devices may keep our
attention so absorbed that we are simply lulled into accepting Dickens's moral positions. But Dickens's use of these repetitive techniques seems natural to his temperament and is reflected in his
personal activities at many stages of his life.

Just as there were two Scrooges, there were multiple Dickenses.
In the engaging essay "How Many Men Was Dickens the Novelist?"
Philip Collins surveys some of the numerous roles Dickens played
in addition to being a prolific novelist: man of business, after-dinner
speaker, journalist, editor of a weekly periodical, social worker, let-
ter-writer, both actor and stage manager in amateur theatricals, public reader of his own fiction (146–47, 158).

Although all of these roles both reflected and shaped Dickens's
personality and influenced his efforts as a writer of fiction, I wish
to emphasize the importance of Dickens's public performances and
to point out, too, the significance of two other areas of activity not
considered by Collins: Dickens as a traveler or tourist (especially in
foreign countries) and Dickens as a secret social rebel. For his trips
within the United Kingdom and his journeys to the Continent and
North America, as well as his clandestine (and unclear) relationship
in later years with Ellen Ternan, combined with his efforts as a
stage performer of plays and of his own fiction to reinforce his

predilection for repeating material and for exploring paradox and diverse perspectives.

When Dickens participated in amateur theatricals, he usually functioned not only as actor but also as stage-manager, assuming responsibility for an extraordinary number of tasks, such as finding a suitable place for the performance, making decisions on casting, and arranging for costumes, props, settings, and lighting, as well as handling publicity and tickets for more ambitious productions. The attention given to Dickens as an actor and stage manager in studies by J. B. Van Amerongen (3–78) and F. Dubrez Fawcett (139–60) is brief. Although details about his engagements in a number of amateur stagings of plays appear in full-length biographies like those by Forster, Edgar Johnson, Fred Kaplan, and Peter Ackroyd, such reports are interspersed with descriptions of Dickens's many other activities, and we may not get a full sense of the extent of his expenditures of time and energy in these histrionic pursuits. A brief overview of this involvement may therefore be useful. Because Johnson usually gives the most detailed and heavily documented accounts of these endeavors, I rely mainly on him for my summation.

Dickens took part in amateur theatricals at different times of his life, but the most sustained and heaviest involvement occurred from July 1845 to September 1852, when acting troupes he had organized put on performances of works like Jonson's *Every Man in His Humour*, Beaumont and Fletcher's *The Elder Brother*, Shakespeare's *The Merry Wives of Windsor*, and Sir Edward Bulwer-Lytton's *Not So Bad as We Seem*, with each play often supplemented by a farce such as *Mr. Nightingale's Diary*, a piece composed by Dickens and his friend Mark Lemon (Johnson 1: 568–72, and 2: 616–18, 644–49, 719–28, 735). These productions, which took place in London and in the provinces, were intended to raise money for philanthropic causes and attracted audiences that at times included members of the royal family as well as other notables. The actors were Dickens himself, some of his relatives, and friends such as Forster, Lemon, Clarkson Stanfield, and John Leech. While by my count the actual performances from 1845 to 1852 added up to a little under forty, we must remember the numerous days of planning, the many lengthy and arduous hours of rehearsal, and also the time and energy spent on travel (Johnson 1: 568–72, and 2: 616–18, 644–49, 719–38).

In 1855 Dickens gathered a group of amateurs to act in Wilkie Collins's melodrama *The Lighthouse* (Johnson 2: 842–43), and in 1857 he arranged a production of another play, *The Frozen Deep*, which

Collins had written with assistance from Dickens (Johnson 2: 863, 866). While the latter work was first put on at Tavistock House, Dickens's home since late 1851, subsequent performances were scheduled for a hall in Manchester, and, because of the large size of the Manchester auditorium, Dickens hired three professional actresses—Mrs. Frances Ternan and two of her daughters, Maria and Ellen (Johnson 2: 876–77).

The meeting with Ellen Ternan was to have great influence on Dickens, but, in addition, his histrionic bent led him not even a year after the Manchester performances of *The Frozen Deep* to begin his professional public readings of his own fiction, ventures that were to include 472 appearances from 1853 to 1870—in London, on provincial tours, and in the United States during his second visit (PR xxvi). The readings stopped in March 1870, a few months prior to Dickens's death, because of concerns over his deteriorating health (Johnson 2: 1106–07, 1109–10, 1144–45). During these public readings Dickens skillfully altered his voice and expressions to suit all the personae being presented. As Philip Collins remarks, Dickens "would in one evening be . . . narrator and take on the voice and visage of as many as twenty characters in an item (and his programmes generally consisted of two, and sometimes three, items)" (PR xvii).

In acting in amateur theatricals, Dickens had performed in a range of roles—from the braggart soldier Captain Bobadil in Jonson's *Every Man in His Humour*, a Falstaffian figure who is dissolute, lazy, pretentious, swaggering, verbose, and cowardly, to the high-minded Lord Wilmot in Sir Edward Bulwer-Lytton's *Not So Bad as We Seem*, a character who pretends to be a rake but is actually benevolent and virtuous.[1] But perhaps the most striking role played by Dickens was that of Richard Wardour in *The Frozen Deep*, an obsessed man who is crazed with jealousy and yet driven by sincere devotion, a figure torn between demonic destructive urges and a noble generosity that leads to a self-sacrificing, heroic rescue of his favored rival in love. In assisting Collins with the script, Dickens shaped this exhausting role as a vehicle for himself as an actor (Ackroyd 771–72).

An actor, except in cases of improvisation, is habitually repeating—speaking words, expressing emotions, and performing actions that have been premeditated and rehearsed and that will in many cases be included in successive (or "repeat") performances. Paradoxically, stage performers are usually at once both themselves and not themselves, as they change identities and assume different personae, for in portraying a given character the performer pretends to adopt that figure's perspective, one that may be alien to that customarily employed by the actor in his or her private life.

Because of these histrionic efforts, many identities coexisted with Dickens's actual self during a major portion of his adult years, for from 1845 until a few months before his death in 1870 he was heavily involved virtually every year in amateur theatricals and in public readings of his own fiction. Moreover, numerous performances called for travel to distant locations. Travel itself, I have earlier suggested, was another major activity in much of Dickens's life. In this case, as with stage performances, the extent of Dickens's travel experiences may not always be apparent in biographies, since accounts of various trips are intermingled with consideration of other matters. Again, a brief overview may be helpful.

In looking at Dickens as a traveler, we may see this as another public role. Indeed, his two long works of nonfiction—*American Notes* and *Pictures from Italy*—are travel books, and in each of his fifteen novels we find important trips undertaken by characters: these range from the treks on foot by Little Nell and her grandfather in *The Old Curiosity Shop* and by Betty Higden in *Our Mutual Friend* to the significant international journeys in *Martin Chuzzlewit, Little Dorrit*, and *A Tale of Two Cities*. In addition, Dickens gave speeches at anniversary celebrations for the Commercial Travellers' Schools, institutions for the children of deceased or needy commercial travellers (*Speeches* 169–76 [30 Dec. 1854], 289–93 [22 Dec. 1859]). The first of these addresses contained comments on the rigors of travel "at home . . . within the limits of the United Kingdom" (*Speeches* 172–73), while in the second Dickens referred figuratively to life as a journey to the grave: "we should remember tonight that we are all Travellers, and that every round we take converges nearer and nearer to our home; that all our little journeyings bring us together to our certain end" (*Speeches* 292–93). He later wrote essays like "Refreshments for Travellers" and "Travelling Abroad," published respectively in March and April 1860 in *All The Year Round* and subsequently included in 1868 in *The Uncommercial Traveller*. Although Dickens in the opening of that volume used the appellation of the title to designate himself (a representative of "the great house of Human Interest Brothers" [1]), his public readings for profit had previously led him to become a kind of commercial traveller. But there were also other reasons leading him to travel.

Despite his penchant for orderliness, Dickens needed stimulation and change, and he often displayed noticeable restlessness. While some of his early trips were imposed on him by his duties as a youthful reporter (Johnson 1: 95, 100–02), nearly all of his subsequent expeditions were voluntary and were much more extensive. He made two long journeys to (and in) America in 1842 and in 1867 to 1868, and various trips to the Continent, including a residence of nearly a year in Genoa from July 1844 to June of the next year, a four-month visit in Switzerland and France in 1846, and a stay of close to a year in France in 1855 and 1856.

Besides the lengthy ventures just mentioned, he undertook shorter journeys for specific purposes, like the visit to Yorkshire in 1838 to learn more about the notorious boarding schools that were to be memorably represented in *Nicholas Nickleby* by Mr. Squeers's Dotheboys Hall (Johnson 1: 217–18). Other travels, however, were intended to provide general stimulation: journeys with friends to Cornwall in 1842 and to the Continent in 1853; excursions with Wilkie Collins in England and abroad from 1855 to 1860; trips for family summer vacations at various English seaside resorts and in Boulogne; and provincial tours with his amateur theatrical groups, as well as for his public readings for profit. Then, too, in the last decade of his life, Dickens's relationship with Ellen Ternan induced him to make frequent trips to France, where he could enjoy more privacy with her than in England.

The amount of time that Dickens spent away from his homes in London and later at Gad's Hill was remarkably extensive. Even with the assistance of servants, much attention had to be given to planning and preparation, and travel itself often proved extremely demanding. By traveling, moving from one location to another, a person usually changes identity: from insider to outsider, neighbor to stranger, native to alien. Our perspectives are necessarily modified as we notice and are influenced by differences in dress and diet, in landscape and language, in architecture and social customs. There is duplication in that we inhabit other dwellings, usually acquire another set of acquaintances, and observe unfamiliar environments.

If Dickens's trips abroad were in some respects dislocating, his involvement with Ellen Ternan caused extraordinary changes in many added ways. He indulged and disguised an obsessive interest in this young woman. As George Woodcock observes in an introduction to *A Tale of Two Cities*, while Dickens "prepared to write on a public revolution" in this novel, he "experienced a private

revolution in which all the circumstances of his life were changed"
(13). The eulogist of family joys and the domestic hearth decided
to separate from his wife and established an unusual, ambiguous
relationship with a young woman twenty-seven years his junior.

Claire Tomalin, who has closely studied the involvement between
Ellen and Dickens during the last thirteen years of his life, observes
that at this time Dickens, because he was unwilling to defy the
rigid social mores of his time (84–85), entered a life of intrigue and
duplicity. Ellen vanished for long stretches of time (Tomalin 135),
and Dickens himself achieved periods "of invisibility" during
which he made frequent, mysterious trips to France, where Ellen
may have been living (Tomalin 138). He later rented a cottage for
her in the village of Slough, near Windsor, but used the pseudonym
"John Tringham" or "Charles Tringham" (Tomalin 157), a practice
he continued when he later took a house for Ellen in Peckham, in
Surrey (Tomalin 172–73, 178). To remain inconspicuous, Dickens
evidently at times did not go by train from London to Slough, but
instead traveled to Windsor or Datchet and then walked to Ellen's
residence (Tomalin 287–88 [n. 12, which quotes Aylmer 15, 38]).
When he considered trying to have Ellen join him in America on
his reading tour, he devised a coded telegram to convey instructions
(Tomalin 179–80). Long before this, after the Staplehurst accident,
he had taken to employing the expression "The Patient" as a covert
name for Ellen (Tomalin 147). Tomalin, after studying the pocket
diary Dickens kept in 1867 between January 1 and November 7,
states that "it reveals with perfect clarity . . . a man intent on a split
life" (168) and goes on to comment, "During the ten months covered
by the diary, he spent one third of his time with, or near, Nelly; one
third at Gad's Hill; and one third serving his other love, the public"
(168) in his readings. Describing the months just prior to the death
of Dickens, Tomalin observes, "he continued to lead his double life
and lay false trails" (194).

Covert trips, attempts to conceal one's identity, deliberately misleading actions, coded messages, pseudonyms, evasion, subter-
fuge—we think of a character in *A Tale of Two Cities* acting as a spy
in alien territory, rather than of a famous and beloved public figure.
Indeed, Dickens was a secret social rebel, taking all kinds of precau-
tions to minimize the risk of exposure.

In reviewing the Pilgrim Edition volume containing Dickens's
letters from 1865 to 1867, John M. L. Drew comments that Dickens
in this correspondence "reappears constantly . . . in a bewildering
multitude of roles" (139), and quotes a passage in which Dickens

observes that his travels had made him "accustomed to view" himself as if he "were another man" (141). Indeed, the letters lead Drew to view Dickens as someone presenting a number of selves, each of which "treads the same boards" as the others (145).

Public performance, travel, and the friendship with Ellen Ternan all overlap, especially since Ellen was an actress and her relationship with Dickens required pretense on her part as well as his. Dickens's life and art seem to interact, each influencing the other, for, despite all the days and hours spent in stage performances or travel and touring or in the relationship with Ellen, the primary involvement of his life was with his fiction. Arnold Goldman and John Whitley, in their edition of *American Notes*, quote from an 1843 review in which James Spedding proposes that Dickens was led by his "habits as a writer of fiction" to "study [American] society, with a view to gathering suggestions and materials for his creative faculty to work upon, rather than simply to consider and understand it" (330).[2] The activity of composing fiction was with him nearly all the time—in planning and anticipation, in the arduous work of writing, in editing, in remembering.

Dickens, in creating his novels and stories, employs duplicating devices to illuminate characters, themes, and situations that contribute to complicated narrative designs, and the intricacies of these patterns often reflect an intriguing moral complexity. The inconsistencies and the instances of moral ambiguity in Dickens's fiction seem to reflect contradictions in Victorian society. Urbanization brings greater freedom, a larger group of persons from whom to select friends, but it also reduces social cohesion and leads to what Friedrich Engels, in a passage describing the hectic pedestrian traffic on London streets, calls a "selfish egotism . . . [that is] blatantly evident . . . in the frantic bustle of the great city" (30–31).

George H. Ford is among the scholars who find in Dickens an ambivalence towards "the new, earnest, hard-working middle class way of life," a style that clashed with "the old easy-going, fun-loving, aristocratic way" ("Self-Help" 95). Generalizing about mid-twentieth-century Western civilization, the sociologist Daniel Bell points to a comparable "extraordinary contradiction within the social structure itself": the same "business corporation [that] wants an individual to work hard, pursue a career, accept delayed gratification" nevertheless endorses "in its products and its advertisements . . . pleasure, instant joy, relaxing and letting go" (71–72). This conflict seems largely rooted in the nineteenth century, although anticipations can be found long before.

Dickens induced his readers to confront their anxieties about ano-
mie, poverty, crime, greed, and cruelty, but he also offered comforting myths, stories to impart hope: the victimized child is rescued
by a generous benefactor, virtuous characters succeed in resisting
predatory villains. As we observed before, the moral stance is clear
in favoring honesty and kindness and attacking deceit and cruelty.

Dickens's appeal was strengthened by his use of serialization,
which extended and intensified his relationship with his readers, as
well as by his activities as an after-dinner speaker, as the editor for
twenty years of popular weekly periodicals, and as a stage performer. His ever-growing fame stimulated public interest in all his endeavors. And the range of his fiction was truly extraordinary, fusing
topical references with his own personal fantasies, impressive realism with striking caricature, simple emotional appeals with com-
plexly interwoven plots, sentiment with satire.

Referring to the Charles Dickens Edition, published in 1867, John
Sutherland remarks, "One effect of this kind of collective issue was
to keep all of Dickens simultaneously before the public," thereby
enabling him to have "a kind of total and continual existence for
the readers of his age" (37). The public readings served to remind
both the novelist and his listeners of earlier works. As Philip Collins
observes, in these performances Dickens assumed that his audience
was familiar with the material: "he does not bother to explain why
Jonas Chuzzlewit acts in a guilty fashion, or who Mr. Pickwick or
Mr. Micawber is or what his relations to the other characters are"
(PR lxiii). To all these factors building his popularity, we must add
Dickens's prolific output and the longevity of his career. For a period of thirty-four years, from the appearance of *Pickwick Papers* in
1836 until the novelist's death in 1870, the percentage of months in
which a reader could purchase new and major fiction by Dickens
was remarkably high, approximately 50%. For an author to be producing and to be widely read over so lengthy a period established
a remarkable sense of continuity. A reader could have a sustained
relationship with Dickens for nearly three and a half decades.

In numerous respects, Dickens provides in his fiction a synthesis
of many perspectives. The novels and stories offer readers both a
confrontation with and an escape from fears and anxieties created
by each person's efforts to achieve a sense of identity, to reconcile
being simultaneously insider and outsider, for as a literary artist
Dickens acts as a discriminating elegist of the England of stage
coaches and a fixed societal order that is passing and also as both
a celebrant and a severe critic of the new time of cities, commercial

expansion, and increased social mobility. A powerful analyst of abuse and rejection, he becomes, by creating comforting responses to loss, a source of hope and optimism, and while the exciting future he looked to has now passed, the social and moral problems he considered seem to remain, as does our need for his stimulation and reassurance.

The duplicating devices so plentifully introduced in the fiction serve to make it more realistic. In discussing Dickens's fascination with "the coincidences, resemblances, and surprises of life," Forster mentions his friend's remarking that "to-morrow bore so close a resemblance to nothing half so much as yesterday" (*Life* 1: 5: 76). Life is repetitious and paradoxical, and in seeking to understand it we resort to diverse perspectives. Writing to Thackeray's friend Mrs. William Henry Brookfield about her own novel, Dickens refers to the difficulties of composing for weekly serialization: "There must be a special design, to overcome that specially trying mode of publication," since an author's story must be planned "patiently and expressly . . . for presentation in these fragments [the weekly parts], and yet for afterwards fusing together as an uninterrupted whole" (PL 11: 160 [20 Feb. 1866]). David Paroissien directs attention to this comment and refers to the need for a "double focus of the instalment and the whole" ("Literature's 'Eternal Duties' " 24). Appropriately, such a "double focus" is asked from all of us if we are to understand the relationship between daily events and the patterns of an entire human life. Like a weaver, the writer of fiction must know when to reveal and when to conceal, how to begin and how to end. In weaving stories, Dickens offers various ways of approaching life and its choices and of comprehending ourselves and others.

Notes

1. In an epilogue to the play, the character Softhead describes his own tendency "to imitate one—," referring to Wilmot, and hears another character complete the construction with the clause, "Who defies imitation" (138), almost certainly an inside joke playing on Dickens's nickname, "the Inimitable."

2. In a letter to the Editor of *The Times*, Dickens objected strenuously to Spedding's remark suggesting that Dickens "went to America as a kind of missionary in the cause of international copyright" (PL 3: 423 [15 Jan. 1843]).

Works Cited

Ackroyd, Peter. *Dickens*. New York: HarperCollins, 1990.

Adrian, Arthur A. *Dickens and the Parent-Child Relationship*. Athens, OH: Ohio UP, 1984.

Altick, Richard D. "Education, Print, and Paper in *Our Mutual Friend*." *Nineteenth-Century Literary Perspectives: Essays in Honor of Lionel Stevenson*. Ed. Clyde de L. Ryalls with the assistance of John Clubbe and Benjamin Franklin Fisher IV. Durham, NC: Duke UP, 1974. 237–54.

Amerongen, J[uda] B. Van. *The Actor in Dickens: A Study of the Histrionic and Dramatic Elements in the Novelist's Life and Works*. 1926. New York: Benjamin Blom, 1969.

Anglo-Jewish Letters (1158–1917). Ed. Cecil Roth. London: Soncino P, 1938.

Arac, Jonathan. *Commissioned Spirits: The Shaping of Social Motion in Dickens, Carlyle, Melville, and Hawthorne*. New Brunswick, NJ: Rutgers UP, 1979.

Armstrong, Nancy. *Fiction in the Age of Photography: The Legacy of British Realism*. Cambridge, MA: Harvard UP, 1999.

Axton, William F. *Circle of Fire: Dickens' Vision & Style & The Popular Victorian Theater*. Lexington: U of Kentucky P, 1966.

———."*Great Expectations* Yet Again." *Dickens Studies Annual* 2 (1972): 278–93.

Aylmer, Felix. *Dickens Incognito*. London: R. Hart-Davis, 1959.

Barreca, Regina. " 'The Mimic Life of the Theatre': The 1838 Adaptation of *Oliver Twist.*" *Dramatic Dickens.* Ed. Carol Hanberry MacKay. New York: St. Martin's, 1989. 87–95.

Bate, Walter Jackson. *The Achievement of Samuel Johnson.* New York: Oxford UP, 1955.

Bates, Catherine. "Weaving and Writing in *Othello.*" *Shakespeare Survey* 46 (1994): 51–60.

Baumgarten, Murray. "Seeing Double: Jews in the Fiction of F. Scott Fitzgerald, Charles Dickens, Anthony Trollope, and George Eliot." *Between "Race" and Culture: Representations of "the Jew" in English and American Literature.* Ed. Bryan Cheyette. Stanford: Stanford UP, 1996. 44–61, 189–91.

Bell, Daniel. *The Cultural Contradictions of Capitalism.* New York: Basic Books, 1976.

Bledsoe, Robert. "Dickens and Opera." *Dickens Studies Annual* 18 (1989): 93–118.

Briggs, Julia. *Night Visitors: The Rise and Fall of the English Ghost Story.* London: Faber, 1977.

Brown, E[dward] K[illoran]. *Rhythm in the Novel.* 1950. Toronto: U of Toronto P, 1963.

Bulwer-Lytton, Sir Edward. *Not So Bad As We Seem; or, Many Sides to a Character.* London: Chapman and Hall, 1851.

Calisch, Edward N. *The Jew in English Literature, as Author and as Subject.* 1909. Port Washington, NY: Kennikat P, 1969.

Caserio, Robert L. *Plot, Story, and the Novel: From Dickens and Poe to the Modern Period.* Princeton, NJ: Princeton UP, 1979.

Cheadle, Brian. "Mystification and the Mystery of Origins in *Bleak House.*" *Dickens Studies Annual* 25 (1996): 29–47.

Chesterton, G. K. *Appreciations and Criticisms of the Works of Charles Dickens.* New York: E. P. Dutton, 1911.

Coleridge, Samuel Taylor. "[Dramatic Illusion]." *Shakespearean Criticism.* Ed. Thomas Middleton Raysor. 2nd Ed. Vol. 1. New York: E. P. Dutton, 1960. 176–83.

Coles, Nicholas. "The Politics of *Hard Times*: Dickens the Novelist versus Dickens the Reformer." *Dickens Studies Annual* 15 (1986): 145–79.

Collins, Philip. *Dickens and Crime.* Bloomington: Indiana UP, 1968.

———."Dickens' Self-Estimate: Some New Evidence." *Dickens the Craftsman: Strategies of Presentation.* Ed. Robert B. Partlow, Jr. Carbondale: Southern Illinois UP, 1970. 21–43.

———."How Many Men Was Dickens the Novelist?" *Studies in the Later Dickens.* Ed. Jean-Claude Amalric. Montpellier: Université Paul Valéry, 1975. 145–68.

Coolidge, Archibald C., Jr. *Charles Dickens as Serial Novelist*. Ames: Iowa State UP, 1967.

Cotsell, Michael. *The Companion to Our Mutual Friend*. Boston: Allen & Unwin, 1986.

Dabney, Ross H. *Love and Property in the Novels of Dickens*. London: Chatto & Windus, 1967.

Daleski, H. M. *Dickens and the Art of Analogy*. New York: Schocken, 1970.

Davies, James A. *The Textual Life of Dickens's Characters*. Savage, MD: Barnes & Noble, 1990.

Davis, Earle. "Dickens and Significant Tradition." *Dickens Studies Annual* 7 (1978): 49–67.

———.*The Flint and the Flame: The Artistry of Charles Dickens*. Columbia: U of Missouri P, 1963.

De Quincey, Thomas. "On the Knocking at the Gate in *Macbeth*." *De Quincey as Critic*. Ed. John E. Jordan. Boston: Routledge & Kegan Paul, 1973. 240–44.

Dickens, Charles. *American Notes for General Circulation*. Ed. John S. Whitley and Arnold Goldman. New York: Penguin, 1989.

———.*Barnaby Rudge*. Ed. Gordon Spence. New York: Penguin, 1966.

———.*Bleak House*. Ed. George Ford and Sylvère Monod. New York: Norton, 1977.

———.*The Christmas Books*. Ed. Michael Slater. 2 vols. Baltimore, MD: Penguin, 1971.

———.*David Copperfield*. Ed. Jerome H. Buckley. New York: Norton, 1990.

———.*David Copperfield*. Ed. Nina Burgis. Oxford: Clarendon, 1980.

———.*Dickens' Working Notes for His Novels*. Ed. Harry Stone. Chicago: U of Chicago P, 1987.

———.*Dombey and Son*. Ed. Peter Fairclough. New York: Penguin, 1985.

———.*Great Expectations*. Ed. Angus Calder. New York: Penguin, 1965, rpt. 1985.

———.*Great Expectations*. Ed. Edgar Rosenberg. New York: Norton, 1999.

———.*Hard Times*. Ed. George Ford and Sylvère Monod. 2nd Ed. New York: Norton, 1990.

———.*The Letters of Charles Dickens*. Vol. 1: 1820–1839. The Pilgrim Edition. Ed. Madeline House and Graham Storey. Oxford: Clarendon, 1965.

————.*The Letters of Charles Dickens.* Vol. 2: 1840–1841. The Pilgrim Edition. Ed. Madeline House and Graham Storey. Oxford: Clarendon, 1969.

————.*The Letters of Charles Dickens.* Vol. 3: 1842–1843. The Pilgrim Edition. Ed. Madeline House, Graham Storey, and Kathleen Tillotson. Oxford: Clarendon, 1974.

————.*The Letters of Charles Dickens.* Vol. 5: 1847–1849. The Pilgrim Edition. Ed. Graham Storey and K. J. Fielding. Oxford: Clarendon, 1981.

————.*The Letters of Charles Dickens.* Vol. 6: 1850–1852. The Pilgrim Edition. Ed. Graham Storey, Kathleen Tillotson, and Nina Burgis. Oxford: Clarendon, 1988.

————.*The Letters of Charles Dickens.* Vol. 8: 1856–1858. The Pilgrim Edition. Ed. Graham Storey and Kathleen Tillotson. Oxford: Clarendon, 1995.

————.*The Letters of Charles Dickens.* Vol. 9: 1859–1861. The Pilgrim Edition. Ed. Graham Storey. Oxford: Clarendon, 1997.

————.*The Letters of Charles Dickens.* Vol. 10: 1862–1864. The Pilgrim Edition. Ed. Graham Storey. Oxford: Clarendon, 1998.

————.*The Letters of Charles Dickens.* Vol. 11: 1865–1867. The Pilgrim Edition. Ed. Graham Storey. Oxford: Clarendon, 1999.

————.*Little Dorrit.* Ed. Stephen Wall and Helen Small. New York: Penguin Books, 1998.

————.*Martin Chuzzlewit.* Ed. P. N. Furbank. Baltimore, MD: Penguin Books, 1968.

————.*Master Humphrey's Clock and A Child's History of England.* Intro. Derek Hudson. New York: Oxford UP, 1958, rpt. 1978.

————.*Nicholas Nickleby.* Ed. Mark Ford. New York: Penguin Books, 1999.

————.*Oliver Twist.* Ed. Fred Kaplan. New York: Norton, 1993.

————.*The Old Curiosity Shop.* Ed. Angus Easson. New York: Penguin, 1972, rpt. 1985.

————.*Our Mutual Friend.* Ed. Adrian Poole. New York: Penguin Books, 1997.

————.*The Pickwick Papers.* Ed. Robert L. Patten. New York: Penguin, 1972.

————.*Pictures from Italy.* Ed. Kate Flint. New York: Penguin, 1998.

————.*The Public Readings.* Ed. Philip Collins. Oxford: Clarendon, 1975.

————.*Sketches by Boz.* Ed. Dennis Walder. New York: Penguin, 1995.

————.*The Speeches of Charles Dickens.* Ed. K. J. Fielding. Oxford: Clarendon, 1960.

————.*A Tale of Two Cities.* Ed. George Woodcock. New York: Penguin, 1970.

————.*The Uncommercial Traveller and Reprinted Pieces.* Intro. Leslie C. Staples. New York : Oxford UP, 1958, rpt. 1964.

Dickens: The Critical Heritage. Ed. Philip Collins. New York: Barnes & Noble, 1971.

Drew, John M. L. "Dickens Reappears." Review of *The Letters of Charles Dickens*, Vol. 11, ed. Graham Storey. *Dickens Quarterly* 18: 1 (Sept. 2001): 139–47.

Dyson, A. E. *The Inimitable Dickens: A Reading of the Novels.* New York: St. Martin's, 1970.

Eigner, Edwin M. *The Dickens Pantomime.* Berkeley: U of California P, 1989.

————.*The Metaphysical Novel in England and America: Dickens, Bulwer, Melville, and Hawthorne.* Berkeley: U of California P, 1978.

————."Shakespeare, Milton, Dickens and The Morality of the Pious Fraud." *Dickens Studies Annual* 21 (1992): 1–25.

Endelman, Todd M. *The Jews of Georgian England, 1714–1830.* Philadelphia: Jewish Publication Society of America, 1979.

Engel, Monroe. *The Maturity of Dickens.* Cambridge, MA: Harvard UP, 1959.

Engels, Friedrich. *The Condition of the Working Class in England* (1845). Tr. and ed. W. O. Henderson and W. H. Chaloner. Oxford: Basil Blackwell, 1958.

Erikson, Erik. *Toys and Reasons: Stages in the Ritualization of Experience.* New York: Norton, 1977.

Ermath, Elizabeth Deeds. *Realism and Consensus in the English Novel.* Princeton: Princeton UP, 1983.

Fawcett, F. Dubrez. *Dickens the Dramatist: On Stage, Screen and Radio.* London: W. H. Alden, 1952.

Felsenstein, Frank. *Anti-Semitic Stereotypes: A Paradigm of Otherness in English Popular Culture, 1660–1830.* Baltimore: Johns Hopkins UP, 1995.

Fisch, Harold. *The Dual Image: The Figure of the Jew in English and American Literature.* New York: KTAV Publishing House, 1971.

Fleissner, Robert. *Dickens and Shakespeare.* New York: Haskell House, 1965.

Flint, Kate. *Dickens.* Atlantic Highlands, NJ: Humanities, 1986.

Ford, George H. "Self-Help and the Helpless in *Bleak House.*" *From Jane Austen to Joseph Conrad: Essays Collected in Memory of James*

T. Hillhouse. Ed. Robert C. Rathburn and Martin Steinmann, Jr. Minneapolis: U of Minnesota P, 1958. 92–105.

Forster, John. *The Life of Charles Dickens.* Ed. J. W. T. Ley. London: Cecil Palmer, 1928.

————.Review of *Our Mutual Friend. The Literary Examiner,* October 28, 1865, 681–82.

Forsyth, Neil. "Wonderful Chains: Dickens and Coincidence." *Modern Philology* 83: 2 (Nov. 1985): 151–65.

Frank, Lawrence. " 'Through a Glass Darkly': Esther Summerson and *Bleak House.*" *Dickens Studies Annual* 4 (1975): 91–112.

Freud, Sigmund. *The Standard Edition of the Complete Psychological Works of Sigmund Freud.* Tr. James Strachey et al. 24 vols. London: Hogarth P, 1953–74.

Friedman, Stanley. "A Considerate Ghost: George Rouncewell in *Bleak House.*" *Dickens Studies Annual* 17 (1988): 111–28.

————."Dickens' Mid-Victorian Theodicy: *David Copperfield.*" *Dickens Studies Annual* 7 (1978): 128–50, 252–57.

————."A Loose Thread in *Our Mutual Friend.*" *Dickens Studies Newsletter* 1: 2 (Sept. 1970): 18–20.

————."The Motif of Reading in *Our Mutual Friend.*" *Nineteenth-Century Fiction* 28: 1 (June 1973): 38–61.

Frost, Robert. "Tree at My Window." *Collected Poems, Prose, & Plays.* Ed. Richard Poirier and Mark Richardson. New York: Library of America, 1995. 230–31.

Frye, Northrop. *Anatomy of Criticism: Four Essays.* 1957. New York: Atheneum, 1966.

Gager, Valerie L. *Shakespeare and Dickens: The Dynamics of Influence.* New York: Cambridge UP, 1996.

Garrett, Peter K. *The Victorian Multiplot Novel: Studies in Dialogical Form.* New Haven: Yale UP, 1980.

Gilmour, Robin. *The Idea of the Gentleman in the Victorian Novel.* London: George Allen & Unwin, 1981.

Glavin, John. *After Dickens: Reading, Adaptation and Performance.* New York: Cambridge UP, 1999.

Gold, Joseph. *Charles Dickens: Radical Moralist.* Minneapolis: U of Minnesota P, 1972.

Golden, Morris. *Dickens Imagining Himself: Six Novel Encounters with a Changing World.* Lanham, MD: UP of America, 1992.

————."Dickens, Oliver, and Boz." *Dickens Quarterly* 4: 2 (June 1987): 65–77.

Goldknopf, David. *The Life of the Novel.* Chicago: U of Chicago P, 1972.

Green, André. *The Tragic Effect: The Oedipus Complex in Tragedy.* Trans. Alan Sheridan. New York: Cambridge UP, 1979.

Greenberg, Robert A. "On Ending *Great Expectations.*" *Papers on Language and Literature* 6: 2 (Spring 1970): 152–62.

Greenstein, Michael. "Mutuality in *Our Mutual Friend.*" *Dickens Quarterly* 8: 3 (Sept. 1991): 127–34.

Gregory, Marshall W. "Values and Meaning in *Great Expectations*: The Two Endings Revisited." *Essays in Criticism* 19: 4 (Oct. 1969): 402–09.

Grob, Shirley. "Dickens and Some Motifs of the Fairy Tale." *Texas Studies in Literature and Language* 5: 4 (Winter 1964): 567–79.

Handley, Graham. *Hard Times.* Oxford: Basil Blackwell, 1969.

Harbage, Alfred. *A Kind of Power: The Shakespeare-Dickens Analogy.* Philadelphia: American Philosophical Society, 1975.

———."Shakespeare and the Early Dickens." *Shakespeare: Aspects of Influence.* Ed. G. B. Evans. Cambridge, MA: Harvard UP, 1976. 109–34.

Hardy, Barbara. "The Complexity of Dickens." *Dickens 1970.* Ed. Michael Slater. London: Chapman and Hall, 1970. 29–53.

———.Introduction. *Daniel Deronda.* By George Eliot. Baltimore, MD: Penguin, 1967. 7–30.

Harte, Bret. *The Condensed Novels of Bret Harte.* 1871. Upper Saddle River, NJ: Literature House, 1969.

Harvey, W. J. *Character and the Novel.* Ithaca, NY: Cornell UP, 1965.

Hayward, Jennifer. *Consuming Pleasures: Active Audiences and Serial Fictions from Dickens to Soap Opera.* Lexington: The UP of Kentucky, 1997.

Haywood, Charles. "Charles Dickens and Shakespeare; or, The Irish Moor of Venice, *O'Thello* with Music." *The Dickensian* 73 (May 1977): 67–88.

Heller, Deborah. "The Outcast as Villain and Victim: Jews in Dickens's *Oliver Twist* and *Our Mutual Friend.*" *Jewish Presences in English Literature.* Ed. Derek Cohen and Deborah Heller. Montreal: McGill-Queen's UP, 1990. 40–60.

Henkle, Roger B. *Comedy and Culture: England 1820–1900.* Princeton: Princeton UP, 1980.

Herbert, Christopher. "The Occult in *Bleak House.*" *Novel: A Forum on Fiction* 17: 2 (Winter 1984): 101–15.

Herst, Beth F. *The Dickens Hero: Selfhood and Alienation in the Dickens World.* New York: St. Martin's, 1990.

Hill, T. W. "Notes to *Our Mutual Friend.*" *The Dickensian* 43 (March 1947): 85–90; 43 (June 1947):142–49; 43 (Sept. 1947): 206–12.

Hollingsworth, Keith. *The Newgate Novel, 1830–1847: Bulwer, Ainsworth, Dickens, & Thackeray*. Detroit: Wayne State UP, 1963.

The Holy Bible. Authorized King James Version. New York: Meridian, New American Library, 1974.

House, Humphry. *The Dickens World*. 2nd ed. London: Oxford UP, 1942.

Irwin, John T. *Doubling and Incest/ Repetition and Revenge: A Speculative Reading of Faulkner*. Baltimore: Johns Hopkins UP, 1975.

Jekels, Ludwig. "On the Psychology of Comedy." *Selected Papers*. New York: International Universities P, 1952. 97–104.

Johnson, Edgar. *Charles Dickens: His Tragedy and Triumph*. 2 vols. New York: Simon and Schuster, 1952.

Kaplan, Fred. *Dickens: A Biography*. New York: William Morrow, 1988.

Kawin, Bruce. *Telling It Again and Again: Repetition in Literature and Film*. Ithaca, NY: Cornell UP, 1972.

Kettle, Arnold. "*Our Mutual Friend*." *Dickens and the Twentieth Century*. Ed. John Gross and Gabriel Pearson. London: Routledge & Kegan Paul, 1962. 213–25.

Korg, Jacob. "The Rage of Caliban." *University of Toronto Quarterly* 37: 1 (Oct. 1967): 75–89.

Kotzin, Michael C. *Dickens and the Fairy Tale*. Bowling Green, OH: Bowling Green U Popular P, 1972.

Kucich, John. "Action in the Dickens Ending: *Bleak House* and *Great Expectations*." *Nineteenth-Century Fiction* 33: 1 (June 1978): 88–109.

Kurrik, Maire Jaanus. *Literature and Negation*. New York: Columbia UP, 1979.

Larson, Janet. *Dickens and the Broken Scripture*. Athens: U of Georgia P, 1985.

Leavis, F. R., and Q. D. Leavis. *Dickens the Novelist*. New York: Pantheon Books, 1970.

Leitch, Thomas. "Closure and Teleology in Dickens." *Studies in the Novel* 18: 2 (Summer 1986): 143–56.

Lindsay, Jack. *Charles Dickens: A Biographical and Critical Study*. New York: Philosophical Library, 1950.

Mack, Maynard. *Everybody's Shakespeare: Reflections Chiefly on the Tragedies*. Lincoln: U of Nebraska P, 1993.

McMaster, R. D. "Birds of Prey: A Study of *Our Mutual Friend*." *The Dalhousie Review* 40: 3 (Fall 1960): 372–81.

Macready, William Charles. *The Diaries of William Charles Macready 1833–1851*. Ed. William Toynbee. 2 vols. London: Chapman and Hall, 1912.

Manning, Sylvia. "Dickens' *Nickleby* and Cavalcanti's: Comedy and Fear." *Dickens Studies Annual* 17 (1988): 47–66.

Marcus, Steven. *Dickens: From Pickwick to Dombey.* New York: Basic Books, 1965.

Mayhew, Henry. *London Labour and the London Poor.* 4 vols. Vol. 2: *The London Street-Folk.* 1861–62; rpt. 1967. London: Frank Cass and Co., 1967.

Meckier, Jerome. "Charles Dickens' *Great Expectations*: A Defense of the Second Ending." *Studies in the Novel* 25: 1 (Spring 1993): 28–58.

———.*Hidden Rivalries in Victorian Fiction: Dickens, Realism, and Revaluation.* Lexington: UP of Kentucky, 1987.

Melville, Herman. *Correspondence.* Ed. Merrell R. Davis and William H. Gilman. Vol. 14 in *The Writings of Herman Melville.* Chicago: Northwestern UP and The Newberry Library, 1993.

Miller, J. Hillis. *Charles Dickens: The World of His Novels.* Cambridge, MA: Harvard UP, 1958.

———.*Fiction and Repetition: Seven English Novels.* Cambridge, MA: Harvard UP, 1982.

Millhauser, Milton. "*Great Expectations*: The Three Endings." *Dickens Studies Annual* 2 (1972): 267–77.

Milton, John. *Paradise Lost.* Ed. Scott Elledge. New York: Norton, 1975.

Miyoshi, Masao. "Resolution of Identity in *Our Mutual Friend.*" *Victorian Newsletter* No. 26 (Fall 1964): 5–9.

Monod, Sylvère. *Dickens the Novelist.* Norman: U of Oklahoma P, 1968.

Morgentaler, Goldie. *Dickens and Heredity: Like Begets Like.* New York: St. Martin's, 2000.

Morse, Robert. "*Our Mutual Friend.*" *The Dickens Critics.* Ed. George H. Ford and Lauriat Lane, Jr. Ithaca, NY: Cornell UP, 1961. 197–213.

Moynihan, Julian. "The Hero's Guilt: The Case of *Great Expectations.*" *Essays in Criticism* 10: 1 (Jan. 1960): 60–79.

Muir, Kenneth. "Image and Structure in *Our Mutual Friend.*" *Essays and Studies Collected for the English Association.* New Series. 19 (1966): 92–105.

Naddaff, Sylvia. *Arabesque: Narrative Structure and the Aesthetics of Repetition in the* 1001 Nights. Evanston, IL: Northwestern UP, 1991.

Naman, Anne Aresty. *The Jew in the Victorian Novel: Some Relationships Between Prejudice and Art.* New York: AMS, 1980.

Nelson, Harland S. "Dickens's *Our Mutual Friend* and Henry Mayhew's *London Labour and the London Poor.*" *Nineteenth-Century Fiction* 20: 3 (Dec. 1965): 207–22.

——."Dickens' Plots: 'The Ways of Providence' or the Influence of Collins?" *Victorian Newsletter* No. 19 (Spring 1961): 11–14.

Newman, S. J. *Dickens at Play.* New York: St. Martin's, 1981.

Newsom, Robert. *Dickens on the Romantic Side of Familiar Things.* New York: Columbia UP, 1977.

——." 'To Scatter Dust': Fancy and Authenticity in *Our Mutual Friend.*" *Dickens Studies Annual* 8 (1980): 39–60.

Oddie, William. *Dickens and Carlyle: The Question of Influence.* London: Centenary Press, 1972.

Orwell, George. "Charles Dickens." *The Collected Essays, Journalism and Letters of George Orwell.* Vol. 1: *An Age Like This 1920–1940.* Ed. Sonia Orwell and Ian Angus. New York: Harcourt Brace Jovanovich, 1968. 413–60.

Panitz, Esther L. *The Alien in Their Midst: Images of Jews in English Literature.* London: Associated U Presses, 1981.

Paroissien, David. *The Companion to* Oliver Twist. Edinburgh: Edinburgh UP, 1992.

——."Literature's 'Eternal Duties': Dickens's Professional Creed." *The Changing World of Charles Dickens.* Ed. Robert Giddings. Totowa, NJ: Barnes and Noble, 1983. 21–50.

Patten, Robert L. "Dickens Time and Again." *Dickens Studies Annual* 2 (1972): 163–96, 362–66.

Pearlman, E. "Inversion in *Great Expectations.*" *Dickens Studies Annual* 7 (1978): 190–202.

Pool, Daniel. *What Jane Austen Ate and Charles Dickens Knew: From Fox-Hunting to Whist — the Facts of Daily Life in Nineteenth-Century England.* New York: Simon and Schuster, 1993.

Pratt, Branwen Bailey. "Dickens and Father: Notes on the Family Romance." *Hartford Studies in Literature* 8: 1 (1976): 4–22.

Ragussis, Michael. "The Ghostly Signs of *Bleak House.*" *Nineteenth-Century Fiction* 34: 3 (Dec. l979): 253–80.

Raina, Badri. *Dickens and the Dialectic of Growth.* Madison: U of Wisconsin P, 1986.

Rank, Otto. *The Double: A Psychoanalytic Study.* Trans. and Ed. Harry Tucker, Jr. Chapel Hill: U of North Carolina P, 1971.

——."The Double as Immortal Self." *Beyond Psychology.* New York: Dover, 1958. 62–101.

Rawlins, Jack P. "Great Expiations: Dickens and the Betrayal of the Child." *Studies in English Literature* 23: 4 (Autumn 1983): 667–83.

Reed, John R. *Victorian Conventions*. Athens: Ohio UP, 1975.

Ricks, Christopher. *"Great Expectations." Dickens and the Twentieth Century*. Ed. John Gross and Gabriel Pearson. Toronto: U of Toronto P, 1962. 199–211.

Rimmon-Kenan, Shlomith. "The Paradoxical Status of Repetition." *Poetics Today* 1: 4 (1980): 151–59.

Rosenberg, Edgar. *From Shylock to Svengali: Jewish Stereotypes in English Fiction*. Stanford, CA: Stanford UP, 1960.

———."Last Words on *Great Expectations*: A Textual Brief on the Six Endings." *Dickens Studies Annual* 9 (1981): 87–115.

Roth, Cecil. *Essays and Portraits in Anglo-Jewish History*. Philadelphia: The Jewish Publication Society of America, 1962.

Rudnytsky, Peter L. *Freud and Oedipus*. New York: Columbia UP, 1987.

Russell, Bertrand. "A Free Man's Worship." *Mysticism and Logic and Other Essays*. London: George Allen & Unwin, 1917. 46–57.

Sadoff, Dianne F. *Monsters of Affection: Dickens, Eliot & Brontë on Fatherhood*. Baltimore: Johns Hopkins UP, 1982.

Sadrin, Anny. *Parentage and Inheritance in the Novels of Charles Dickens*. Cambridge, UK: Cambridge UP, 1994.

Scheid, John, and Jesper Svenbro. *The Craft of Zeus: Myths of Weaving and Fabric*. Tr. Carol Volk. Cambridge, MA: Harvard UP, 1996.

Scott, Sir Walter. *The Lives of the Novelists*. Everyman's Library. New York: E. P. Dutton, n.d.

Senelick, Laurence. "Traces of *Othello* in *Oliver Twist*." *The Dickensian* 70 (May 1974): 97–102.

Shakespeare, William. *The Riverside Shakespeare*. 2nd ed. Ed. G. Blakemore Evans. Boston: Houghton Mifflin, 1997.

Shea, F. X. "No Change of Intention in *Our Mutual Friend*." *The Dickensian* 63 (Jan. 1967): 37–40.

Shores, Lucille P. "The Character of Estella in *Great Expectations*." *Massachusetts Studies in English* 3: 4 (Fall 1972): 91–99.

Slater, Michael. *Dickens and Women*. Stanford, CA: Stanford UP, 1983.

———.Introduction. *Nicholas Nickleby*. By Charles Dickens. New York: Penguin, 1978. 13–31.

Smith, Grahame. *Dickens, Money, and Society*. Berkeley: U of California P, 1968.

Smith, Marion Bodwell. *Dualities in Shakespeare*. Toronto: U of Toronto P, 1966.

Spevack, Marvin. *The Harvard Concordance to Shakespeare*. Cambridge, MA: Belknap P of Harvard UP, 1973.

Stewart, Garrett. *Death Sentences: Styles of Dying in British Fiction.* Cambridge: Harvard UP, 1984.

———."The New Mortality of *Bleak House.*" *ELH* 45:3 (Fall 1978): 443–87.

Stone, Harry. *Dickens and the Invisible World: Fairy Tales, Fantasy, and Novel-Making.* Bloomington: Indiana UP, 1979.

———."Dickens and the Jews." *Victorian Studies* 2: 3 (March 1959): 223–53.

———."The Love Pattern in Dickens' Novels." *Dickens the Craftsman: Strategies of Presentation.* Ed. Robert B. Partlow, Jr. Carbondale: Southern Illinois UP, 1970.

Stone, Lawrence. *The Family, Sex and Marriage in England: 1500–1800.* New York: Harper & Row, 1977.

Storey, Gladys. *Dickens and Daughter.* London: Muller, 1939.

Sucksmith, Harvey Peter. *The Narrative Art of Charles Dickens: The Rhetoric of Sympathy and Irony in his Novels.* Oxford: Clarendon, 1970.

Sulloway, Frank J. *Freud, Biologist of the Mind: Beyond the Psychoanalytic Legend.* New York: Basic Books, 1979.

Sutherland, J. A. *Victorian Novelists and Publishers.* Chicago: U of Chicago P, 1976.

Tambling, Jeremy. Introduction. *David Copperfield.* By Charles Dickens. New York: Penguin, 1996. vii–xxii.

Tatar, Maria M. "The Houses of Fiction: Toward a Definition of the Uncanny." *Comparative Literature* 33: 2 (Spring 1981): 167–82.

Tillotson, Geoffrey. *A View of Victorian Literature.* Oxford: Clarendon, 1978.

Tillotson, Kathleen. Introduction. *Oliver Twist.* By Charles Dickens. Oxford: Clarendon, 1966. xv–xlvii.

———."The Middle Years from the *Carol* to *Copperfield.*" *Dickens Memorial Lectures 1970.* The Dickensian 65 supplement (Sept. 1970): 7–19.

———."Writers and Readers in 1851." *Mid-Victorian Studies.* By Geoffrey and Kathleen Tillotson. London: Athlone P of the U of London, 1965. 304–28.

Tolstoy, Leo. *Anna Karenina.* 2nd ed. Trans. and ed. George Gibian. New York: Norton, 1995.

Tomalin, Claire. *Invisible Woman: The Story of Nelly Ternan and Charles Dickens.* New York: Knopf, 1991.

Tracy, Robert. " 'The Old Story' and Inside Stories: Modish Fiction and Fictional Modes in *Oliver Twist.*" *Dickens Studies Annual* 17 (1988): 1–33.

Twain, Mark. "Concerning the Jews." *Collected Tales, Sketches, Speeches, & Essays 1891–1910*. New York: Library of America, 1992. 354–70.

Van Ghent, Dorothy. "The Dickens World: A View from Todgers's." *The Sewanee Review* 58: 3 (July-Sept. 1950): 419–38.

———.*The English Novel: Form and Function*. 1953. New York: Harper, 1961.

Vogel, Jane. *Allegory in Dickens*. University, AL: The U of Alabama P, 1977.

Walder, Dennis. *Dickens and Religion*. Boston: George Allen & Unwin, 1981.

Walpole, Horace. *Horace Walpole's Correspondence with Sir Horace Mann*. Vol. 7. Vol. 23 in The Yale Edition of Horace Walpole's Correspondence. Ed. W. S. Lewis. New Haven: Yale UP, 1967.

Warner, Marina. *From the Beast to the Blonde: On Fairy Tales and Their Tellers*. New York: Farrar, Straus and Giroux, 1994.

Watkins, Gwen. *Dickens in Search of Himself: Recurrent Themes and Characters in the Work of Charles Dickens*. Totowa, NJ: Barnes & Noble, 1986.

Webber, Joan. "*Hamlet* and the Freeing of the Mind." In *English Renaissance Drama: Essays in Honor of Madeleine Doran & Mark Eccles*. Carbondale: Southern Illinois UP, 1976. 76–99.

Wentersdorf, Karl P. "Mirror-Images in *Great Expectations*." *Nineteenth-Century Fiction* 21: 3 (Dec. 1966): 203–24.

Westburg, Barry. *The Confessional Fictions of Charles Dickens*. De Kalb: Northern Illinois UP, 1977.

Wheeler, Burton M. "The Text and Plan of *Oliver Twist*." *Dickens Studies Annual* 12 (1983): 41–61.

Wilson, Edmund. "Dickens: The Two Scrooges." *The Wound and the Bow: Seven Studies in Literature*. New York: Oxford UP, 1947; 2nd printing, 1959. 1–104.

Winters, Warrington. "Dickens' *Hard Times*: The Lost Childhood." *Dickens Studies Annual* 2 (1972): 217–36.

Wolgast, Elizabeth Hankins. *Paradoxes of Knowledge*. Ithaca, NY: Cornell UP, 1977.

Woolf, Virginia. "*David Copperfield*." *Collected Essays*. Vol. 1. New York: Harcourt, Brace & World, 1967. 191–95.

Wordsworth, William. Preface to *Lyrical Ballads, with Pastoral and Other Poems* (1802). *Literary Criticism of William Wordsworth*. Ed. Paul M. Zall. Lincoln: U of Nebraska P, 1966. 38–62.

Young, Melanie. "Distorted Expectations: Pip and the Problems of Language."*Dickens Studies Annual* 7 (1978): 203–20.

Zabel, Morton Dauwen, ed. Introduction. *Charles Dickens' Best Stories*. Garden City, NY: Hanover House, 1959. 9–28.

Zwerdling, Alex. "Esther Summerson Rehabilitated." *PMLA* 88: 3 (May 1973): 429–39.

Index

Stanley Friedman, who received his doctorate from Columbia University, is Associate Professor Emeritus at Queens College, CUNY, where he taught in the English Department for over thirty-six years. Since 1996 he has been one of the editors of *Dickens Studies Annual.* Dr. Friedman has published numerous articles on Dickens in *Dickens Studies Annual, Dickens Quarterly, The Dickensian, Nineteenth-Century Fiction,* and other periodicals.